# Collected Works of
# Nassau William Senior

## Volume 5

Edited with a new Introduction by
### Donald Rutherford
University of Edinburgh

OVERSTONE

# Collected Works of Nassau William Senior

Edited and Introduced by Donald Rutherford,

*University of Edinburgh*

Printed in England by Antony Rowe Ltd., Chippenham

# Miscellaneous Writings on Economics

NASSAU WILLIAM
SENIOR

THOEMMES PRESS

KYOKUTO SHOTEN LTD

This edition co-published in 1998 by

**THOEMMES PRESS**
11 Great George Street, Bristol BS1 5RR, United Kingdom

**KYOKUTO SHOTEN LTD**
12, Kanda-Jimbocho 2-Chome, Chiyoda-Ku, Tokyo, Japan

COLLECTED WORKS OF NASSAU WILLIAM SENIOR
6 volumes : ISBN 1 85506 617 3

PUBLISHER'S NOTE

The publisher has gone to great lengths to ensure the quality of this reprint but
points out that some imperfections in the original book may be apparent.
This book is printed on acid-free paper, sewn, and cased in a durable buckram cloth.

● Overstone is an imprint of Thoemmes Press.

# Contents

# Report on the State of Agriculture

*Quarterly Review* (July 1821)

ART. IX.—1. *Report from the Select Committee to whom the several Petitions complaining of the Depressed State of the Agriculture of the United Kingdom were referred. Ordered by the House of Commons to be Printed, 18th June, 1821.* pp. 56. London: Sherwood, Neely and Jones.

2. *Essay*

2. *Essay on the Application of Capital to Land, with Observations showing the Impolicy of any great Restriction of the Importation of Corn, and that the Bounty of* 1680 *did not lower the Price of it.* By a Fellow of University College, Oxford. pp. 69. London. 1815.

CONSIDERING the extent of the subjects referred to the Agricultural Committee, the eagerness with which they have been discussed—an eagerness not disproportioned to their importance—and the practical weight, which the talents and station of many of the members of the Committee must give to the Report, we have been anxious, at any sacrifice, not to let a Number elapse before we gave some account of its contents. For this purpose we have been forced to consider the Report without the Minutes of Evidence, which do not seem likely to be published before this Article is in the press, and to write somewhat more rapidly than we could have wished on so difficult a subject. The first we have found a less inconvenience than we expected. The Report consists so much of inferences from acknowledged principles and facts, and is so little founded on information derived from the witnesses, that it may well be treated, as we have treated it, as an independent work. The second we have felt severely; but we hope that in the wide circulation of this Journal our errors will not escape detection, and that we shall be able, when we recur to the subject, (for it is one that must often engage our attention,) to correct those which are important.

The branch of political economy which is the principal subject of this Report, the effect of the employment of capital in obtaining raw agricultural produce, is one on which writers and speakers are in general guilty of so many errors, and seem so little aware of their ignorance, that we may, perhaps, be forgiven if we endeavour to explain at some length the mistake, by which those errors appear to us to have been principally occasioned. That mistake consists in applying to the employment of capital in obtaining raw produce, the maxims which regulate the employment of capital in manufacturing raw produce, or, to use a more convenient though less accurate expression, in considering agriculture and manufactures as governed by the same rules. They are in fact the subjects of one fundamental distinction, which opposes them to one another in all their details, and renders almost every proposition, which is true as to one, false as to the other. The distinction may be thus stated: every additional capital employed in manufactures produces a greater proportionate net return, while every additional capital employed in agriculture produces a smaller proportionate net return; or thus—every additional quantity of manufactured produce

is

is obtained, so far as the manufacturing it alone is concerned, at a smaller respective expense, while every additional quantity of agricultural produce is obtained at a greater respective expense.

The first branch of the distinction is too obvious to require more than to be stated. It is the necessary consequence of the division of labour. The second, though less obvious, will perhaps appear equally clear when we consider that the soil of every country is of various degrees of fertility, and that the most fertile portions of it are the first occupied; that these portions are of small comparative extent, and that every additional quantity of agricultural produce must be obtained, either by the cultivation of lands less fertile than those formerly occupied, or by applying additional capital to the lands already in cultivation. In the first case the net return is obviously diminished;—and that the net return is diminished when additional capital is applied to land already in cultivation, notwithstanding the improvement in skill and in division of labour with which it is applied, appears from the mere fact that lands less fertile than the very best are cultivated; for if fresh capital could be applied to the more fertile land already in cultivation, with the same return as was afforded by the capital previously employed on them, no man would employ it (necessarily to less advantage) in the cultivation of less fertile land. The principle, however, is now so generally admitted that we will not detain our readers with a more detailed proof of it. That proof they will find, where the principle first was stated, in the ' Essay on the Application of Capital to Land,' with which we have headed our Article—a work of which Mr. West, a barrister, is now, we believe, known to be the author, and which contains more valuable and more original instruction on the subject than we have ever seen condensed into so small a space. We ought, however, when we refer our readers to Mr. West, to observe that we think him wrong in absolutely excluding the competition of capitalists from the causes which diminish the profits of capital, and in his supposition that tithes have a constant tendency to increase upon rents ; and also in his view of the effect which a diminished agricultural capital would have upon rent. We say this, not intending at present to engage in an argument, however interesting, for which we have not room, but to avoid any inference which might have been drawn from our silence.

The effect of the two opposite rules, which we have pointed out, may be traced in the variation to which the price of every commodity that we buy is subject. So far as the price of any commodity consists of the value of the raw material, of which it is composed, it has a tendency to rise as the consumption increases; so far as it consists of the alteration in form, which that material has undergone, it has a tendency to fall. The ore of which a watch-spring

is

is formed makes so small a part of its value that we may expect to see watch-springs of the same quality cheaper and cheaper as the demand for them increases; but the raw material of beef, whether we consider it as consisting of the beast, or of the grass and hay that has been employed in feeding it, makes so large a part of its value, and the alteration in form produced by cutting up and cooking it, so small, that an increased price seems the necessary consequence of an increased demand. No improvement of skill, or of division of labour, in butchery or cooking, will ever make roast beef as cheap in England as in South America. The two rules are sometimes so balanced that at different stages of the manufacture, the one, and then the other, preponderates; and the coarser the manufacture the more it is subject to the first rule, the finer it is, to the second. The raw material of cloth is dearer in England now than it was 100 years ago, and dearer than it is now in Russia; and perhaps the coarsest cloths might have been more cheaply manufactured in England then, or might be in Russia now, than by our present manufacturers. But the finer the cloth, the cheaper it will become in proportion to that which is coarse, and we have no doubt that an English lady's habit now does not cost her half the price which it would have cost Queen Ann, or would cost the Empress of Russia. It is probable that a person acquainted with the history and details of the manufacture might be able to point out the stages at which, in the preparation of the same piece of cloth, improvement of skill gradually compensates, and at last overbalances, increased expense of material. Supposing the wool to be 20 per cent. dearer, the cloth, in the rough state in which it leaves the loom, may bear the same price as it did 100 years ago: in its finished state it may be 20 per cent. cheaper. We may apply the same reasoning to man, considered as a commodity. So far as the commodities he consumes consist of manufactures he becomes cheaper; so far as they consist of raw produce he becomes dearer. His clothing and furniture belong principally to the first class; his food to the second. The real wages of labour, therefore, so far as they consist of food, will have a tendency to rise, as respects the employer, though they remain stationary, or fall, as respects the labourer. Though he is not better, or is even worse, fed, his food will cost more; but so far as they consist of clothing and furniture they have a tendency to rise, as respects the labourer, though they remain stationary, or fall, as respects the employer. The clothing of a respectable day labourer, and of his wife and children, and the linen and bedding and household furniture of his cottage, including, perhaps, ' the wooden clock that clicks behind the door,' and a Bible and Prayer Book, the Pilgrim's Progress, and two or three other books on a shelf near it, though

saved

saved without any great sacrifice out of his wages, would have
been worth a little fortune in the reign of Henry VIII. But as
food is the principal commodity consumed by the ordinary labourer, his employer is on the whole a loser, and the ordinary labourer is a commodity constantly increasing in price. The proprietor of 500 acres cannot maintain double the retinue which
followed his ancestor 300 years ago, though he has ten times the
amount of all other comforts and luxuries. But the gentleman
labourer is a consumer of manufactures; he does not consume
more raw produce than the ordinary labourer—perhaps not so
much. What he wants are books and clothes, and those decen-
cies of life which enable him to mix with the opulent class of society, and acquire their tone and feelings. He is a commodity,
therefore, constantly diminishing in price. The fees of physicians
have not been raised since the reign of Charles II. when money
was treble or quadruple its present value. You may get a clerk in
a public office, with an education and feelings equal, perhaps, to
those of the head of his department, at a less expense than that of
your butler. You may not only get him, but the instant the va-
cancy is known there will be a hundred applicants, and the privilege of filling it will be a valuable piece of patronage.

But, to return from this long digression: though we think we may
consider the principle of this distinction as acknowledged, there are
many deductions from it, which do not appear to us to be generally
perceived. Among the most important are the following.

In all manufactured articles of the same kind, the natural price,
so far as the manufacturer is concerned, that is, the price which replaces the capital, which he has expended in their manufacture, including the wages he has paid to his workmen, with the average
profit of capital at that time and place, is the same. And their
natural price is their market price; with this exception, that if the
natural price should, as to some of them, sink, the market price
will sink too, and draw with it the market price of those other
articles of the same kind of which the natural price has not sunk.
But on the contrary, the natural price of each individual article
of raw agricultural produce of the same kind, is different, and the
market price and the natural price are never the same; except as
to the individual article, which has been produced at the greatest
expense, with the natural price of which the market price of the
whole roughly coincides.

To express the distinction more concisely, the price of manufactures, as manufactures, is governed generally by the cost of
production, and only as an exception, by supply and demand.

The price of raw produce is governed by supply and demand, and
only

only as an exception, by the cost of production. An increased demand will eventually sink the former and raise the latter.

We will endeavour to illustrate both propositions somewhat in detail. Suppose the raw material, of which a particular sort of knife is formed, to cost the cutler 5*d.*—the expense of manufacturing it, supposing him to manufacture 1000, to be 5*d.* more—and the average profit of capital to be 10 per cent. Every such knife will be at the same natural price, 11*d.* But suppose the expense of manufacturing 5000, to be 4½*d.* a piece; and that, by reducing the price of his knives one farthing, he can extend his sale from 1000 to 5000, it will clearly be his interest to do so. The natural price of the knives made by him subsequently to this extension of sale, will be, within a minute fraction, 10½*d.*, that of those made by him previously, and still made by others, being 11*d.* Until the example of our supposed manufacturer has been followed by others, he will be able to get a monopoly price of 10¾*d.* for his subsequently made knives, to which the price of his previously made knives, and that of those made by others, must be accommodated. His capital therefore will return him 12½ per cent. while that of the other persons engaged in the same trade will only return them 7½ per cent. But it is impossible that this state of things should continue. Before our cutler could quintuple his knife-making, he must have withdrawn part of his capital from other branches of the cutlery business. Among his brother cutlers, some will follow his example, and by diminishing the price of their knives, endeavour still further to increase their sale, while others will withdraw their capital from knife-making, now become (at the old prices) an unprofitable business, and employ it in an increased manufacture of those articles which the makers of knives have relinquished. The same consequences will re-appear. The increased capital in these branches will yield an increased proportionate return, the advantage of which will at first go to the cutlers, and the capital in their business will yield a profit above the general average ; until the competition, occasioned by the general influx into that trade of the disengaged capital of the country, reduces their profits to the common level, and the whole advantage is felt, in diminution of price, by the public.

We hope our readers will forgive us the roughness of these details, into which we have been led by an attempt to show practically something like the method, by which the market price of manufacturing industry is adjusted, and its tendency to follow the natural price in the fall occasioned by the increasing division of labour. Every fall in price, the demand continuing the same, is occasioned by some manufacturer's underselling his neighbours ; and his motive to do so is always to employ a larger capital in that specific manufacture, with an increased division of labour, and consequently an increased net profit.

We will now endeavour practically to illustrate our proposition as to raw produce.  Suppose a man to inherit £20,000 in money, invested in manufactures, and returning, as the average profits of capital at that time and place, 10 per cent. and 1000 acres, the first 100 highly fertile, and each successive 100 diminishing in fertility one tenth, but the worst capable of producing corn, with a great deal of dressing, and consequently of some use, as natural pasture, without any.  Were he to employ £500 in cultivating, in the least expensive manner, his most fertile 100 acres, the natural price of his corn, that is the price which would replace his £500, with 10 per cent. profit, would probably be not one fourth of the market price.  But he would have no temptation to sell it at that price: for the motive to sell at a less price than the market price, that of employing a larger capital at an increased net profit, would not exist.  He would sell at the market price, and instead of a profit of 10, get perhaps a profit of 100 per cent.  The next year we will suppose him to employ an additional £500 on the 100 acres of the next rank in fertility.  The produce being smaller in proportion, the natural price would be nearer to the market price, he would obtain on his £500, only 90 per cent.  The next year we will suppose him to employ another £500, not perhaps in the cultivation of a third 100 acres, but in additional cultivation of his first. This additional £500 would yield him a still less net return than the last, perhaps 85 per cent.—the next year he perhaps would take in his third 100 acres at 80 per cent.—the next year employ another £500 on his second 100 acres at 75 per cent.—and we can conceive him in this manner going on, both his gross and his net return increasing in amount, but the net constantly bearing a less proportion to the gross, till he reached a point at which his land, remaining uncultivated, was so barren, and his land already in cultivation had received so much capital, that the additional corn produced, by bringing into cultivation the former, or by applying additional capital to the latter, would at the market price only replace the £500 employed in raising it, with 10 per cent. profit.  At this point, the natural price and the market price coincide.  The proprietor might employ two additional sums of £500 each on his land with a profit of 10 per cent.  The one in additional cultivation of his land, already in cultivation, the other in breaking up the barren land still uncultivated.  The first he will probably do, by transferring to it the least productive or most transferable £500 of his manufacturing capital.  The other he will not do, for he would only obtain the same profit as his £500 previously gave him as manufacturing capital, and would lose the advantage which the land

gave

gave him as natural pasture. The rest of his capital he will retain in manufactures, until a diminution in the profits of manufacturing industry, or an increased price of corn, occasioned by the demands of an increased population, gives him a motive for investing new capital in the cultivation of his land already in cultivation, and of breaking up a portion of his uncultivated land, with a return, equal in the first instance to the average profit of capital, and in the second, to that profit, and to the advantages which he derived from the land in its uncultivated state.

The point which we have supposed our proprietor to have reached, when he ceased to increase his agricultural investment, is that at which his whole land and his whole manufacturing capital would be most profitably employed. To this point cultivation is always intended to go, for if it were to go less far, a portion of capital would be employed in manufactures, which might be more profitably employed on the land—and at this point it is always intended to stop —for were it to go farther, a portion of capital would be employed on the land, which might be more profitably employed in manufactures.

And if we suppose the proportion of land to manufacturing capital prodigiously increased, the periods much longer, and the profits of manufacturing capital at first much higher, and gradually diminishing with its increased abundance, and with the increased expense of obtaining raw produce, and that diminution, together with the growing demands of a population increasing in numbers and wealth, occasioning each successive investment in the land, this is the picture, not of an individual, but of a nation.

But let us suppose the same course as before run by two individuals instead of one, and that the proprietor of the land is one person, and the proprietor of the capital another. It is clear that the landed proprietor will not permit the capitalist to obtain from his land more than the average profit of capital. When the first £500 returns a net profit of £500, he will allow the capitalist to retain £50, being as much as he could have made by any other investment, and demand the remaining £450, being the surplus profit produced by the investment, for having afforded the land, out of which the whole £500 was gained ; and he will obtain his demand; because if the supposed capitalist would not give it, somebody else would. Out of the £450 profit produced by the second £500, he will demand and obtain £400. And out of the £400 produced by the third £500, though employed on land already in cultivation, he will obtain £350, and so on for each successive investment of capital, always leaving the capitalist the £50 profit, which he would have made in any other investment of capital, and taking all the surplus profit himself. But the last £500 invested by the capitalist

1 1 2                                                              would

would produce only £50; and there being no surplus, the landed proprietor would receive nothing for having permitted its investment. The sums thus received by the landed proprietor are, of course, what is called rent. They are the surplus profit obtained from the investment of capital in land over that obtained from its investment in any other business; and they are occasioned by each portion of raw agricultural produce being raised at a different expense, and each portion, except that raised at the greatest expense, selling at a monopoly price, the difference between which price, and the natural price, is taken by the proprietor of the land, in return for the privilege of using it.

We shall perhaps best show the importance of keeping steadily in view the true nature of rent, by a reference to some of the errors which have arisen from a neglect of it. One of the principal of these consists in attributing the whole difficulty, which the British finds in competing with the foreign grower, to the exorbitant rents of our landlords. The first contest must lie between the growers of that British corn and that foreign corn which are respectively grown at the greatest expense, including, as to the foreign corn, the expense of carriage. But the corn grown at the greatest expense is that grown by an application of capital, for the privilege of which application the grower pays no rent. Rent therefore cannot enter into its price—and were the landlord to remit the whole of his rent, that price would not be altered, nor could the grower compete better with his foreign rival than before.—While the importation lasts, the only remedy is that which the grower himself must apply, the removal of that portion of capital which has ceased to return the average profit of capital: and this he will do, notwithstanding any reduction of the rent, which he has paid in respect of his other capital. It is true that the landlord might make the retaining of the whole of the existing capital on the land, the condition on which he remitted the rent, on that part of it which paid rent: and it might be worth the tenant's while to comply with the condition; but it never could be worth the landlord's to impose it.

To the same cause may be traced the use of a term which has occasioned so much petitioning and legislation—a remunerating price. In its proper sense the remunerating price of any thing is its natural price—the price which replaces the capital employed in its production with the average profit of capital at the same time and place. In this sense the remunerating price of every quarter of wheat may differ from that of every other, according to the infinite varieties of soil, situation, mode of cultivation, and weather. But the agriculturists add that it must likewise repay the rent, which has been paid for the land on which it has been raised. If

our

our reasonings be correct, it is clear that no corn can ever pay rent, which has not previously paid a remunerating price to the grower —for rent is the excess of price above that remunerating price. But that is not what the agriculturist means by rent. He means the actual sum of money which each individual tenant has agreed to pay to each individual landlord. We are forced to answer that it is impossible to form any calculation in which so vague a term is to be admitted—a term depending on the providence or improvidence—the harshness, or negligence, or partiality of all the tenants and landlords in the kingdom. The *real* or *mean rent*, the surplus profit obtained by the investment of capital in land over other investments of capital, is the only standard by which the conventional rent, except in individual cases, can be estimated. It is to this standard that it is always meant to be adjusted; never of course with complete success—for the real rent must fluctuate from year to year, and even from month to month—it must vary with all the accidents of weather, and the success or failure of every bargain: but as the landlord is anxious not to receive less, and the tenant not to pay more, the real and the conventional rent, though never for an instant the same, will at the long run pretty nearly coincide. If then by rent we mean the real rent, that, wherever it exists, presupposes a remunerating price. And what *is* a remunerating price will be a question as much depending on the accidental circumstance of every different quarter of corn, and as incapable of a general answer, as before. If, on the other hand, we mean conventional rent, and conventional rent as differing from real rent, then a remunerating price will be an expression still more vague. To the variations of soil and climate we shall have to add those of human conduct, and of human conduct, by the supposition itself, governed by mistake, for it is only through a mistake, in the landlord or the tenant, that the conventional rent can differ from the real rent. Were a farmer with £10,000 to lay it out in cultivating the shingles of Eastbourn, or the rocks of Dartmoor, or were he to turn Bond Street or Grosvenor Square into corn-fields, or even to employ the whole of his capital in the experiment how far the produce of ten fertile acres could be carried; one hundred, or five hundred guineas, a quarter might not be a remunerating price. But were a lease of 10,000 fertile acres to be granted him at 5s. per acre, it is probable that he would be well remunerated by 10s. or 15s. a quarter. Nothing but experience could convince us that legislation, intended to be permanent, has been attempted on data such as these.

We have observed that there is a portion of corn, that raised at the greatest expense, of which the price roughly coincides with the cost of production. And it has been said, that as it is the price of

this

this portion which governs that of all the remainder, the price of
that remainder is likewise governed by the cost of production. But
first, when we say that the price of any thing is governed by the
cost of production, we mean the cost of its own production,—not
of the production of any thing else. And, secondly, to say that it
is the price of this last portion of corn, which governs that of the
remainder, is to mistake the effect for the cause. The price of other
corn does not rise because the last portion has been produced at a
greater expense, but the last portion is produced, because the proportion of demand to supply has previously occasioned such a rise
in the price of the corn already produced, that additional capital
laid out in producing additional corn, at a greater proportionate
expense, will return the average profit of capital. Corn does not
become dear because a portion is raised at a great expense, but a
portion is raised at a great expense because corn has already become dear.

The last step in agriculture will always be the application of
fresh capital to land already in cultivation. The corn produced by
it is intended to sell at its natural price: and this price must previously have been, and must continue to be, that of all other corn,
or the last application of capital would not have been made,—would
have been greater,—or would not be continued. And it is in this
sense only, (and it must be acknowledged to be very obscurely
pointed out,) that the corn raised at the greatest expense can be said
to fix, or govern, or regulate the price of all other corn : not as
an efficient cause, for it must always be subsequent in time, but as
an index. All corn of the same quality will sell for the same price :
and, therefore, if you find the natural price of the corn which is
produced, and continued to be produced, at the greatest expense,
you will find the market price both of that corn and of all other
corn. But this index will be correct only in a stationary country,
a market neither rising nor falling. If the market price be rising
from an increased demand, it will outrun the natural price even of
the corn produced at the greatest expense. A constantly increasing
price, followed by a constantly increasing production, may continue for a long period of years, during no part of which will the
natural and market price of any portion of corn coincide. This
is the state of an advancing country. But if the wealth or number
of the consumers diminishes, the diminution of price may outrun
the diminution of production. Both may diminish : but from the
difficulty, often the impossibility, of removing some portions of
capital from the land, the supply may not diminish so rapidly as the
demand. Every year there will be less produced, and the expensiveness of the most expensive corn will be every year less, but the
fall of price may be still greater. This is the state of a declining
country.

country. And as every country is, in fact, either advancing or declining, (for the few which are said to be stationary can be so only
by the compensation of successive periods of advance and decline,)
there is no country in which the cost of the production of any portion of corn can be said correctly, even to indicate, much less to
govern, or regulate, or fix, that of the rest.

Our readers will perceive that we are opposed on this point, as
well as on some others, to Mr. Ricardo. We trust that distinguished economist will believe that we differ from him with great
reluctance, and, as far as there is doubt as to matters of science,
with great hesitation : but he would be the last person to wish,
that our expression of opinion should be restrained by deference
to his authority, or even by gratitude for the instruction we owe to
him.

We are now come to the Report itself, and we hope that our
previous discussion will be found to have saved time on the whole,
by clearing the way for its consideration.

The duties of the Committee were so indefinite—their subject-
matter so difficult in its nature, and so perplexed by conflicting interests and obstinate prejudices, and the body itself so large and
heterogeneous, that they could scarcely have been expected to produce a very clear and consistent report. It might have been expected to consist, either of a statement of the opinions and wishes
on the subject of one of the two great parties who speak and think
on it as partizans, or of truisms on matters not in dispute, and vague
generalities, and propositions so qualified as to be nugatory, on the
debateable points; or of a discordant mixture of true and false,—
good theory to be followed at some indefinite future period,—and
mischievous practice for the present,—and full acknowledgments of
contradictory propositions scattered throughout. But none of these
characters applies to the present Report as a whole—great judgment has been shown in selecting the topics on which the opinion
of the Committee was most desirable, and great manliness in fairly
discussing them. The reader of the Report must, we think, be convinced that it is the work of very able and well-informed men. He
will, unless his knowledge on the subject far exceeds ours, receive
much valuable instruction, and he will be struck by the absence of
system, and the desire of truth and practical utility, by which it is
distinguished. He will, if he thinks with us, disagree with much
of it ; but was there ever a collection of dicta and reasonings on
disputed points, with much of which every different reader did not
disagree?—and if he find inconsistency in many parts, and a want
of arrangement and unity in the whole, he will only wonder that
under the circumstances of its composition, these faults are not
still more observable. We will endeavour, although it has the last

fault

fault in a degree peculiarly inconvenient for our purpose, to give, as far as we are able, a connected view of its contents.

They may be divided into, 1st. a statement of the substance of the corn laws. 2d. Of the opinion of the Committee as to the existence of agricultural distress. 3d. Of their opinion as to the nature of its causes, and the manner in which they are likely to operate in future. 4th. A proposal for a prospective and for an immediate alteration of the corn laws. And 5th. An answer to the reasonings of some of the agricultural petitions. And as this arrangement is, with some deviations, that of the Report, we will adopt it in our remarks.

We will give the first two heads in the words of the Committee.

' Your Committee do not think it necessary to preface the observations which they have to make, upon the important matters referred to them by the House, by a recapitulation of the numerous laws which have been passed, at different periods, for regulating the trade in Corn. The most material of those laws have been brought under the consideration of the House by the reports of former Committees on this subject. It is, therefore, sufficient to remark, that by the salutary law of 1806, a free interchange in grain of every description, was established between Great Britain and Ireland ; and that the trade in foreign corn is altogether governed by the provisions of the Acts of 54 and 55 Geo. III. by which were, for the first time, enacted ;—first, a constantly free exportation from the United Kingdom, without reference to price, or without such exportation being either encouraged by any bounty, or restrained by any duty whatsoever ;—secondly, an absolute prohibition against the introduction of every description of foreign grain, meal, or flour, into the consumption of the United Kingdom, when the average prices, ascertained according to the mode established by former Acts, are below certain specified rates ;—thirdly, an unlimited freedom of importation, from all parts of the world, without any duty whatever, when the prices are above those specified rates.

' Such being the state of the law which affects, so far as legislative interference can affect, the important interests brought under the consideration of the House by the numerous petitions presented in this session, your Committee proceeded, in the first instance, to inquire into the allegations of those petitions. It is with deep regret that they have to commence their Report by stating, that, in their judgment, the complaints of the petitioners are founded in fact, in so far as they represent that, at the present price of corn, the returns to the occupier of an arable farm, after allowing for the interest of his investment, are by no means adequate to the charges and outgoings: of which a considerable proportion can be paid only out of the capitals, and not from the profits of the tenantry.

' This pressure upon the farmer is stated by some of the witnesses to have materially affected the retail business of shopkeepers in country towns connected with the Agricultural districts. But notwithstanding
this

this diminution of demand in particular parts of the country, it appears, by official returns, that the total consumption of the principal articles subject to duties of excise and customs has increased in the last year, compared with the average of the three preceding years ; and also, that the quantity of cotton wool used for home consumption, and of cloth manufactured in Yorkshire, was greater last year than in the year preceding, although the export of woollens in 1820 appears to have diminished. Your Committee have not the same authentic means of ascertaining the consumption of iron, but there appears every reason to believe that it has also increased.

' The opinion of your Committee, in respect to the present pressure upon the tenantry, is formed upon the best documentary evidence which the nature of the case admits of, confirmed by the testimony of many respectable witnesses, as well occupiers of land as surveyors and land agents : and it is further strengthened by a comparison of the difference between the existing price and the average price of the last ten years, the period within which most of the present engagements, affecting the tenant of the soil, may be supposed to have been contracted. If the present price could, under all the present circumstances, be remunerative, the average price of that period must have afforded an excessive profit; which does not appear probable, nor warranted by any facts. The only fair inference, perhaps, to be drawn from such a comparison, and from the state of our agriculture during the last war, is, that for a considerable part of that period, the returns of farming capital somewhat exceeded the ordinary rate of profit, and that at this time they are considerably below it.'—*Report*, p. 3—5.

Want of the Minutes prevents our inquiry into the evidence, on which the Committee ground their belief of the existence of great agricultural distress. We fear, however, that there is no reason to doubt its truth ; we only regret that they have used expressions which might appear to admit the existence of a general remunerating price. We believe that, putting rent out of the question, there is, and always must be when the price of corn is falling, a portion of the capital employed in growing it as to which the price for the time being is not remunerative, a portion as to which it is precisely remunerative, and that as to all the rest, it is more than remunerative. And we put rent out of the question, because real rent, the excess of agricultural profit over the average profit of capital, *must* exist as to this last portion, and *cannot* as to the two others; and conventional rent will at the long run correspond with real rent, and therefore is too temporary, and in the mean time depends upon all the accidents of human conduct, and therefore is too indefinite a term to enter into the definition.

This indeed the Committee seem to have felt, and therefore disguise rent under the expressions ' charges and outgoings,' ' present engagements' and ' present circumstances.' It is only when they proceed to apologize for its present amount that they call it rent.
But

But though we think that the expression ' a remunerative price,' in the unexplained manner in which it is used by the Committee, is likely to lead, and indeed has led, to the most dangerous errors, it may, perhaps, be used with convenience if solely intended to signify the price which, at a given time and place, replaces to the grower of the corn grown at the greatest expense, the capital employed in growing it, with the average profit of capital. As to this corn, it will exclude rent; as to all other corn grown at the same time and place, it will imply real rent; and as real rent is the only standard by which we can estimate conventional rent, we may, generally speaking, consider it as implying conventional rent. Through their apology for rent the Committee slide into the third branch of their subject, the nature of the causes of the present distress, and the manner in which they are likely to operate in future. A want of distinctness in the Report makes it difficult to ascertain the opinion of the Committee on the former point; but we think they mean to refer the agricultural distress to four principal heads:— 1st. To the alteration in the value of our currency. 2d. To an excess of supply as compared with demand. 3d. To ' the general derangement which the convulsions of the last thirty years have produced in all the relations of commerce, in the application of capital, and in the demand for labour ;' and, 4th. To the operation of the present corn laws.

We fully agree with the Committee that the alteration which has taken place in the value of our currency must have occasioned, and must continue for a time to occasion, great injury to the occupiers of land. Its effect is, to injure all those who have definite sums to pay out of indefinite receipts—the latter diminishing while the former remain fixed, and this is the situation of those occupiers of land (by far the greatest portion) who are lessees or mortgagers. And we join in the conviction expressed in the Report that the evil is temporary in the one case, and in the hope that it will be so in the other.

On recurring to the Report we are not quite sure that it bears us out as to the second and third causes which we have represented the Committee as assigning; but there is so much excellent sense in the whole passage which refers to them, that we will prevent all chance of misrepresentation by extracting it.

' Your Committee feel it an important part of their duty to recall to the recollection of the House, and the Country, that, in the years 1804 and 1814, a depression of prices,—principally caused by abundant harvests, and a great extension of tillage, excited by the extraordinary high prices of antecedent years,—appears to have produced a temporary pressure and uneasiness among the owners and occupiers of land, and a corresponding difficulty in the payment of rents and the letting

of

of farms, in some degree similar to the apprehensions and embarrassments which now prevail; and also, that in many earlier periods, similar complaints may be traced in the history of our agriculture.

' Among numerous instances of these complaints, which may be found in other publications between the middle of the 17th century and the beginning of the late reign, two have been pointed out by one of the witnesses, in which the House will not fail to remark the great similarity between the arguments and alarms which were then current, with those which prevail in many quarters at this period.

' That in these earlier and more remote stages of our agriculture these alarms were only temporary, and that the fears of those who reasoned upon their continuance and increase, were ere long dissipated by the natural course of seasons and events, is now matter of history. And it is impossible to look back to the discussions of the years 1804 and 1814, and more especially to the evidence taken before the Committee appointed by the House on the latter occasion, without being forcibly struck with the conformity of the statements and opinions, then produced, respecting the ruinous operation and expected continuance of low prices, with those which will be found in the evidence now collected. Indeed these statements, in some instances, come from the mouths of the same witnesses.

' Your Committee trust that this reference to past experience will not be altogether useless and unavailing to allay the alarm, and to dispel some of the desponding predictions which, by unnecessarily increasing anxiety for the future, tend to aggravate the severe pressure of our present difficulties;—that the reflections which such a retrospect is calculated to excite, may lead the occupiers of the soil, as it has led your Committee, to infer that in agriculture, as in all other pursuits in which capital and industry can be embarked, there have been, and will be, periods of reaction; that such reaction is the more to be expected in proportion to the long continued prosperity of the pursuit, and to the degree of previous excitement and exertion which that prosperity had called forth. They must add, as a further inference from the experience of former periods, to which the present crisis bears no distant resemblance, that there is a natural tendency in the distribution of capital and labour to remedy the disorders which may casually arise in society from such temporary derangement, and (without at all meaning to deny that it is the duty of the legislature to do every thing in its power to shorten the duration, and to palliate the evils of the crisis) that it often happens that these disorders are prolonged, if not aggravated, by too much interference and regulation.

' It is by no means with the expectation that the suffering of our own community can be alleviated by the contemplation of a corresponding pressure upon other nations that your Committee find themselves called upon to state that many commodities of general and extensive demand, the staple productions of other countries, such as corn, cotton, rice and tobacco in the United States of America; sugar and rum in the West Indies; tallow, flax, hemp, timber, iron, wool and corn, on the continent of Europe, appear to have fallen in price, in some instances more,

and

and scarcely in any less, in proportion to the prices of those articles prior to 1816, than the fall in the price of grain in this country; with regard to several of which articles, and the countries producing them, some of the causes which have principally affected the value of grain in this country cannot be considered as operating.

' The proofs of this great revulsion of prices, in other parts of the world, may be found, as to most of those articles, in the evidence collected by your Committee, and the remainder in other authentic information now before the House. The facts indeed are, from their nature, matter of such notoriety to the commercial classes of the community, that they cannot admit of a doubt. So far as this state of things tends to involve other countries in embarrassment, it must be matter not of satisfaction, but of regret; and this natural feeling of every liberal mind will only be confirmed by reflecting upon the intimate connection which must exist between the advancement of other nations towards wealth and improvement, and the growing prosperity of our own. Entertaining this feeling, your Committee trust, that their motive for noticing the present state of the markets in other parts of the world will not be misconceived. The fact is one which naturally came within the scope of their inquiry, as tending to affect the markets of this country, and it appeared not unessential to advert to it for the further object of showing that the causes which have produced this great change are not confined to any one country. It would seem that the influence of that general derangement which the convulsions of the last thirty years have produced in all the relations of commerce, in the application of capital, and in the demand for labour, is not yet spent and exhausted, and that neither the habits and dealings of individuals, members of the same community, nor the transactions and intercourse of different communities with one another, have hitherto altogether adjusted themselves to that more natural state of things which we may now hope is likely to become again the more habitual and permanent condition of society.'—pp. 10—14.

There appears some doubt whether the Committee attribute the present redundance of supply to the unusual abundance of the late harvest, or generally to too great an extension of tillage; but as they contemplate a gradual remedy, which the former would not require, we think they must mean the latter. It appears doubtful, too, whether they refer to the state of foreign markets as an illustration, or as an efficient cause, of that of our own.

We believe ourselves that the deterioration of our foreign market, occasioned partly by the causes alluded to by the Committee, and partly by the loss of the monopoly which we possessed in it, has produced great distress among our manufacturers, (including under that name those who live by circulating as well as by working up commodities,) and that the distress of our agriculturists is, in a great measure, caused by that of their customers, the manufacturers; that an inability in the manufacturers to buy has produced

duced an inability in the agriculturists to sell, at its natural price; that part of their produce which has been produced at the greatest expense; and that that part of their produce is, therefore, to use the expression of the Committee, redundant—that is, meets with no demand *at its natural price.* We are anxious to insert this qualification of price, when we speak of the want of demand, be-. cause we are far from believing that, at a price below the natural price, there is any want of demand. We are far from believing that more corn is produced in this country than the inhabitants wish to consume, or, in fact, than they do consume; and we believe they could, with great pleasure, consume much more. All that they want is the money to pay for it, or, in more accurate language, a sufficiency of equivalents to replace to the producer of corn the whole capital which he has employed in its production, with the average profit of capital. We believe, in short, the redundancy to be not positive, but relative, and that positive redundancy, if it can ever exist in any article which is limited in quantity, is peculiarly improbable in the case of corn, from the tendency of corn, as affording the great necessary of life, to produce its own demand. The Committee, however, appear to consider corn as peculiarly liable, if not to positive redundancy, yet to an approach to it.

‘ In the article of corn, however, there is one consideration to be constantly borne in mind, most material to enable the House and the Country to arrive at sound and safe conclusions on this important subject, namely, that the price of corn fluctuates more than that of any other commodity of extensive consumption, in proportion to any excess or deficiency in the supply. The truth of this proposition had not escaped several writers on this subject, and has been confirmed by many of the witnesses who have been examined; although it may be doubted whether, generally, they were aware of its extent and practical operation in the present state of this country and of our corn laws.

‘ The cause which produces this greater susceptibility in the corn market cannot be better explained by your Committee than in the following extract from the answers of Mr. Tooke, one of the witnesses who was particularly examined to this point:—“ Why should a dif“ ferent principle apply to corn than to any other general production? “ —Because a fall in the price of any other commodity not of general “ necessity, brings the article within the reach of the consumption of a “ greater number of individuals, whereas in the case of corn, the “ average quantity is sufficient for the supply of every individual; all “ beyond that is an absolute depression of the market for a great length “ of time, and a succession of even two or three abundant seasons must “ evidently produce an enormously inconvenient accumulation.”—“ Is “ there not a greater consumption of corn when it is cheap than when “ it is dear, as to quantity?—There may be, and possibly must be, a “ greater consumption; but it is very evident that if the population “ was before adequately fed, the increased consumption from abundance
“ can

" can amount to little more than waste; and this would be in a very
" small proportion to the whole excess of a good harvest or two."—
" The whole population of this country and others do not subsist upon
" wheat; therefore, when wheat becomes cheaper, those who were for-
" merly fed upon other corn may take to feeding upon wheat?—My
" remark was general as applying to corn. There is no doubt that if
" there is one description of corn applicable to human food which is
" abundant, and another that is deficient, then the principle does not
" apply; my principle applies to corn generally applicable to human
" food. It may be observed that abundant seasons generally extend to
" the leading articles of consumption, and that it seldom happens, that
" in what are called commonly good years, there is a complete failure
" in any one great article."

   ' In the substance of this reasoning your Committee entirely concur;
and it appears to them that it cannot be called in question, without
either denying that corn is an article of general necessity and universal
consumption among the population of this country, or [affirming] that
the demand is materially varied by the amount of the supply. This
latter proposition, except within very narrow limits, altogether disproportioned to the fluctuations in production, is not warranted by experience. The general truth of the observation remains, therefore, unaltered by any small degree of waste on the one side, or of economy on
the other; neither of which are sufficient to counteract the effect which
opinion and speculation must have upon price, when it is felt how little
demand is increased by redundancy, or checked by scantiness of supply.'—pp. 14—16.

   We are sorry that we cannot feel all the concurrence which the
Committee express in the substance of Mr. Tooke's reasoning—we
are sorry, because it proceeds on a premise in which it must be de-
lightful to believe:—that the average quantity of corn is sufficient
for the supply of every individual;—that it so adequately feeds our
whole population that the increased consumption from abundance
is little more than waste. But we fear that, so far from its being
true that every person in this country has as much bread as he
wants, it will be found that, even in the most favourable seasons,
not six, not four, out of our twelve millions, are in this situation.
Mr. Tooke can scarcely have seen the cottages of our poor, where
the loaf is the *food* only of the man, and the LUXURY of his wife and
children. He can scarcely have recollected the immense consumption of flour in puddings and pastry of every description, and that
that consumption is kept within the limits of the existing supply,
in the bulk of our population, only by the most painful economy;
and above all he must have forgotten the elasticity with which population, supposing the resources of the country to be uninjured,
expands whenever the force that limits it is relaxed by an increased
supply of the great necessary of life. So far from the demand of
corn being little increased by redundancy and checked by scantiness

ness of supply, and the former only producing a small degree of waste, and the latter of economy, we believe that it is more susceptible of variation from these causes than the demand for the non-necessaries of life. If the supply of hats be doubled there will not be more heads, and the existing heads will not wear more hats at a time, though they may wear them out a little sooner; but if the supply of corn be doubled there will be more mouths, and the existing mouths will consume more than before. Every such increase will produce immediately an improvement of habits, and, if permanent, an increase of numbers in the labouring part of the population; and every diminution in the supply of corn will produce immediately a deterioration of their habits, and, if permanent, a diminution of their numbers. A positive redundancy of corn could exist, even for a time, only in a society without a wish to increase its consumption; it could permanently exist only in a society without a tendency to increase its numbers. The former state of society is improbable—the latter impossible.

We are now come to the fourth head of the causes of the present agricultural distress—the Corn Laws. It is prefaced by some remarks of the Committee, with the substance of which we agree, and to which we may have occasion to recur, on the danger to which a price habitually and considerably exceeding the prices of the remainder of the world, would expose the grower, notwithstanding his monopoly of the home market, and on the probable course which legislation on what is called a remunerative price, may be expected to take. The sentence with which they begin would not prepare us for the admirable good sense of what follows it.

'Taking as the basis of all wise regulations on the subject of the corn laws, the undeniable positions,—that the landlord, the tenant, and the consumer, have one great and common interest in maintaining a permanent and adequate supply of corn at prices as steady as possible,—and that steadiness of price must depend on guarding, as much as legislative interference can guard, against the effects of fluctuation of seasons,— your Committee have examined the practical operation of the present system of our foreign trade in corn with a reference to these two points.' —pp. 21, 22.

A more deniable position than that it is the tenant's interest to maintain steadiness of price by preventing, through legislative interference, the natural effect on price of fluctuating seasons, that is, to keep the price of his produce the same, while its quantity is necessarily varying, never was propounded. As the tenant's principal payments are *fixed*, it must be to his interest to have *fixed* returns; and as the *quantity* of his produce varies with the variations of season this can only be effected by an inverse variation of price.

price. It is true that if the variations of price were to exceed those
of the season, they would be injurious even to the tenant; and it is
true that if a steady price were maintained, notwithstanding the
variations of season, as might be done in a small territory by a free
corn trade, the tenant's gains and losses would at the long run be
even, and he might save from the former to meet the latter.  But
if he began with a succession of bad crops he might be ruined before the time of compensation should arrive; if his lease ended
with a series of good ones the rent of his new one might be assessed on an extravagant basis; and putting these contingencies out
of the question, it will always be better for a man to have prudence
provided for him by causes out of his controul, than to have to
furnish it himself.  The landlord's interest, as landlord, in all questions between the tenant and the consumer, is with the tenant—on
whose success his rent depends; so that the ' undeniable position'
of the Committee fails as to two of the three classes whose identity
of interest they have asserted.

But we will no longer detain our readers from the excellent view
which the Committee have given of the practical operation of the
corn laws.

' To prohibit the foreign supply altogether, so long as, from the ca-
sualty of seasons, we are subject to years of deficient or damaged produce, has at all times been felt to be impossible.  But, since the year
1815, we have had recourse to an absolute prohibition up to a certain
price, and an unlimited competition beyond that price.

' This system is certainly liable to sudden alterations, of which the
effect may be at one time to reduce prices already low, lower than
they would probably have been under a state of free trade, and at another, unnecessarily to enhance prices already high;—to aggravate the
evils of scarcity, and to render more severe the depression of prices
from abundance.  On the one hand, it deceives the grower with the
false hope of a monopoly, and, by its occasional interruption, may lead
to consequences which deprive him of the benefits of that monopoly
when most wanted:—on the other hand, it holds out to the country the
prospect of an occasional free trade, but so regulated and desultory as
to baffle the calculations, and unsettle the transactions, both of the
grower and the dealer at home;—to deprive the consumer of most of
the benefits of such a trade, and to involve the merchant in more than
the ordinary risks of mercantile speculation.  It exposes the markets
of the country, either to be occasionally overwhelmed with an inundation of foreign corn altogether disproportionate to its wants; or, in the
event of any considerable deficiency in our own harvest, it creates a
sudden competition on the continent, by the effect of which the prices
there are rapidly and unnecessarily raised against ourselves.  But the
inconvenient operation of the present Corn Law, which appears to be
less the consequence of the quantity of foreign grain brought into this
country, upon an average of years, than of the manner in which that
grain

grain is introduced, is not confined to great fluctuations in price, and consequent embarrassment, both to the grower and the consumer; for the occasional prohibition of import has also a direct tendency to contract the extent of our commercial dealings with other states, and to excite in the rulers of those states a spirit of permanent exclusion against the productions or manufactures of this country and its colonies. In this conflict of retaliatory exclusion, injurious to both, the two parties, however, are not upon an equal footing;—on our part, prohibition must yield to the wants of the people; on the other side, there is no such over-ruling necessity. And inasmuch as reciprocity of demand is the foundation of all means of payment, a large and sudden influx of corn might, under these circumstances, create a temporary derangement of the course of exchange, the effects of which (after the resumption of cash payments) might lead to a drain of specie from the Bank, the consequent contraction of its circulation, a panic among the country banks,—all aggravating the distress of a public dearth, as has been experienced at former periods of scarcity.

' That the present system of our Corn Law has a tendency, according to circumstances, at one time to reduce prices lower than they would probably have been under a state of free trade; and at another time, to enhance those prices, when already perhaps too high, will not appear paradoxical to the House, if it be considered that the practical operation of this system, in its sudden and desultory transitions, may be not only slightly at variance with, but in direct opposition to, the principle on which it is founded;—that principle being, to shut out foreign corn from home consumption in seasons of sufficient or abundant crops, and to give every facility to its introduction in years of scarcity. For example: let it be supposed that on the 15th of August next, the average price of wheat, ascertained in the usual mode, should be 79s. 11d. per quarter, whatever may be the possible scantiness of the forth-coming harvest, (a fact not then capable of being ascertained,) the ports will remain shut till the 15th of November: but if that average should be 80s. 1d., whatever may be the abundance of the forth-coming harvest, the ports and the warehouses of foreign corn will be opened at least for six weeks; and, in reference to the principal exporting countries, for three months. Pursuing the supposition a little further,—if the first case should occur when there was no accumulation of foreign corn in the warehouses of this country, and very little at the shipping ports of the continent, (a state of things by no means rare,) the prices at home, after a failing harvest, would rise very rapidly, and become very high, before any material supply could be drawn from the north of Europe, as both the passage down the rivers, and the navigation of the Baltic, would be interrupted during the winter. In the meantime the prices on the continent would be regulated by those of this country, rising as our prices rose. In the spring there would be a great demand for shipping to bring over the supplies purchased during the winter, by which the charge of bringing the corn to our market would be still further increased; and thus, in various ways, prices would unnecessarily be enhanced in this country; first, during the most distressing period of the year, from the want of a timely and regular supply from abroad; secondly, from the eager and general competition to procure that supply upon the sudden opening of our ports, a competition which will immediately raise the price on the continent against ourselves, until, together with the charges of conveyance, and the probable loss upon the fall of exchange, it becomes upon a level with the scarcity price of this country; and, thirdly, by the direct tax which may be laid upon the export from countries to which we resort for our supplies. This tax, in the Prussian dominions, was about 10s. a quarter during the extreme scarcity which prevailed in this country in the years 1800 and 1801; and it was expressly declared that the continuance or removal of this tax would depend altogether upon the continuance or cessation of the wants of this kingdom.

' But if the second supposed case (that of our ports being opened at a fraction above 80s.) should arise, when there was a great stock of foreign corn in the warehouses of this country, and at the shipping ports of the continent (which is the present state of things), in proportion to the low and ruinous price to which that corn, from long accumulation and want of vent, would be reduced, would be the temptation, and consequent eager competition, and simultaneous effort, to pour it upon this country; where, in the case supposed of an abundant harvest, no part of it would be wanted, and its rapid influx would not fail to lower the prices to a pitch which they never would have reached had the trade not been liable to such sudden alternations.'—pp. 22—25.

The Committee, after illustrating the case last supposed, by a reference to the effects of the importation of oats in August, 1820, add—

' If such be the consequences of the present system, they sufficiently point out the nature of those inconveniences to which it may expose the grower, the dealer at home, and the foreign importer in his speculations abroad. When your Committee find, for instance, in the seventeen months which passed between January, 1816, and June, 1817, the price of wheat varying from 53s. 1d. to 112s. 7d.; and again, in the three months which ensued from June to September, 1817, from 112s. 7d. to 74s., they cannot but ask whether fluctuations so rapid and extensive have existed in any other commodity of universal supply and demand, or in any other country? and whether these fluctuations may not have been aggravated by some of the effects of the present law?

' With respect to the effects which may be produced in this country, all the internal and commercial transactions of which so mainly depend on circulating credit, by a sudden revulsion in the foreign exchanges, the experience of the last thirty years is a sufficient warning. Your Committee, therefore, feel a confident assurance, that when the attention of the House is called to the subject, it will examine with a jealous care for the public interest, how far the present system of the corn trade has a tendency to bring upon the country the renewal of this calamity.'—pp. 27, 28.

With the substance of these reasonings we fully concur; and it
would

would not be easy to add to the force and the clearness with which they are expressed. The Committee then show that the system they have been reprobating has not the sanction of long usage in its favour; that from 1773 to 1814 the ports have been constantly open and the trade free, with the exception of a few short intervals, when the high duty of 24s. 3d. a quarter was demandable, and operated as a prohibition.

' The necessary consequence of the trade in corn having been virtually open with the continent, and the importation allowed at duties merely nominal, during this period of forty years, has been, that the general price, at the shipping ports on the continent, has not, upon an average, been materially lower than the price in England, except to the amount of the charges to be incurred in bringing the foreign corn to the markets of this country. The price, at a distance from those shipping ports, and in the districts which have not the benefit of good roads or internal navigation, it is true, has been much lower, but this difference was absorbed in the expense and risk of transporting it from those districts. The quantity that can be supplied, without incurring that expense, is limited ; and in proportion as the prices in England have been high, has the interior circle on the continent from which the supplies have been drawn, been extended.

' The severe scarcities which we have experienced have furnished us, therefore, with something like a measure of the degree in which they could be relieved from the surplus produce of the continent within the prices which those scarcities respectively occasioned ; whilst the mode in which every rise in the price at home adds to the power and inducement of increasing the foreign importation, shows that any increase of the rates, at which the import commences under the present system, would only tend, whenever the ports should open, to aggravate the fluctuation, and the other inconveniences which appear to your Committee to appertain to the principle of alternate monopoly and free importation.'—pp. 30, 31.

As the country would expect of them, the Committee have followed their remarks on the impolicy of the law, by proposing an alteration. They propose, indeed, two—one temporary, until the present continental glut shall have been dispersed ; and the other permanent. The temporary one, which consists in a relaxation of the present import price, and the imposition of a fixed duty on importation, so much resembles in principle the other, that we need not discuss it independently. We proceed to their permanent plan.

' Your Committee are the more anxious to impress upon the attention of the House the real state of our trade in foreign corn, between the years 1773 and 1814, as it appears to them, taken in connection with the progress of general prosperity in the country, and more especially with the great improvements in agriculture, and its highly flourishing condition during that period, to suggest to Parliament, as a matter highly deserving of their future consideration, whether a trade in corn, constantly open to all nations of the world, and subject only to such a fixed duty as might compensate to the grower the loss of that encouragement which he received during the late war from the obstacles thrown in the way of free importation, and thereby protect the capitals now vested in agriculture from an unequal competition in the home market,—is not, as a permanent system, preferable to that state of law by which the corn trade is now regulated. It would be indispensable, for the just execution of this principle, that such duty should be calculated fairly to countervail the difference of expense, including the ordinary rate of profit, at which corn, in the present state of this country, can be grown and brought to market within the United Kingdom, compared with the expense, including also the ordinary rate of profit, of producing it in any of those countries from whence our principal supplies of foreign corn have usually been drawn, joined to the ordinary charges of conveying it from thence to our markets.'—p. 31.

' It is not the province of Your Committee to specify any precise permanent duty for the protection of the British grower; nor should they, perhaps, be adequately prepared so to do without further inquiry; nor until the obstacle to that inquiry, created by the present accumulation and glut, shall be removed. At the same time, they incline to the opinion, that leaving to every part of the United Kingdom the inestimable public benefit of the most full and free competition in the home market, without regard to the difference of fertility in the soil, or of expense in its cultivation, either from a difference in the price of labour, or in the amount of local and public burthens directly affecting the land; it may, perhaps, be difficult, if not impossible, putting rent out of the question, for the occupiers of some of the poorest and most expensive soils now under tillage in Great Britain, to bring their produce to market in competition with the more fertile lands of this country, and especially of Ireland. Your Committee would be anxious to suggest, for the consideration of Parliament, as the principle and basis of the trade in foreign corn, such a protecting duty upon the produce of other countries, as would not aggravate to the occupiers of such soils the present difficulty of that competition. The general question, How far the forced cultivation of some of those inferior lands may have been expedient or advantageous for the public interest, is one upon which it is unnecessary to offer a positive opinion. They can, however, have no difficulty in stating that, within the limits of the existing competition at home, the exertions of industry and the investment of capital in Agriculture, ought to be protected against any revulsion, but that the protection ought not to go farther;—and that, if protected to that extent, the growth of our population, the accumulation of our internal wealth, affording increased employment to that population, and consequently increased means of purchasing all those articles of consumption and enjoyment, which must be derived from the soil of this country, will continue to give, as they have given during the last sixty years, the most effectual stimulus and encouragement to the progressive improvement of our Agriculture, and to the consequent value

value of the landed property of the kingdom ;—that, under such a system, there can be no apprehension that either will permanently retrograde, (except in so far as rents may be nominally affected by the resumption of cash payments,) or even be for any time stationary,—so long as our institutions continue to afford, to capital and industry, that superior degree of security and protection which they have hitherto found in this country,—so long as public credit and good faith keep pace with that security and protection, and as we avoid any course which, in a time of peace, and possibly of improving confidence in the stability of the institutions of other countries, might drive capital to seek a more profitable employment in foreign states. It is under the impression that the present Corn Law, together with the amount of our taxation, by diminishing the profits of capital, have such a tendency, that Your Committee suggest the modifications which have been pointed out, as fit for further inquiry and investigation ; and that they feel it their duty, also, to accompany that suggestion with a most earnest recommendation, that every opportunity should be watched, and every practical measure adopted, for reducing the amount of the Public Expenditure; as the only means of approximating to a state of Finance, which, without impairing the credit of the country, may lead to a diminution of the existing burthens of the People.'—pp. 34, 35.

We agree fully with the Committee that our present corn laws ought to be abolished. We agree with them as to the propriety both of constantly permitting importation, and of subjecting it at present to a duty. With the principle on which they propose to assess that duty, we utterly disagree; but with less pain, as it appears to us the necessary consequence of our agreement with other parts of the Report. That principle, under different disguises, is throughout the same—prohibition—a monopoly of the home market until the indefinite period shall come, when that market shall be so much improved, as to afford to the capitals now invested in the cultivation of the poorest and most expensive soils now under tillage, the average profit of capital ; that is, until prices rise, or nearly rise, to those of the last years of the war, as expressed in our altered currency.

The duty is to be such, first, as will protect the capitals now vested in agriculture from an unequal competition in the home market. All that distinguishes such a protection from the strictest monopoly, is the word ' unequal.' And we can allow it to produce such a distinction, only, by supposing it to express a competition which reduces the profit of the capital against which it operates, below the average profit of capital in other employments. But until the period we have alluded to shall have arrived, any competition whatever with our agricultural capitalists would reduce their profits further than they now are below the average profit of capital in other employments. If the present supply finds

no demand at a price which remunerates the grower of the most
expensive part of it, much less would an increased supply find such
a demand. The proposed duty, therefore, must be, until that
period shall have arrived, prohibitive.

The next rule by which the Committee propose to assess the
duty is,

‘ That it should be calculated fairly to countervail the difference of
expense, including also the ordinary rate of profit, at which corn, in
the present state of this country, can be grown and brought to market
within the United Kingdom, compared with the expense, including the
ordinary rate of profit, of producing it in any of those countries from
whence our principal supplies of foreign corn have usually been drawn,
joined to the ordinary charges of conveying it from thence to our markets.’

That is, that it should be equal to the difference of price, deducting the expense of carriage, and calculating the British price not
at its existing amount, but at that which would replace the capital
now employed in the cultivation of the most expensive British
corn, with the average profit of capital in other employments—
that price being the measure, in a stationary market, of the expense
of growing and bringing to market with the average profit, the corn
which does not pay rent, and of that expense and profit, together
with the real rent, of that corn which does pay rent. Such a duty,
like the last, would be prohibitive until the arrival of the time, if
ever it is to arrive, when the British price reaches the supposed
amount. It would then remain prohibitive if the price of foreign
corn were to rise; that price necessarily *would* rise, as the exportation would both diminish the supply and increase the demand, in
the foreign market. And though that rise would be created only
in the shipping ports, whence our supplies were derived, yet, as
the Committee have well observed, in the passage already extracted, p. 30., the difference between the prices of those ports,
and of the districts less advantageously situated for exportation,
would be absorbed in the expense and risk of transportation
from those districts.

The last principle upon which the Committee calculate their
duty, is nearly a repetition of the first. It is to be such a duty as
would not aggravate, to the occupiers of the poorest and most ex
pensive soils now under tillage in Great Britain, the present difficulty of competing with the more fertile lands;—that is, which
should prohibit importation, for all importation necessarily *would*
aggravate that difficulty. The difficulty exists, because the supply
is so great that there is no demand at a price, by which the occupiers of the soils in question are remunerated. Increase the supply by importation, and of course the difficulty is increased. It

appears,

appears, from the remarks of the Committee, p. 22. 33. 47., that they propose, in seasons of scarcity, to relax or suspend the duty.

Our readers may be amused, we do not wish to use a graver expression, by recurring to the reprobation with which the Committee have treated the present system of our corn laws, and then examining the practical effect of their own. The effect of the present system is, prohibition under 80s. a quarter; and then, unlimited importation. The effect of the committee's system will be, prohibition under a price, which, to answer their proposed end, must, we fear, be little less than 80s. a quarter, if not more; then importation of that small quantity, which foreign growers can give us without an increase of their own price, until corn shall reach some further very high price, when the relaxation or suspension of the duty renders the importation nearly, or entirely free. The only difference in theory, is, the additional restraint between the period, when the duty ceases to be prohibitive, and that at which it is to be relaxed or suspended. The only differences in practice will be, a diminution of the evils which arise from fluctuation, and an aggravation of those which arise —

' From the hazardous and embarrassing situation of the grower of corn in a country where the lowest price, which is considered to afford him a remuneration, shall habitually and considerably exceed the prices of the remainder of the world, although, up to that price, he should be secured in the complete monopoly of that country;' p. 17. ' from the manner in which the produce of the poorer soils in England is liable to be affected by ungenial seasons;' p. 21. 'from the consequences of a retaliatory exclusion of our own manufactures in foreign countries;' p. 23. ' from a great difference between the cost of subsistence here, and in other countries, not only in regard to the people themselves, but also from the risk which must be in proportion to that difference, of deriving much of the capital by which their industry and labour are supported, to seek employment in other countries. For there cannot be a doubt that this difference operates in the same manner as taxation, to diminish the profits of capital in this country, and there can be as little doubt that, though capital may migrate, the unoccupied population will remain, and remain to be maintained by the landed interest, upon whose resources, diminished in proportion to diminished demand, this additional burthen would principally fall.'—p. 41.

If our readers wish still further to examine the antidote, which the committee have furnished, against their own suggestions, let them read the enlightened passage, in which the effects, on agriculture, of freedom and protection are contrasted.

' In comparing the two periods, each of nearly equal duration, between the peace of Utrecht and the commencement of the Seven Years war,— and between the years 1773 and 1814,—and recollecting that the first period was one of almost uninterrupted peace; and that nearly thirty

years

years of the latter have passed away in the exertions of two most expensive wars;—that, during the former period, the market interest of money was generally much below, and during the latter, frequently as much above the rate fixed by law;—that during the former, the aim of the Legislature was, by artificial means, to divert the application of capital from other employments to that of agriculture, as well by positive bounties which forced an export of grain to other countries, as by duties which generally altogether precluded its import either from the continent or from Ireland;—that during the latter, agriculture has, in point of fact, been without either of those stimulants;—your Committee cannot look at these contrasted circumstances, coincident, during the first period, with a comparative stagnation of our agriculture; and during the second, with its most rapid growth and improvement, without acknowledging that there was nothing in the system pursued up to 1773, which necessarily promoted this most essential branch of public industry and national wealth; and also, that there is nothing incompatible with the success of both these objects in the system which has practically prevailed since that date. If the quantity of wheat, the growth of Great Britain, was truly estimated, as it was estimated in 1773, at four millions of quarters, and if it cannot now be stated so low as at double that amount, it is evident that the change of system has been attended with no defalcation of produce. If, since that year, the number of cattle and sheep has been vastly augmented, their breeds improved, and, by those improvements, their size and aptness to fatten, and in sheep their fleeces greatly increased; if, by this augmentation of live stock, a greater quantity of manure has been produced; if all the most important but expensive meliorations of modern husbandry have been introduced; if scientific drainages have been undertaken, and extensive wastes inclosed, to augment the produce of the land,—it cannot be said that there has been a want of encouragement to invest large and adequate capitals in this branch of national industry.

' If, from agriculture, your Committee look to the permanent improvements which have been made in the country itself within the same period, the bridges which have been built, the roads which have been formed, the rivers which have been rendered navigable, the canals which have been completed, the harbours which have been made and improved, the docks which have been created,—not by the public revenue, but by the capitals and enterprize of individuals; if they look, at the same time, to the unexampled growth of manufactures and commerce—in the contemplation of this augmentation of internal wealth, which defies all illustration from comparison with any former portion of our history, or of the history of any other state;—your Committee may entertain a doubt, (a doubt, however, which they wish to state with that diffidence which a subject so extensive naturally imposes upon their judgment,) whether the only solid foundation of the flourishing state of agriculture is not laid in abstaining, as much as possible, from interference, either by protection or prohibition, with the application of capital, in any branch of industry?—whether all fears for the decline of agriculture, either from temporary vicissitudes to which all
                                                    speculations

speculations are liable, or from the extension of other pursuits of general industry, are not, in a great degree, imaginary?—whether commerce
can expand, manufactures thrive, and great public works be undertaken, without furnishing to the skill and labour which the capitals
thus employed put in motion, increased means of paying for the productions of the land—whether the principal part of those productions
which contribute to the gratification of the wants and desires of the different classes of the community must not necessarily be drawn from
our own soil, the demand increasing with the population, as the population must increase with the riches of the country?—whether, in our
own country in former times, and in other naturally fertile countries up
to the present time, agriculture has not languished from the want of
such a stimulus?—and whether, in those countries, the proprietors of
the land are not themselves poor, and the people wretched, in proportion as, from want of capital, their labour is more exclusively confined
to raising from their own soil the means of their own scanty subsistence?

' If these questions should be answered in the affirmative, it follows,
that the present solidity and future improvement of our national wealth
depend on the continuance of that union by which our agricultural prosperity is so closely connected with the preservation of our manufacturing and commercial greatness.'—pp. 38—41.

We wish that, besides these questions, the Committee could have
been asked how they reconciled their practical advice, with their
opinions, p. 14. that the present distress has partly been occasioned by redundant production, and so far 'admits of no adequate
remedy, except that which must arise from the progressive adjustment of the supply to the demand, either by the diminution of the
one, or the increase of the other, or, more probably, by the combined operation of both?' Whether the supply will be diminished
by protecting the capitals now vested in the cultivation of the
poorest and most expensive soils?—whether the demand will be
increased by a system which 'has a direct tendency to contract the
extent of our commercial dealings,' and ' to diminish the profits of
capital?' And whether the only means of enabling the agricultural
part of the community to obtain a higher price, are not, previously,
to enable the non-agricultural part to give it? The last question
has indeed been put to the agriculturists, and their answer to it,
though unnoticed by the Committee, ought not we think to be passed
over by us. Like most bad reasoners they assume some true premises, that the prosperity of our manufacturers depends on the goodness of their markets; that the home market is far the most valuable, and that it is much injured by the agricultural distress. To
restore, therefore, prosperity to the manufacturer, they propose to
improve his home market, and to do this, by raising the price of
corn, till it shall reach a point which shall put an end to the agricultural distress, which, by deteriorating the home market, has
occasioned

occasioned that of the manufacturers. Now granting the possibility of thus raising the price of corn by legislative interference (which we believe in, much as we do in the Turkish plan of sinking it, by hanging a baker) the plan is, to give prosperity to the manufacturer, by obliging him to pay a larger price for his corn, in consideration that, that excess of price being in return laid out with him, he will retain a *portion* of it as profit.  Give me 80s. a quarter for my corn instead of 50s., says the agriculturist to the cotton-spinner, and your market shall be prodigiously improved; I will lay out 80s. instead of 50s. in buying your stockings, and instead of a profit of 5s. you will get one of 8s. :—though to be sure, you will have given 30s. for the privilege of getting this additional profit of 3s.  We may put the transaction into a still simpler form, by leaving out, (what only perplexes it,) the intervention of money, and supposing it to be carried on, as practically it is, by barter.  Suppose the cotton-spinner, instead of paying 80s. for his corn, and having that 80s. returned to him in exchange for his stockings, were directly to exchange his stockings for his corn.  The proposal then is, to improve his situation by obliging him to give eight pair of stockings for a given quantity of corn instead of five.  But even this is far too favourable a statement of the agricultural argument.  It supposes all that is lost by the manufacturer to be gained by the agriculturist, and all that is gained by the agriculturist to be laid out with the manufacturer.  A great portion of the increased price which the monopoly enabled the agriculturist to receive, would be laid out on horses and servants, in residence abroad, and in all the other modes of expense which are useless to the productive labourers of the community. And a great portion of the remainder would be absorbed by the diminished fertility of the soil of which it forced the cultivation. It is in this manner that all attempts to favour one part of the community at the expense of the other, not by a direct transfer of revenue, but by interfering with the natural application of capital, where they succeed, add waste to injustice.  To put 5s. into the pocket of the agriculturist, they would force the manufacturer to pay him 80s. for a quarter of corn, which he has raised at the expense of 75s. but which might have been raised elsewhere for 50s.  It was on this principle that the Turks refused to introduce printing, because it would interfere with the profits of copyists,—and that the watermen of the Thames requested that Westminster bridge might not be built, because it would interfere with their fares.  It would have been much cheaper to give the copyists and the watermen salaries to the amount of their loss, and leave them to employ themselves in some other occupations.

We have ourselves, however, admitted the propriety of a duty; but it is as a temporary, not a permanent measure, that we approve
of

of one. We are anxious, to use the words of the Committee, ' to spare vested interests, and to deal tenderly with those obstacles to improvement which the long existence of a vicious system too often creates:'—and which in the present instance have been created even by the *short* existence of such a system, operating on the interests, and still more on the prejudices, of a powerful body. But we do not wish to make the use, which is so often made of this argument, and to treat the obstacles to improvement with a tenderness which will make them eternal. We wish to protect the agriculturists from the effects of the sudden alteration of prices which might follow an unrestrained corn trade. Where such a trade will render a part of our agricultural capital unproductive, we wish to give time for the removal of the portion which can be removed, and to soften the loss on what cannot be removed, by making it gradual. For this purpose we would willingly consent to the imposition of any duty the agriculturists should require, if provision were made for its gradual termination. Suppose the duty, which the Committee describe as having been always prohibitive, of 24s. 3d. to be imposed, with a proviso that it should be reduced by 2s. every year. In twelve years a return to true principles would be effected, and the evils attendant on the execution of the measure much mitigated.

It may be feared that the distinguishing quality of such a duty, its gradual operation, will not facilitate its adoption. Legislators are in general far too anxious for immediate results, to make laws of which the full effect is reserved for posterity. The common impatience of human nature is heightened in them by a consciousness that the credit is seldom bestowed till the object is fully attained, and by a well grounded fear, that any measure which is to be completed by a successor, will be mismanaged or neglected, when he who planned it is removed. It has been said, that no architect should ever design a building too vast to be finished in his life-time,—since he may rely on its being spoilt by those who follow him. And the consciousness that his power is more precarious than even his life, and that habits of systematic opposition are likely to prejudice against his views any rival who may displace him, must strengthen in the minister of a popular government, the eagerness to make complete at once, beyond the danger of alteration or repeal, the measures which he has triumphantly carried. But every change, however permanently beneficial, must be attended with immediate injury. If we resolve that it shall at once produce its full effects of good, we must resolve to suffer it at once, to produce, not merely its full effects of evil, but probably much more evil than if we had been content to receive its benefits gradually. And evils of execution, thus concentrated and aggravated, may often make a

wise

wise legislator refuse, or a weak one delay, measures, which, if gradually insinuated, might, in time, have produced all their good, and little of their injury. The only mode by which it was ever proposed to reform the calendar was, by leaving out at once the excessive days.—Fear of the confusion and inconvenience which this would occasion, made us suffer under the evils of a vicious calendar for a century longer, till after all we reformed it at once, at the expense of those of a sudden alteration, increased by the additional excess of a day, which had been created by the delay. All the advantages might have been obtained with scarce any of the evils, if we had merely left out the leap years for forty years. But this would have been a *gradual* measure, and the motives which we have suggested, probably prevented its adoption.*

We hope, however, that they do not apply with their usual force to the case before us. Among the characteristics of the body of statesmen who now govern this country, are, permanence in power, and consistency of plans.—And they mutually re-act on one another. Nothing but a general conviction that a certain system of measures and tone of government is dependant on their continuing at the head of affairs, would have enabled them to keep their station, through so shifting a series of events: to weather the hazards of so much war, and, what is still more dangerous to an administration, of so much peace. And the habit of consistency will of course be strengthened, if it appear to be the tenure of power. We think therefore that the present ministry might originate a plan of gradual operation, with much less than the ordinary chance of its being ultimately abandoned. The measure too, which we propose, is perhaps less likely to be affected by a change of the hands in which power is deposited, than most others. It is not a political measure, intended to rectify or alter the balance of the constitution, by taking from the power of one class, or adding to that of another. Our object is to extricate the agricultural and the non-agricultural classes of the community from a situation, which cramps the resources, and injures the happiness, of both; and to replace them in that natural state, in which the prosperity of the one will constantly produce and re-produce that of the other. And we wish to do it gradually, in order to mitigate the evils with which the most beneficial alteration of an existing system must necessarily be attended.

And evils of execution are all that we anticipate. The Committee, it is true, see danger from ' the dependence of this country for subsistence upon other, possibly hostile, countries.' And ' from

---

* Hence the remark of Bacon, ' Quis novator tempus imitatur, quod novationes ita insinuat ut sensus fallant?'

a diminution

a diminution of the weight, station, and ascendency, which the landed interest has enjoyed so long, and used so beneficially.' p. 36. As to the first, when we recollect from how many sources our supplies of corn may be drawn, and that among them are Canada, the United States, the Baltic, France, the Mediterranean, and the Cape, countries so opposed to one another, in climate, position, and political interests ; and when we consider the nature of commerce, so fertile in resources, and irrepressible by obstacles, we must conclude that a combination of circumstances, natural and political, which should prevent our deriving sufficient supplies from all these sources, or of supplying the deficiency by other means, is one of those remote contingencies, theoretically possible, and therefore fit materials for insincere argument, on which no man of practical wisdom would act, still less make important sacrifices.

As to the other danger, we too are anxious to support the landed interest ;—we only differ from those who think themselves its warmer friends, as to the mode in which that support may best be afforded. We believe that the value of land depends on the quantity of its raw produce, and on the quantity and quality of the accumulated and unaccumulated labour, for which a given portion of that raw produce will exchange; that as the accumulated and unaccumulated labour, that is, the productive population and capital in a country, can be augmented in an increasing ratio, and the raw produce of its land only in a diminishing ratio, the best mode of increasing the value of land is to endeavour to increase, not the quantity of its raw produce, but the quantity and quality of the equivalents for which that raw produce is exchanged; and that from the bulky and perishable nature of raw agricultural produce, the increased difficulty with which every additional quantity of it is obtained, and its tendency, as affording the great necessary of life, to create its own demand, no monopoly can be permanently useful, no free importation permanently injurious, to the landholder. The tendency of a monopoly must be, by cramping the trade, and diminishing the quantity of the great necessary of life, in the country where it exists, to diminish, keep stationary, or retard in increase its productive population and capital, and consequently to diminish, keep stationary, or retard in increase the equivalents which can be exchanged for its raw produce. The deterioration of the market will more than compensate for its exclusive possession. The tendency of free importation must be, by enlarging the trade, and increasing the quantity of the great necessary of life, in the country where it exists, to increase its productive population and capital. There will be more consumers of raw produce, and those consumers will have more to exchange for it. As soon as these effects are felt, as soon (and it will be very soon)

soon) as the non-agricultural part of the community has had time
to increase its numbers and wealth, the improvement in their
market will more than compensate to the agriculturists, for the
competition to which they will be exposed, limited as that must
be, by the nature of the commodity. All experience shows that
great agricultural prosperity must always be the effect of great
commercial and manufacturing prosperity; all reasoning proves
that it can never be the effect of measures, which tend to diminish
the wealth, or limit the number, of consumers.

The remainder of the Report is occupied in remarks on the allegations of some of the agricultural petitions. The first mentioned
are those in which ' the depression and distress of all those concerned in agriculture are mainly ascribed to the extent of our
public burthens, coupled with their diminished means of bearing
them.' And which insist that the price of corn must rise, in order
to remunerate the grower, in the same ratio as the amount of the
public revenue. To this the Committee answer, that

' Without denying that the price of corn may be in some degree
affected by adding to our general taxation, and that any charges particularly paid by the farmer, such as tithes and poor rates, must tend
more directly to raise that price; it is obvious, from what has been
already stated, that the cost of growing corn in any country is regulated
by the amount of capital necessary to produce it upon lands paying no
rent, and that it is the price of the portion of corn which is so raised
that determines the price of all other corn; and that an increase of
general taxes, affecting alike the profits of capital in all the different
branches of industry, would not necessarily raise the price of the particular produce of any one.'—p. 43, 44.

We agree with the Committee, that general taxation falls equally
upon general capital, and that the increased amount of public
revenue affords no reason for an increased price of corn. We are
disposed indeed to go much farther; and to believe that an increase of taxation, instead of raising (which the Committee appear,
from the context, to mean by ' affecting,') must have a tendency
to sink, the price of corn, by diminishing the equivalents, which
the remaining part of the society have to exchange for it; and
that, as no legislative interference can increase those equivalents,
no such interference can prevent corn from falling, in a period of
war and consequent taxation. Other causes, indeed, may, and
such a cause was the commercial monopoly enjoyed by us during
the war: but the general truth of our proposition is strikingly
illustrated by the fall in the price of corn, which the Committee
remark to have been occasioned by the waste of capital and
revenue in the American war. As to specific taxation on the
farmer, such as tithes and poor rates, we have already stated our
                                                                    reasons

reasons for thinking that the price of corn is determined by supply and demand, and not, as the Committee suppose, ' by the price of the portion which is raised on lands paying no rent;' or, to use a more correct expression, which is raised by an application of capital, for the privilege of which application, no rent is paid:— and we believe that tithes and poor rates, so far as they are specific taxes on agricultural produce, have a tendency to diminish both the supply and the demand, without altering their relative proportions, and therefore without increasing the price. We think therefore that they must fall, and must remain, a burthen on the agriculturist, and will be felt first by the tenant, and ultimately by the landlord. But this no legislative interference can prevent, while the tax continues. Whether there are any means of commuting the first which we have mentioned, and removing the second, without incurring still greater inconveniences, we cannot now inquire. But as to general taxation, every reader will agree with the Committee, that

' However sanguine may be the hope that peace will afford increased facility and encouragement to further accumulation, it is not less the duty of Government directly to aid that accumulation, by diminishing our expenditure, and thus both to improve the comforts and to stimulate the skill and enterprize of those classes, by whose industry and savings the capital of the whole kingdom is augmented. This duty, important at all times, appears to Your Committee to be still more so, under the present circumstances of the country; for, whilst they are desirous of correcting the mistaken opinion, that the depression under which our Agriculture now labours, is either exclusively or principally to be attributed to taxation, they cannot disguise from themselves, that the weight of the public burthens of the country, their nominal amount remaining the same, must be more severely felt, in proportion as the money-incomes derived from trading, farming, and manufacturing capital and industry, are diminished. No exertion, therefore, should be omitted to endeavour to reduce those burthens, as nearly as circumstances will permit, in the degree in which such incomes may have been reduced : for, in considering this subject, it is important to bear in mind, that the general amount and real pressure of taxation have been positively increased in the proportion of the improved value of our currency.'—p. 45, 46.

The Committee next consider the prayer, to be found in most of the petitions, for protection for all the productions of agriculture, equal to the protection given to the manufacturers of this country.

To this the Committee reply; first, that the duty by which the petitioners wish that protection to be extended, would be prohibitory; and therefore that the principle, if acted upon, would go far to annihilate commercial intercourse altogether. Secondly,

that

that what the petitioners suppose to be a protecting duty, is often, as in the case of glass, a financial regulation to give effect to the heavy duty of excise imposed on it in this kingdom. Thirdly, that these protecting duties, as to our considerable manufactures, with the exception of silk, are in fact obsolete; our own superiority having made foreign competition in the home market impossible; and lastly, by an argument which we feel so difficult of comprehension, that we shall extract it.

' There exists this most essential difference between the effect of protection given to the manufacturer, (even if he did not enjoy, from natural causes, a preference in the home market,) and the attempt at a similar protection and monopoly to the produce of the soil ; that in all employment of capital, either in trade or manufactures, profits are limited by competition. If, for any length of time, or from any circumstances, profits are increased, in any particular branch, above the accustomed average, additional capital seeks employment in that branch, and profits are again speedily reduced to their former level. This would equally be the case if the demand for that particular article *were doubled;* and it may further frequently happen, as we have witnessed of late years, (in all goods, for instance, wrought of iron and cotton,) that, owing to discoveries in mechanical and chemical science, and improvements in the manufacture, an immense increase of consumption may be concomitant with, and probably, in a great degree, the result of, a great fall in price.

' The same principle, it is true, applies to the capital and business of the farmer; but with this important distinction, that the price of corn, taken for any series of years, is necessarily regulated by the expense of production upon the lands which, at that price, make no return beyond the charge of raising it, together with the ordinary profit of the capital employed upon those lands. The cultivator of such lands, for the time, is upon a footing with the merchant and the manufacturer; but if the demand *for corn were doubled* it would force into cultivation poorer lands, requiring a larger capital to raise the same quantity of produce; the price of that produce would determine the price of the whole, or those poorer lands could not be maintained in cultivation; for there cannot permanently be two rates of profit in the same occupation. It is sufficient for your Committee to point out this ground of difference, and to leave it to the judgment of the House, in connection with the observations which they have already submitted in a former part of this Report.'—p. 48, 49.

We think that the argument which the Committee mean to employ is this;—that if the effect of the monopoly were, by confining the operation of the whole demand for any manufactured article within the home market, to make it more intense in that market, yet that the influx of capital into that manufacture, which the competition of capitalists would occasion, would create a proportionate increase of supply, and prevent the price from rising;
but

but that an increased demand for corn in the home market must be met by an increase of supply, raised from poorer lands at a greater expense, and, on their principle, that the corn raised at the greatest expense regulates the price of the whole, occasioning, as to the whole quantity raised, an increase of price.

Without attempting to separate the truth and falsehood, which are so blended in the last argument, we will mention an answer to the prayer of the petitioners, which appears to us more satisfactory than any, except the first, of those used by the Committee : it is, that, supposing the protection intended to be afforded to one branch of our manufacturing industry to be effectual, it can be so only by being injurious to another. As foreigners will not give us their goods for nothing, the prohibition of the importation of foreign silk is a prohibition of the exportation of those articles of home production which must have been exported to obtain the silk, either in direct exchange, or in exchange for the bullion, or other commodities, for which the silk *was* directly exchanged. And as all interference renders the application of capital less profitable, the general result of our protecting duties upon our manufacturers must be injurious—and must tend to diminish their power, and certainly not to increase their obligation, to pay more for their subsistence.

The Committee lastly consider, p. 50. the objections of the petitioners against the warehousing system ;—1st. as employing in the foreign, capitals which would be employed in the British, corntrade; and 2dly, as depressing the market, by the notoriety that large quantities of foreign corn are already in the country ready to be poured in, when the price rises to 80s. The Committee answer, very sensibly, to the first objection, that they see no reason for supposing either that the capital engaged in the foreign corn-trade is large, or that any part of that capital is withdrawn from the British trade. And to the second, that whatever depression is produced by the accumulation in English warehouses, would be produced by an accumulation in Dutch, with this difference only, that the British grower would not have equally accurate information to guide his proceedings. And they add that the correspondence of this system with our general practice, the security it affords against the aggravation of our wants by foreign states, and the commercial advantages which it may afford, are sufficient reasons for not abandoning it, without further proof of its prejudicial effects on agriculture. They add' that the supposition, that it has afforded a means for the fraudulent introduction of foreign corn into home consumption, appears (except to an inconsiderable, if any, extent) to be without foundation.

This is the last topic considered by the Committee. They end their Report with the following observations, with which, as they express in better language our own feelings and sentiments, we, too, shall conclude :—

' Instead of expressing doubts with respect to the remedies which have been suggested by others, it would have been far more satisfactory to your Committee, to have been enabled to conclude their labours by pointing out some immediate measure of alleviation, which would have been efficacious at once to mitigate the distress, and to allay the alarm which prevail among the agricultural classes of the community.

' If such an expedient could have been found, even in a temporary departure from any sound and recognized principle of general policy on this subject, or in any modification of the existing law which could now be attempted, they might have been disposed to submit it to the favourable consideration of the House; but when, after a long and anxious inquiry, they have not been able to discover any means, which, in their estimation, are calculated immediately to remove the present pressure, they know too well their own duty to the House, and feel too much respect for the manly character of that class of the community whose difficulties have been the object of their investigation, either to attempt to disguise the view which they have taken of the origin and nature of those difficulties, or to recommend that specific plan of relief pointed out by the suffering parties, which, however sanctioned by the arguments and prayer of their Petitions, appears to be founded in delusion, and likely therefore to lead only to disappointment.

' So far as the present depression in the markets of Agricultural produce is the effect of abundance from our own growth, the inconvenience arises from a cause which no legislative provision can alleviate ; so far as it is the result of the increased value of our money, it is one not peculiar to the farmer, but which has been and still is experienced by many other classes of society.'—p. 53.

' 'The difficulties, great as they are, in which it has involved the farming, the manufacturing and trading interests of the country, must diminish in proportion as contracts, prices, and labour, adjust themselves to the present value of money. That this change is now in progress, and has already taken place to a considerable degree, is in evidence before your Committee. They are satisfied that it will continue until that balance is restored, which will afford to labour its due remuneration, and to capital its fair return. And, although they deeply lament the derangement which the fluctuations of the last ten years in the value of the currency have occasioned in all the transactions of life, together with the individual loss and suffering unavoidably produced by the return to a fixed standard, they are satisfied that this was the only course which it was in the power of Parliament to adopt,—as well to prevent the continuance of a derangement, leading, as it must have led, to the aggravation of those losses and sufferings, as to manifest to the world the inflexible determination of this country, rigidly to adhere to that good faith of which the moral character of the people is the sure guardian, and which, with that character, has placed our greatness and our power upon the foundation, hitherto unshaken amidst all our vicissitudes, of public credit and national honour.'—p. 56.

ART.

# THREE LECTURES

ON THE

# RATE OF WAGES,

DELIVERED BEFORE THE UNIVERSITY OF OXFORD,
IN EASTER TERM 1830.

WITH A PREFACE

ON THE

CAUSES AND REMEDIES OF THE PRESENT
DISTURBANCES.

Bellique causas et vitia et modos
Tractas, et incedis per ignes
Suppositos cineri doloso.

By NASSAU WILLIAM SENIOR,

OF MAGDALEN COLLEGE, A. M.;
LATE PROFESSOR OF POLITICAL ECONOMY.

*THE SECOND EDITION.*

LONDON:
JOHN MURRAY, ALBEMARLE-STREET.
MDCCCXXXI.

LONDON:
PRINTED BY WILLIAM CLOWES,
Stamford Street.

# PREFACE.

THE following Lectures contain little that is not well known to many of my readers, and still less that is peculiarly and exclusively appropriate to the present emergency. They were written and delivered in a period of profound tranquillity ; but we are now in a state which may require the exertions of every individual among the educated classes, and many may have to assist in executing, or even in originating measures for the relief of the labouring population, who are not yet sufficiently familiar with the principles according to which that relief is to be afforded.

Under such circumstances, it has appeared to me that advantage might be derived from a short explanation of the ambiguities and fallacies which most obscure the subject of wages—the most difficult and the most important of all the branches of political economy.

My principal object, however, has been to draw attention to the elementary proposition, that *the rate of wages depends on the extent of the fund for the maintenance of labourers, compared with the number of labourers to be maintained.* This proposition is so nearly self-evident, that it may appear scarcely to deserve a formal statement ; still less to be dwelt on as if it were a discovery. It is true that it is obvious and trite; but, perhaps, on that very account, its practical consequences have been neglected. In the first place, if this proposition be admitted, many prevalent opinions respecting the effects of unproductive consumption, of machinery, and of free-trade, must be abandoned ; and to show this, is the object of the second and third of the following Lectures. And in the second place, it must also follow that the rate of wages can be raised, or, what is nearly the same, the condition of the labouring classes improved, only by either increasing the fund for their maintenance, or diminishing the number to be maintained.

The principal means by which the fund for the maintenance of labourers can be increased, is by increasing the productiveness of labour. And this may be done,—

*First,* By allowing every man to exert himself in the way which, from experience, he finds most beneficial; by freeing industry from the mass of restrictions, prohibitions, and protecting duties, with which the Legislature, sometimes in well-meaning ignorance, sometimes in pity, and sometimes in national jealousy, has laboured to crush or misdirect her efforts ; and,

*Secondly*, By putting an end to that unhappy sys- tem which, in the southern counties, has dissociated labour from subsistence—has made wages not a matter of contract between the master and the work- man, but a right in the one, and a tax on the other ; and, by removing the motives for exertion, has ren- dered, as far as it has been possible, the labourer unworthy of his hire.

The only effectual and permanent means of pre- venting the undue increase of the number to be maintained, is to raise the moral and intellectual character of the labouring population ; to improve, or, I fear we must say, to create habits of prudence, of self-respect, and of self-restraint ; to equalize, as by nature they are equal, the wages of the single and the married, and no longer to make a family the passport to allowance. But these are necessarily gradual measures—they are preventive, not reme- dial. The only *immediate* remedy for an actual ex- cess in one class of the population, is the ancient and approved one, *coloniam deducere*.

It is of great importance to keep in mind, that not only is emigration the sole immediate remedy, but that it is a remedy preparatory to the adoption and necessary to the safety of every other.

The principal cause of the calamities that we are witnessing, has been the disturbance which the

poor-laws, as at present administered in the south
of England, have created in the most extensive and
the most important of all political relations, the relation between the employer and the labourer.

The slave (using that word in its strict sense)
cannot choose his owner, his employment, or his
residence ; his whole services are the property of
another, and their value, however high, gives him
no additional claim.  On the other hand, he is
entitled to subsistence for himself and his family :
clothing, lodging, food, medical attendance—every-
thing, in short, which is necessary to keep him in
health and strength is provided for him, from the
same motives, and with the same liberality, that they
are provided for the other domestic animals of his
master.  He is *bound* to labour, and has a *right* to
be maintained.  Extreme idleness may subject him
to the lash, but extraordinary diligence cannot better
his condition.  He is equally incapable of being
benefited by self-restraint, or injured by improvidence.  While single, he receives a bare subsistence ; if he have a family, his maintenance rises in
precise proportion to his wants : the prudential
check to population does not exist—it is kept down,
if at all, by oppression on the part of the master, or
vice on that of the slave.  This, notwithstanding
the various degrees of mitigation which have been
introduced by custom or by law, is in substance the
condition of slaves, wherever slavery exists.

In such a country distress begins, not, as in the case of a free country, with the lower orders, but with the higher. A bad system, therefore, can continue there much longer, because the class affected have farther to fall; and, for the same reason, the ruin, when it does come, is sudden and irretrievable. While misgovernment, by excessive or ill-placed taxation, by commercial restrictions, by allowing insecurity of person or property, by applying any artificial stimulus to population, or under any other of its numerous forms, is gradually wasting the surplus that belongs to landlords and capitalists, the slave population may scarcely feel its effects. Subsistence is all they are entitled to, and *that* they must receive as long as their labour produces it. But the instant that surplus is gone, and distress reaches those whose previous maintenance was only equal to their necessities, what is there between them and absolute destruction? If the evils which have been so long accumulating in some of our West Indian islands had affected a free country, the whole population would, long ago, have risen to redress them. But as yet, they have reached only the slave-owner. He has found his property gradually wasting away; he has found that his slaves every year consume a larger and a larger proportion of what they produce; but even still he has something to lose: and while that is the case, *their* situation is unaffected. When the whole produce has

become only sufficient to feed the negroes,—a time
which, under the present system, is rapidly advancing
in some of the older islands,—the whites must abandon them as a field for all the moral and physical
evil that slaves, helpless by education and despe-
rate from want, will mutually suffer and inflict *.

The freeman (using that term in its full meaning)
is the master of his exertions, and of his residence.
He may refuse to quit the spot, or to change the
employment, in which his labour has become unprofitable. As he may refuse to labour at all, he
may ask for his services whatever remuneration he
thinks fit ; but as no one is bound to purchase those
services, and as no one is obliged to afford him food,
clothing, or any of the necessaries of life, he is
forced, if he would subsist, to follow the trade,
and dwell in the place, and exert the diligence
which will make his services worth purchasing ; and
he is forced to offer them for sale, by the same
necessity which forces the capitalist to offer him
wages in exchange for them. And the bargain is
settled, like all other free bargains, by the respective market values of the things exchanged. As
marriage has no tendency to increase the value of
his labour, it has no tendency to increase his remuneration. He defers it, therefore, till the savings
made while he was single afford a fund to meet the

---

* This is one of the modes in which slavery may be extinguished,
but it is a dreadful abuse of language to call it euthanasia.

expenses of a family; and population is kept down by the only check that is consistent with moral or physical welfare—the prudential check.

To this state of things there is a near approach among the labouring classes in the most advanced districts of the continent of Europe, in the lowlands of Scotland, and even throughout the British empire, among the best educated of those classes who derive their chief subsistence from their exertions, including professional persons, domestic servants, skilled artisans, and that portion of the shopkeepers whose profits are, in fact, principally the wages of their labour.

The poor-laws, as administered in the southern districts of England, are an attempt to unite the irreconcilable advantages of freedom and servitude. The labourer is to be a free agent, but without the hazards of free agency; to be free from the coercion, but to enjoy the assured subsistence of the slave. He is expected to be diligent, though he has no fear of want; provident, though his pay rises as his family increases; attached to a master who employs him in pursuance of a vestry resolution; and grateful for the allowance which the magistrates order him as a right.

In the natural state of the relation between the capitalist and the labourer, when the amount of wages to be paid, and of work to be done, are the subjects of a free and open bargain; when the labourer obtains, and knows that he is to obtain just what his services are worth to his employer, he must feel any fall in the price of his labour to be an evil, but is not likely to complain of it as an injustice. Greater exertion and severer economy are his first resources in distress ; and what they cannot supply, he receives with gratitude from the benevolent. The connexion between him and his master has the kindliness of a voluntary association, in which each party is conscious of benefit, and each feels that his own welfare depends, to a certain extent, on the welfare of the other. But the instant wages cease to be a bargain—the instant the labourer is paid, not according to his *value*, but his *wants*, he ceases to be a freeman. He acquires the indolence, the improvidence, the rapacity, and the malignity, but not the subordination of a slave. He is told that he has a *right* to wages, but that he is *bound* to work. Who is to decide how hard he ought to work, or how hard he does work? Who is to decide what amount of wages he has a *right* to? As yet, the decision has been made by the overseers and the magistrates. But they were interested parties. The labourer has thought fit to correct that decision. For the present he thinks that he has a *right* to 2*s*. 3*d*. a day in winter, and 2*s*. 6*d*. in summer. And our only hope seems to be, that the promise of such wages will bribe him into quiet. But who can doubt that he will measure his rights by his wishes,

or that his wishes will extend with the prospect of
their gratification ?   The present tide may not complete the inundation, but it will be a dreadful error
if we mistake the ebb for a permanent receding of
the waters.   A breach has been made in the sea-
wall, and with every succeeding irruption they will
swell higher and spread more widely.   What we are
suffering is nothing to what we have to expect.
Next year, perhaps, the labourer will think it *unjust*
that he should have less than 4*s*. a day in winter, and
5*s*. in summer;—and woe to the tyrants who deny
him his *right!*

It is true, that such a right could not be permanently enforced;—it is true, that if the labourer
burns the corn-ricks in which his subsistence for
the current year is stored—if he consumes in idleness or in riot the time and the exertions on which
next year's harvest depends—if he wastes in extravagant wages, or drives to foreign countries, the
capital that is to assist and render productive his
labour, *he* will be the greatest sufferer in the common ruin.   Those who have property may escape
with a portion of it to some country in which *their
rights* will be protected; but the labourer must
remain to enjoy his own works—to feel that the
real rewards for plunder and devastation are want
and disease.

But have the consequences of the present system ever been explained to the labourer?   Is not

his right to good wages re-echoed from all parts of
the country? Is he not told—' Dwell in the land,
and verily thou shalt be fed?' Does not the Honourable Member who has affixed this motto to
his work, assume, that the fund out of which the
labourer is to be fed is practically inexhaustible?
And can words more strongly imply that his sufferings arise from the *injustice* of his superiors?
Have not even magistrates and landlords recommended the destruction, or, what is the same, both in
principle and effect, the disuse of the very machines
of which the object is to render labour more efficient
in the production of the articles consumed by the
labourer—in the production of that very fund on
the extent of which, compared with the number to
be maintained, the amount of wages depends? And
is there any real difference between this conduct and
the burning of a rick-yard? Threshing-machines
are the present objects of hostility, ploughs will
be the next; spades will then be found to diminish
employment; and when it has been made penal to
give advantage to labour by any tool or instrument
whatever, the last step must be to prohibit the use
of the right-hand.

Have sufficient pains been taken even to expose
the absurdity of what appears so obvious to the po-
pulace—that the landlords ought to reduce their
rents and the clergy their tithes, and then the farmer
would give better wages? If the farmer had his

land for nothing, still it would not be his interest to
give any man more wages for a day's work than his
day's work was worth. He could better *afford* it,
no doubt, to be paid as a *tax;* but why should the
farmer pay that tax more than the physician or the
shopkeeper? If the farmer is to employ, at this
advanced rate of wages, only whom he chooses, the
distress will be increased, since he will employ only
that smaller number whose labour is worth their
increased pay. If he is to employ a certain proportion of the labourers, however numerous, in his
parish, he is, in fact, to pay rent and tithes as
before, with this difference only, that they are to be
paid to paupers, instead of to the landlord and the
parson ; and that the payment is not a fixed but an
indefinite sum, and a sum which must every year
increase in an accelerated ratio, as the increase
of population rushes to fill up this new vacuum, till
rent, tithes, profit, and capital, are all eaten up,
and pauperism produces what may be called its
natural effects—for they are the effects which, if un-
checked, it must ultimately produce—famine, pestilence, and civil war.

That this country can preserve its prosperity, or
even its social existence, if the state of feeling
which I have described becomes universal among
the lower classes, I think no one will be bold
enough to maintain. That it is extensively prevalent, and that, under the present administration of

the poor-laws, it *will*, at no remote period, become universal in the southern districts, appears to me to be equally clear. But who, in the present state of those districts, will venture to carry into execution a real and effectual alteration of the poor-laws? Remove, by emigration, the pauperism that now oppresses those districts, and such an alteration, though it may remain difficult, will cease to be impracticable.

Again, the corn-laws, by their tendency to raise the price of subsistence, by the ruin which they have inflicted on the internal corn-trade, and the stimulus which they have given to the increase of the agricultural population, have without doubt been amongst the causes of the present distress ; and if, while the population of England and Wales continues to increase *at the rate of* 500 *persons a day*, the introduction of foreign corn is subject, under ordinary prices, to a prohibitive duty, those laws will become every day more mischievous, and less remediable. But the repeal of those laws, however gradual (and only a gradual repeal can be thought of), would, under the present pressure of pauperism, tend to aggravate the agricultural distress. Lighten that pressure, and we may gradually revert to the only safe system—the system of freedom.

This observation, indeed, is only one example of a general rule. Nature has decreed that the road to good shall be through evil—that no improvement

shall take place in which the general advantage shall
not be accompanied by partial suffering. The obvious remedy is to remove those whose labour has
ceased to be profitable, to a country that will afford
room for their exertions. Few inventions, during
the present century, have conferred greater benefits
on the labouring classes than that of the power-loom.
By diminishing the expense of clothing, it has been
a source, not merely of comfort, but of health and
longevity. But its proximate effect was to spread
ruin among the hand-weavers ; to reduce almost all
of them to a mere subsistence, and many to the
most abject want. Ever since its introduction,
thousands have been pining away under misery, not
alleviated even by hope ; with no rational expectation, but that the ensuing year would be more
calamitous than the passing one : and this without
fault, without even improvidence. If it had been
thought that the removal of a fellow-creature from
misery to happiness is worth 12*l.*, they might now
have formed a flourishing settlement in British
America.

The hostility of many, coupled with the indifference of almost all others, to any systematic plan of
emigration, is a ground for regret and alarm, considered not only as a cause, but as a symptom. It
is a lamentable proof of ignorance as to the real
state of the country, or of carelessness as to its welfare, or of a determination to make no sacrifice for
its relief.

We are told that emigration would be expensive, and again we are told that the vacuum would be filled up.

It is true, that to remove a million of persons might, perhaps, cost 12,000,000*l.* sterling; that is to say, might cost as much as the direct expenditure of THREE MONTHS' WAR ; and that an expenditure of 12,000,000*l.* sterling is an evil. But in the first place, it has been demonstrated * that the expense of keeping paupers at home is far greater than that of their removal. It may be necessary to repeat, though it has often been remarked before, that the relief is afforded not only to those individuals who emigrate, but to the much greater number who remain. If there are 450 labourers in a district which requires the full employment, and affords the full subsistence of only 400, all, or nearly all, will be in distress, and by the emigration of fifty all will be relieved. And, in the second place, even if the balance of expense were on the side of removing a portion of our surplus population, is no expense beyond that of their mere keep to be feared from their presence? If the present insurrection spread (and it will spread if the peasantry are told, as practically they have been told, that for riot and rebel-

---

* See Mr. Wilmot Horton's ' Causes and Remedies of Pauperism, fourth series.

Hic etiam fatis aperit Cassandra futuris
Ora Dei jussu non unquam credita Teucris.

lion three days' imprisonment is the punishment, and
a rise of wages the REWARD); if the ravage of the
country reacts, as it will react, on the towns; if,
when trade begins to languish, the master manufacturers, according to their late practice, dismiss their
workmen, and the manufacturing workmen, in their
turn, d stroy machinery; if the foundations, not
merely of our wealth, but of our existence, are thus
impaired, will twelve millions, or twenty millions, or
even a hundred millions sterling represent the loss?

It is true, that if we adopt no preventive measures, if we persist blindly in our course of error,
the temporary relief afforded by emigration will
come to an end, and the vacuum will, in sixteen or
seventeen years, be filled up. But is it certain that
we shall not profit by experience? Have we a right,
or, rather, are we compelled, to assume, as a link in
the argument, that we and our successors must be
madmen? If a man has been outrunning his income,
is it quite certain that we can do him no good by
paying his debts, on the ground that *if he goes on*
in the same thoughtless expenditure, he will again
be involved as deeply as ever? And even granting
that the vacuum will be filled up, will it be nothing
to have obtained sixteen years' respite?—to have
weathered the existing storm?—to have adjourned
the crisis to a period which may be more favourable,
and cannot possibly be less so?

We are told that the labourers form the strength

of the country, and that to diminish their number is to incur voluntary feebleness. But does the pauper, —the man whose labour is not worth his subsistence, who consumes more than he produces,—does he add to the strength of the country? When I hear such remarks, I fancy myself standing by the bedside of an apoplectic patient, and hearing the nurse and the friends prohibit the lancet. ' The blood,' says one, ' is the support of life : how can you think of dimi- ' nishing it in his present state of weakness ?' ' If ' you do diminish it,' cries out another, ' with his ' habits of free living, it will be renewed ; in a year ' the vacuum will be filled up.' But is it impossible that the blood can be in excess ? Is it certain that his habits are unchangeable ? Shall we let him die now, lest we should have to bleed him again a year hence ?

It will be observed, that I have assumed that the paupers are willing to emigrate. That they have been so as yet, is unquestionable : I hope, I had almost said I trust, that they still continue to be so. But if they are allowed to fix the labour they are to give, and the wages they are to receive ; if they are to help themselves, while it lasts, from the whole property of the country, it is too much to expect that they will not prefer idleness, riot, and plunder at home, to subsistence, however ample, to be earned by toil and hardship abroad. But this only shows the danger, the madness of delay. While we are

deliberating, or even before we have begun to de-
liberate, the moment for applying the remedy is
passing away.

Hitherto, it has been common to defend every
existing practice as agreeable to common sense, in
opposition to the visionary schemes of political
theorists ; to plead experience in behalf of every-
thing that has long prevailed, and to deprecate new
experiments. It is high time that those who profess to venerate experience should now, at length,
show that they can learn from it. To what has
common prejudice, reigning under the title of common sense, brought us? Have the *practical* men
who have hitherto administered our system of poor-
laws saved us from being brought to the very brink
of ruin? Or have they suggested any effectual
means for stopping our downward career? Surely
common sense, if there be any such thing in the
country, will now, at last, bear witness to the truth
of Bacon's maxim, that ' he who dreads new reme-
' dies, must expect new evils ! '

*Lincoln's Inn, December* 3, 1830.

# LECTURE I.

## DEFINITION OF HIGH AND LOW WAGES.

THE labourers form the mass of every community. The inquiry into the causes affecting wages is, therefore, the most important branch of political economy. In the following Lectures I propose, first, to explain some ambiguities in the terms high and low wages ; secondly, to state the proximate cause which regulates the amount of wages; and, lastly, to expose some prevalent errors respecting that cause; leaving the remoter causes, the causes of the proximate cause, for discussion in a subsequent course.

Wages are the remuneration received by the labourer in recompense for having exerted his faculties of mind and body; and they are termed high or low, in proportion to the extent of that remuneration. That extent has been estimated by three different measures ; and the words high and low wages have, consequently, been used in three different senses.

*First.* Wages have been termed high or low, according to the amount of *money* earned by the labourer within a given period, without any reference to the commodities which that money would purchase ; as when we say that wages have *risen* since the reign of Henry VII., because the labourer now receives 1*s*. 6*d*. or 2*s*. a day, and then received only 4½*d*.

*Secondly.* They have been termed high or low, according to the *quantity and quality of the commodities* obtained by the labourer, without any reference to his receipts in money ; as when we say that wages have *fallen* since the reign of Henry VII., because the labourer then earned two pecks of wheat a day, and now earns only one.

*Thirdly.* They have been termed high or low, according to the share or proportion which the labourer receives of the produce of his own labour, without any reference to the total amount of that produce.

The first nomenclature, that which measures wages simply by their amount in money, is the popular one. The second, that which considers wages simply with reference to the quantity and quality of the commodities received by the labourer, or to speak more correctly, purchaseable with his money wages, was that generally adopted by Adam Smith. The third, that which considers wages as high or low, simply with reference to the labourer's share or proportion of what he produces, was introduced by Mr. Ricardo, and has been continued by many of his followers.

This last use of the words high and low wages has always appeared to me one of the most unfortunate of Mr. Ricardo's many innovations in the language of political economy. In the first place, it has a tendency to withdraw our attention, even when we are considering the subject of wages, from the facts which most influence the labourer's condition. To ascertain whether his wages are high or low, we are desired to inquire, not whether he is ill or well paid,—not whether he is well or ill fed, or clothed, or lodged, or warmed, but simply what proportion of what he produces comes to his share. During the last four or five years, many a hand-weaver has received only 8s. 3d. for producing, by a fortnight's exertion, a web that the capitalist has sold for 8s. 4d. A coal-merchant often pays his men two guineas a week, and charges his employers for their services two guineas and a half. But, according to Mr. Ricardo's nomenclature, the wages of the weaver, at 4s. 1½d. a week, are much higher than those of the coal-heaver at two guineas, since the weaver receives 99 per

cent. of the value of his labour, while the coal-
heaver had only 80 per cent.

And, even if the nomenclature in question
were free from this objection—even if the point
on which it endeavours to fix the attention were
the most important, instead of being the least
important incident to wages, it still would be
inconvenient from its obscurity. No writer can
hope to be consistent in the use of familiar
words in a sense always different from their
established meaning, and often directly opposed
to it; still less can he hope to be always understood. Even Mr. Ricardo, though he professes
to mean by high wages a *great proportion*, has in
several places considered them as productive of
consequences which would follow only if they
signified a *great amount*. And his followers and
opponents have, almost uniformly, supposed
those words to mean a great amount. Since the
publication of Mr. Ricardo's work, it has been
received as an axiom, among the dabblers in
political economy, that, according to the established doctrines of the science, high wages and
high profits are incompatible ; and, therefore,
that either the leading doctrines of political
economy are false, or the interests of the labourer and the capitalist are always directly
opposed to one another. The former opinion
has been adopted by the large class who do

not attend to what they read ; the latter, by
the still larger class who do not attend to what
they see.

The two other meanings of the words high
and low wages, that which refers to the money,
and that which refers to the commodities, received by the labourer, are both equally convenient, if we consider the rate of wages *at the
same time and place ;* for then they both mean the
same thing. At the same time and place, the
labourer who receives the highest wages necessarily receives the most commodities. But
when we refer to different places, or different
times, the words high or low wages direct the
attention to very different subjects, as we understand them to mean more or less in money, or
more or less in commodities. The differences
which have taken place in the amount of money
wages at different times, inform us of scarcely
any thing but the abundance or scarcity of the
precious metals at those times : facts which are
seldom of much importance. The differences
in the amount of money wages in different
places at the same time, are of much more importance, since they indicate the different values
of the labour of different countries in the general market of the world. But even these differences afford no premises, from which the positive condition of the labouring classes, in any

country, can be inferred, and but imperfect grounds for estimating their relative condition. The only data which enable us to ascertain the actual situation of the labourers at any given time and place, or their comparative situation at different times and places, are the quantity and quality of the commodities which form their wages, if paid in kind, or are purchaseable with their wages, if paid in money. And as the actual or comparative situation of the labourer is the principal object of the following inquiry, I shall use the word wages, to express, not the money, but the commodities, which the labourer receives ; and I shall consider wages to rise as the quantity or quality of those commodities is increased or improved, and to fall as that quantity or quality is diminished or deteriorated.

It is obvious, too, that the labourer's situation does not depend on the amount which he receives at any one time, but on his average receipts during a given period—during a week, a month, or a year ; and that the longer the period taken, the more accurate will be the estimate. Weekly wages have, of course, more tendency to equality than daily ones, and annual than monthly ; and, if we could ascertain the amount earned by a man during five, or ten, or twenty years, we should know his situation better than if we confined our attention to a single year. There is, however, so much difficulty in ascertaining the amount of wages during very long periods, that, I think, a single year will be the best that we can take. It comprehends what, in most climates, are very different, summer and winter wages; it comprehends also the period during which the most important vegetable productions come to maturity in temperate climates, and on that account has generally been adopted by political economists as the average period for which capital is supposed to be advanced.

I should observe, that I include, as part of the wages of the married labourer, those of his wife and unemancipated children. To omit them would lead to inaccurate estimates of the comparative situation of the labourers in different countries, or in different occupations. In those employments which are carried on under shelter, and with the assistance of that machinery which affords power, and requires human aid only for its direction, the industry of a woman, or a child, approaches in efficiency to that of a full-grown man. A girl of fourteen can manage a power-loom nearly as well as her father; but where strength, or exposure to the seasons, are required, little can be done by the wife, or the girls, or even by the boys, until

they approach the age at which they usually
quit their father's house. The earnings of the
wife and children of many a Manchester weaver
or spinner exceed, or equal, those of himself.
Those of the wife and children of an agricultural labourer, or of a carpenter, or a coal-
heaver, are generally unimportant—while the
husband, in each case, receive 15s. a week;
the weekly income of the one family may be
30s., and that of the other only 17s. or 18s.

It must be admitted, however, that the workman does not retain the whole of this apparent
pecuniary advantage. The wife is taken from
her household labours, and a part of the increased wages is employed in purchasing what
might, otherwise, be produced at home. The
moral inconveniences are still greater. The
infant children suffer from the want of mater-
nal attention, and those who are older from the
deficiency of religious, moral, and intellectual
education, and childish relaxation and amuse-
ment. The establishment of infant and Sunday schools, and laws regulating the number of
hours during which children may labour, are
palliatives of these evils, but they must exist, to
a certain degree, whenever the labour of the
wife and children is the subject of sale; and,
though not, perhaps, strictly within the province
of political economy, must never be omitted in

any estimate of the causes affecting the welfare of the labouring classes.

The last preliminary point to which I have to call your attention is, the difference between the *rate of wages* and *the price of labour*.

If men were the only labourers, and if every man worked equally hard, and for the same number of hours, during the year, these two expressions would be synonymous. If each man, for instance, worked three hundred days during each year, and ten hours during each day, one-three-thousandth part of each man's yearly wages would be the price of an hour's labour. But neither of these propositions is true. The yearly wages of a family often include, as we have seen, the results of the labour of the wife and children. And few things are less uniform than the number of working days during the year, or of working hours during the day, or the degree of exertion undergone during those hours.

The established annual holidays in Protestant countries, are between fifty and sixty. In many Catholic countries they exceed one hundred. Among the Hindoos, they are said to occupy nearly half the year. But these holidays are confined to a certain portion of the population ; the labour of a sailor, or a soldier, or a menial servant, admits of scarcely any distinction of days.

Again, in northern and southern latitudes, the hours of out-door labour are limited by the duration of light; and in all climates by the weather. When the labourer works under shelter, the daily hours of labour may be uniform throughout the year. And, independently of natural causes, the daily hours of labour vary in different countries, and in different employments in the same country. The daily hours of labour are, perhaps, longer in France than in England, and, certainly, are longer in England than in Hindostan. In Manchester, the manufacturer generally works twelve hours a day; in Birmingham, ten: a London shopman is seldom employed more than eight or nine.

There is still more discrepancy between the exertions made by different labours in a given period. They are often, indeed, unsusceptible of comparison. There is no common measure of the toils undergone by a miner and a tailor, or of those of a shopman and an ironfounder. And labour which is the same in kind, may vary indefinitely in intensity. Many of the witnesses examined by the Committee on Artisans and Machinery (Session of 1824) were English manufacturers, who had worked in France. They agree as to the comparative indolence of the French labourer, even during

his hours of employment. One of the witnesses, Adam Young, had been two years in
one of the best manufactories in Alsace. He is
asked, ' Did you find the spinners there as
industrious as the spinners in England?' and
replies, ' No; a spinner in England will do
twice as much as a Frenchman. They get up
at four in the morning, and work till ten at
night; but our spinners will do as much in six
hours as they will in ten.'

' Had you any Frenchmen employed under
you?'—' Yes; eight, at two francs a day.'

' What had you a day?'—' Twelve francs.'

' Supposing you had had eight English carders under you, how much more work could
you have done?'—' With one Englishman, I
could have done more than I did with those
eight Frenchmen. It cannot be called work
they do : it is only looking at it, and wishing it
done.'

' Do the French make their yarn at a greater
expense?'—' Yes; though they have their
hands for much less wages than in England.'
—pp. 580, 582.

Even in the same country, and in the same
employments, similar inequalities are constantly
observed. Every one is aware that much more
exertion is undergone by the labourer by task-
work than by the day-labourer; by the inde-

pendent day-labourer than by the pauper; and
even by the pauper than by the convict.

It is obvious that the rate of wages is less
likely to be uniform than the price of labour, as
the amount of wages will be affected, in the first
place, by any variations in the price, and, in
the second place, by any variations in the
amount, of the labour exerted.

The average annual wages of labour in England, are three times as high as in Ireland; but
as the labourer in Ireland is said not to do more
than one-third of what is done by the labourer
in England, the price of labour may, in both
countries, be about equal.   In England, the
labourer by task-work earns much more than
the day-labourer; but as it is certainly as profitable to employ him, the price of his labour
cannot be higher.   It may be supposed, indeed,
that the price of labour is everywhere, and at
all times, the same; and, if there were no disturbing causes,—if all persons knew perfectly
well their own interest, and strictly followed it,
and there were no difficulties in moving capital
and labour from place to place, and from employment to employment,—the price of labour,
at the same time, *would* be everywhere the same.
But these difficulties occasion the price of
labour to vary materially, even at the same time
and place; and variations, both in the amount

of wages and in the price of labour at different times, and in different places, are occasioned, not only by these causes, but by others which will be considered in a subsequent course.

These variations affect very differently the labourer and his employer. The employer is interested in keeping down the price of labour; but while that price remains the same, while at a given expense he gets a given amount of work done, his situation remains unaltered. If a farmer can get a field trenched for 12*l*. it is indifferent to him whether he pays the whole of that sum to three capital workmen, or to four ordinary ones. The three would receive higher wages than the four, but as they would do proportionably more work, their labour would come just as cheap. If the three could be hired at 3*l*. 10*s*. a-piece, while the four required 3*l*. a-piece, though the wages of the three would be higher, the price of the work done by them would be lower.

It is true that the causes which raise the amount of the labourer's wages often raise the rate of the capitalist's profits. If, by increased industry, one man performs the work of two, both the amount of wages and the rate of profits will generally be raised. But the rate of profit will be raised, not by the rise of wages, but in consequence of the additional supply of labour having diminished its price, or having diminished the period for which it had previously been necessary to advance that price.

The labourer, on the other hand, is principally interested in the amount of wages. The amount of his wages being given, it is certainly his interest that the price of his labour should be high, for on that depends the degree of exertion imposed on him. But if the amount of his wages be low, he must be comparatively poor, if that amount be high, he must be comparatively rich, whatever be his remuneration for each specific act of exertion. In the one case he will have leisure and want,—in the other, toil and abundance. I am far from thinking that the evils of severe and incessant labour, or the benefits of a certain degree of leisure, ought to be left out in any estimate of happiness. But it is not with happiness, but with wealth, that I am concerned as a political economist ; and I am not only justified in omitting, but, perhaps, am bound to omit, all considerations which have no influence on wealth. In fact, however, wealth and happiness are very seldom opposed. Nature, when she imposed on man the necessity of labour, tempered his repugnance to it by making long-continued inactivity painful, and by strongly associating with exertion the idea of its reward. The poor and half-employed Irish labourer, or the still poorer and less industrious savage, is as inferior in happiness as he is in income to the hardworked English artisan. The Englishman's industry may sometimes be excessive, his desire to better his condition may sometimes drive him on toils productive of disease ill recompensed by the increase of his wages, but that such is not generally the case may be proved by comparing the present duration of life in England with its former duration, or with its duration in other countries. It is generally admitted, that during the last fifty years, a marked increase has taken place in the industry of our manufacturing population, and that they are now the hardest working labourers in the world. But during the whole of that period the average duration of their lives has been constantly increasing, and appears still to increase: and notwithstanding the apparent unhealthiness of many of their occupations, notwithstanding the atmosphere of smoke and steam in which they labour for seventy-two hours a week, they enjoy longer life than the lightly-toiled inhabitants of the most favoured soils and climates. The average mortality among savage nations is the greatest that is known. In the continent of Europe it is about one in thirty-four. In England, about a century ago, when more than half of our population was agricultural, it was supposed to be one in thirty ; fifty years ago it was calculated at one in forty ; thirty years ago at one in forty-seven ; twenty years ago at one in fifty-two.  Now, when two-thirds of our labourers are manufacturers, and more than one-third dwell in cities, it is estimated at one in fifty-eight.

# LECTURE II.

## POPULAR ERRORS ON THE CAUSES AFFECTING WAGES.

HAVING in the last Lecture marked the distinction which really exists between the price of labour and the amount of wages, I shall for the future consider every labouring family as consisting of the same number of persons, and exerting the same degree of industry. On that supposition, the distinction between the price of labour and the amount of wages will be at an end ; or rather, the only distinction will be, that the former expression designates the remuneration for each specific exertion : the latter, the aggregate of all those separate remunerations, as summed up at the end of each year. And the question to be answered will be, what are the causes which decide what in any given country, and at any given period, shall be the quantity and quality of the commodities obtained by a labouring family during a year? The proximate cause appears to me to be clear. The quantity and quality of the commodities obtained by each labouring family during a year, must depend on the quantity and quality of the commodities directly or indirectly appropriated during the year to the use of the labouring population, compared with the number of labouring families (including under that term all those who depend on their own labour for subsistence); or, to speak more concisely, on the extent of the fund for the maintenance of labourers, compared with the number of labourers to be maintained. This proposition is so nearly self-evident, that if political economy were a new science, I should assume it without further remark. But I must warn you, that this proposition is inconsistent with opinions which are entitled to consideration, some from the number, and others from the authority of those who maintain them.

*First.* It is inconsistent with the doctrine, that the rate of wages depends on the proportion which the number of labourers bears to the amount of *capital* in a country. The word capital has been used in so many senses, that it is difficult to state this doctrine precisely; but I know of no definition of that term which will not include many things that are not used by the labouring classes; and if my proposition be correct, no increase or diminution of *these* things can directly affect wages. If a foreign merchant were to come to settle in this country, and bring with him a cargo of raw and manufactured silk, lace, and diamonds, that cargo would increase the capital of the country; silks, lace, and diamonds, would become more abundant, and the enjoyments of those who use them would be increased; but the enjoyments of the labourers would not be directly increased : indirectly, and consequentially, they might be increased. The silk might be re-exported in a manufactured state, and commodities for the use of labourers imported in return ; and then, and not till then, wages would rise; but that rise would be occasioned, not by the first addition to the capital of the country, which was made in the form of silk, but by the substituted addition made in the form of commodities used by the labourer.

*Secondly.* It is inconsistent with the doctrine, that wages depend on the proportion borne by the number of labourers to the *revenue* of the society of which they are members. In the example last suggested, of the introduction of a new supply of lace or diamonds, the *revenues* of those who use lace or diamonds would be increased ; but as wages are not spent on those articles, *they* would remain unaltered. It is possible, indeed, to state cases in which the revenue of a large portion of a community might be increased, and yet the wages of the labourers might fall without an increase of their numbers. I will suppose the principal trade of Ireland to be the raising produce for the English market ; and that for every two hundred acres ten families were employed in raising, on half the land, their own subsistence, and on the remainder corn and other exportable crops requiring equal labour. Under such circumstances, if a demand should arise in the English market for cattle, butchers'-meat, and wool, instead of corn, it would be the interest of the Irish landlords and farmers to convert their estates from arable into pasture. Instead of ten families for every two hundred acres, two might be sufficient: one to raise the subsistence of the two, and the other to tend the cattle and sheep. The revenue of the landlords and the farmers would be increased, but a large portion of the labourers would be thrown out of employment ; a large portion of the land formerly employed in producing commodities for their use would be devoted to the production of commodities for the use of England ; and the fund for the maintenance of Irish labour would fall, notwithstanding the increase of the revenue of the landlords and farmers.

*Thirdly.* It is inconsistent with the prevalent

opinion, that the non-residence of landlords, funded proprietors, mortgagees, and other unproductive consumers, can be detrimental to the labouring inhabitants of a country *that does not export raw produce.*

In a country which exports raw produce, wages may be lowered by such non-residence. If an Irish landlord resides on his estate, he requires the services of certain persons, who must also be resident there, to minister to his daily wants. He must have servants, gardeners, and perhaps gamekeepers. If he build a house, he must employ resident masons and carpenters; part of his furniture he may import, but the greater part of it must be made in his neighbourhood ; a portion of his land, or, what comes to the same thing, a portion of his rent, must be employed in producing food, clothing, and shelter for all these persons, and for those who produce that food, clothing and shelter. If he were to remove to England, all these wants would be supplied by Englishmen. The land and capital which was formerly employed in providing the maintenance of Irish labourers, would be employed in producing corn and cattle to be exported to England to provide the subsistence of English labourers. The whole quantity of commodities appropriated to the use of Irish labourers would be diminished, and that appropriated to the use of English labourers increased, and wages would, consequently, rise in England, and fall in Ireland.

It is true that these effects would not be co-extensive with the landlord's income. While, in Ireland, he must have consumed many foreign commodities. He must have purchased tea, wine, and sugar, and other things which the climate and the manufactures of Ireland do not afford, and he must have paid for them by sending corn and cattle to England. It is true, also, that while in Ireland he probably employed a portion of his land and of his rents for other purposes, from which the labouring population received no benefit, as a deer park, or a pleasure garden, or in the maintenance of horses or hounds. On his removal, that portion of his land which was a park would be employed, partly in producing exportable commodities, and partly in producing subsistence for its cultivators ; and that portion which fed horses for his use might be employed in feeding horses for exportation. The first of these alterations would do good ; the second could do no harm. Nor must we forget that, through the cheapness of conveyance between England and Ireland, a portion, or perhaps all, of those whom he employed in Ireland might follow him to England

and, in that case, wages in neither country would be affected. The fund for the maintenance of labourers in Ireland, and the number of labourers to be maintained, would both be equally diminished, and the fund for the maintenance of labourers in England, and the number of labourers to be maintained, would both be equally increased.

But after making all these deductions, and they are very great, from the supposed effect of the absenteeism of the Irish proprietors on the labouring classes in Ireland, I cannot agree with Mr. M'Culloch that it is immaterial. I cannot but join in the general opinion that their return, though it would not affect the prosperity of the British empire, considered as a whole, would be immediately beneficial to Ireland, though perhaps too much importance is attached to it.

In Mr. M'Culloch's celebrated examination before the committee on the state of Ireland, (4th Report, 814, Sess. 1825,) he was asked, ' Supposing the largest export of Ireland were ' in live cattle, and that a considerable portion ' of rent had been remitted in that manner, does ' not such a mode of producing the means of ' paying rent contribute less to the improve- ' ment of the poor than any extensive employ- ' ment of them in labour would produce?'—He replies, ' Unless the means of paying rent are

' changed when the landlord goes home, his re-
' sidence can have no effect whatever.'

' Would not,' he is asked, ' the population of
' the country be benefited by the expenditure
' among them of a certain portion of the rent
' which (if he had been absent) has (would have)
' been remitted (to England)?' ' No,' he replies, ' I do not see how it could be benefited
' in the least. If you have a certain value laid
' out against Irish commodities in the one case,
' you will have a certain value laid out against
' them in the other. The cattle are either ex-
' ported to England, or they stay at home. If
' they are exported, the landlord will obtain an
' equivalent for them in English commodities ;
' if they are not, he will obtain an equivalent
' for them in Irish commodities ; so that in both
' cases the landlord lives on the cattle, or on the
' value of the cattle : and whether he lives in
' Ireland or in England, there is obviously just
' the very same amount of commodities for the
' people of Ireland to subsist upon.'

This reasoning assumes that the landlord,
while resident in Ireland, himself personally de-
vours all the cattle produced on his estates ; for
on no other supposition can there be the very
same amount of commodities for the people of
Ireland to subsist upon, whether their cattle are
retained in Ireland or exported.

But when a country does *not* export raw produce, the consequences of absenteeism are very different. Those who derive their incomes from such a country cannot possibly spend them abroad until they have previously spent them at home.

When a Leicestershire landlord is resident on his estate, he employs a certain portion of his land, or, what is the same, of his rent, in maintaining the persons who provide for him those commodities and services, which must be produced on the spot where they are consumed. If he should remove to London, he would want the services of Londoners, and the produce of land and capital which previously maintained labourers resident in Leicester, would be sent away to maintain labourers resident in London. The labourers would probably follow, and wages in Leicestershire and London would *then* be unaltered; but until they did so, wages would rise in the one district and fall in the other. At the same time, as the rise and fall would compensate one another, as the fund for the maintenance of labour, and the number of labourers to be maintained, would each remain the same, the same amount of wages would be distributed among the same number of persons, though not precisely in the same proportion as before.

If he were now to remove to Paris, a new distribution must take place. As the price of raw produce is lower in France than in England, and the difference in habits and language between the two countries prevents the transfer of labourers from the one to the other, neither the labourers nor the produce of his estates could follow him. He must employ French labourers, and he must convert his share of the produce of his estates, or, what is the same thing, his rent into some exportable form in order to receive it abroad. It may be supposed that he would receive his rent in money. Even if he were to do so, the English labourers would not be injured, for as they do not eat or drink money, provided the same amount of commodities remained for their use, they would be unaffected by the export of money. But it is impossible that he could receive his rent in money unless he chose to suffer a gratuitous loss. The rate of exchange between London and Paris is generally rather in favour of London, and scarcely ever so deviates from par between any two countries, as to cover the expense of transferring the precious metals from the one to the other, excepting between the countries which do, and those which do not possess mines. The remittances from England to France must be sent, therefore, in the form of manufactures, either directly to France, or to some country with which France has commercial relations. And how would these manufactures be obtained? Of course in exchange for the landlord's rent. His share of the produce of his estates would now go to Birmingham or Sheffield, or Manchester or London, to maintain the labourers employed in producing manufactures, to be sent and sold abroad for his profit. An English absentee employs his income precisely as if he were to remain at home and consume nothing but hardware and cottons. Instead of the services of gardeners and servants, upholsterers and tailors, he purchases those of spinners, and weavers, and cutlers. In either case his income is employed in maintaining labourers, though the class of labourers is different; and in either case, the whole fund for the maintenance of labourers, and the number of labourers to be maintained, remaining unaltered, the wages of labour would not be affected.

But, in fact, that fund would be rather increased in quantity and rather improved in quality. It would be increased, because land previously employed as a park, or in feeding dogs and horses, or hares and pheasants, would now be employed in producing food or clothing for men. It would be improved, because the increased production of manufactured commodities would occasion an increased division of labour, the use of more and better machinery, and the other improvements which we long ago ascertained to be its necessary accompaniments.

One disadvantage, and one only, it appears to me would be the result. The absentee in a great measure escapes domestic taxation. I say in a great measure, because he still remains liable, if a proprietor of houses or of land, to those taxes which fall upon rent : he pays, too, a part of the taxes on the materials of manufactures ; and if it were our policy to tax income or exported commodities, he might be forced to pay to the public revenue even more than his former proportion. But, under our present system, which throws the bulk of taxation on commodities produced for internal consumption, he receives the greater part of his revenue without deduction, and instead of contributing to the support of the British Government, contributes to support that of France or Italy. This inconvenience, perhaps, about balances the advantages which I have just mentioned, and leaves a community which exports only manufactures, neither impoverished nor enriched by the residence abroad of its unproductive members.

I ought, perhaps, on this occasion again to remind you, that it is to wealth and poverty

that my attention is confined. The *moral* effects
of absenteeism must never be neglected by a
writer who inquires into the causes which promote the *happiness* of nations, but are without
the province of a political economist. Nor do
I regret that they are so, for they form a subject on which it is far more difficult to obtain
satisfactory results. In one respect, indeed,
the moral question is the more simple, as it is
not complicated by the consideration whether
raw produce or manufactures are exported, or
whether the non-resident landlord is abroad, or
in some town within his own country. If his
presence is to be morally beneficial, it must be
his presence on his own estate. To the inhabitants of that estate, the place to which he ab-
sents himself is indifferent. Adam Smith believed his residence to be morally injurious.
The residence of a court, he observes (book ii.
chap. 3), ' in general makes the inferior sort of
people dissolute and poor. The inhabitants of
a large village, after having made considerable
progress in manufactures, have become idle in
consequence of a great lord having taken up his
residence in their neighbourhood.' And Mr.
M'Culloch, whose fidelity and intelligence as
an observer may be relied on, states, as the
result of his own experience, that in Scotland
the estates of absentees are almost always the

best managed. Much, of course, depends on individual character; but I am inclined to believe, that in general the presence of men of large fortune is morally detrimental, and that of men of moderate fortune morally beneficial, to their immediate neighbourhood. The habits of expense and indulgence which, in different gradations, prevail among all the members of a great establishment, are mischievous as examples, and perhaps still more so as sources of repining and discontent. The drawing-room and stable do harm to the neighbouring gentry, and the housekeeper's room and servants' hall to their inferiors. But families of moderate income, including under that term incomes between 500*l.* and 2000*l.* a year, appear to be placed in the station most favourable to the acquisition of moral and intellectual excellence, and to its diffusion among their associates and dependents. I have no doubt that a well-regulated gentleman's family, removing the prejudices, soothing the quarrels, directing and stimulating the exertions, and awarding praise or blame to the conduct of the villagers round them, is among the most efficient means by which the character of a neighbourhood can be improved. It is the happiness of this country, that almost every parish has a resident fitted by fortune and education for these services;

and bound, not merely by feelings of propriety, but as a matter of express and professional duty, to their performance. The dispersion throughout the country of so many thousand clerical families, each acting in its own district as a small centre of civilization, is an advantage to which, perhaps, we have been too long accustomed to be able to appreciate its extent.

Still, however, I think that even the moral effects of absenteeism have been exaggerated. Those who declaim against the 12,000 English families supposed to be resident abroad, seem to forget that not one-half, probably not one-quarter, of them, if they were to return, would dwell anywhere but in towns, where their influence would be wasted, or probably not even exerted. What does it signify to the Connaught, or Northumbrian, or Devonshire peasant, whether his landlord lives in Dublin, or London, or Cheltenham, or Rome? And even of those who would reside in the country, how many would exercise that influence beneficially? How many would be fox-hunters or game-preservers, or surround themselves with dependents whose example would more than compensate for the virtues of their masters? Nothing can be more rash than to predict that *good* would be the result of causes which are quite as capable of producing evil.

The economical effects have been still more generally misunderstood; and I have often been tempted to wonder that doctrines so clear as those which I have been submitting to you, should be admitted with reluctance even by those who feel the proofs to be unanswerable, and should be rejected at once by others, as involving a paradox too monstrous to be worth examination.

Much of this, probably, arises from a confusion of the economical with the moral part of the question. Many writers and readers of political economy forget that wealth only is within the province of that science; and that the clearest proof that absenteeism diminishes the virtue or the happiness of the remaining members of a community is no answer to arguments which aim only at proving that it does not diminish their wealth.

Another source of error arises from the circumstance, that when the landlord is present, the gain is concentrated, and the loss diffused; when he is absent, the gain is diffused, and the loss concentrated. When he quits his estate, we can put our finger on the village tradesman and labourer who lose his custom and employment. We cannot trace the increase of custom and employment that is consequently scattered among millions of manufacturers. When he

returns, we see that the expenditure of 2000*l*.
or 3000*l*. a year in a small circle gives wealth
and spirit to its inhabitants. We do not see,
however clearly we may infer it, that so much
the less is expended in Manchester, Birmingham, or Leeds. The inhabitants of his village
attribute their gain and their loss to its causes;
and their complaints and acknowledgments are
loud in proportion to the degree in which they
feel their interests to be affected. No single
manufacturer is conscious that the average
annual export of more than forty millions sterling has been increased or diminished to the
amount of two or three thousand pounds. And
even if aware of that increase or diminution, he
would not attribute it to the residence in Yorkshire or Paris of a given individual, of whose
existence he probably is not aware. When to
obvious and palpable effects nothing is to be
opposed but inferences deduced by a long,
though perfectly demonstrative reasoning process, no one can doubt which will prevail,
both with the uneducated and the educated
vulgar.

Many persons, also, are perplexed by the
consideration, that all the commodities which
are exported as remittances of the absentee's
income are exports for which no return is
obtained; that they are as much lost to this

country as if they were a tribute paid to a
foreign state, or even as if they were thrown
periodically into the sea. This is unquestionably true; but it must be recollected, that
whatever is unproductively consumed, is, by
the very terms of the proposition, destroyed,
without producing any return. The only difference between the two cases is, that the resident landlord performs that destruction here;
the absentee performs it abroad. In either
case, he first purchases the services of those
who produce the things which he, for his benefit,
not for theirs, is to consume. If he stays here,
he pays a man to brush a coat, or clean a pair
of boots, or arrange a table—all which in an
hour after are in their former condition. When
abroad, he pays an equal sum for the production of needles, or calicoes, which are sent
abroad, and equally consumed without further
benefit to those who produced them. The income of unproductive consumers, however paid,
is a tribute; and whether they enjoy it here or
elsewhere, is their own concern. We know that
a man cannot eat his cake and have it; and it
is equally true that he cannot sell a cake to
another and keep it for himself.

The last cause to which I attribute the slow
progress of correct opinions on this subject, is
their distastefulness to the most influential

members of the community. Nothing can be more flattering to landlords, annuitants, mortgagees, and fundholders, than to be told that their residence is of vital importance to the country. Nothing can be more humiliating than to be assured that it is utterly immaterial to the rest of the community whether they live in Brighton, or London, or Paris. Those who are aware how much our judgment, even in matters of science, is influenced by our wishes, will not be surprised at the prejudices against a doctrine which forbids the bulk of the educated class to believe that they are benefactors to their country by the mere act of residing within its shores.

I may appear, perhaps, to have dwelt too much on a single subject; but no prevalent error can be effectually exposed until its prevalence has been accounted for. And these are errors which are to be heard in every society, and often from those whose general views in political economy are correct. They may be called harmless errors, but no error is, in fact, harmless; and when there is so much in our habits that really requires alteration, we may lose sight of the real and the remediable causes of evil, while our attention is misdirected to absenteeism.

# LECTURE III.

## POPULAR ERRORS ON THE CAUSES
## AFFECTING WAGES, (*concluded.*)

I STATED in the last Lecture, that the quantity
and quality of the commodities obtained by
each labouring family during the year, must
depend on the quantity and quality of the commodities directly or indirectly appropriated
during the year to the use of the labouring
population, compared with the number of labouring families : or, to speak more concisely,
on the extent of the fund for the maintenance
of labourers, compared with the number of labourers to be maintained ; and I observed, that
this proposition is inconsistent with many opinions entitled to consideration. Three of those
opinions I then examined ; in the present Lecture I shall consider the remainder.

*Fourthly.* It is inconsistent with the doctrine
that the general rate of wages can, except in
two cases, be diminished by the introduction of
machinery.

The two cases in which the introduction of machinery can produce such an effect, are— first, when labour is employed in the construction of machinery, which labour would otherwise have been employed in the production of commodities for the use of labourers; and, secondly, when the machine itself consumes commodities which would otherwise have been consumed by labourers, and *that* to a greater extent than it produces them.

The first case is put by Mr. Ricardo, in his chapter on Machinery; but in so detailed a form, that, instead of reading it, I will extract its substance, with a slight variation of the terms. He supposes a capitalist to carry on the business of a manufacturer of commodities for the use of labourers; or, to use a more concise expression, the business of a manufacturer of wages. He supposes him to have been in the habit of commencing every year with a capital consisting of wages for a certain number of labourers, which we call twenty-six, and of employing that capital in hiring twenty men, to reproduce, during the year, wages for the whole twenty-six, and six to produce commodities for himself. He now supposes him to employ ten of his men during a year in producing, not wages, but a machine, which, with the aid of seven men to keep it in repair and work it, will produce every year wages for thirteen men.

At the end of the year the capitalist's situation
would be unaltered : he would have wages for
thirteen men, the produce of the labour of his
other ten men during the year—and his machine, also the produce of the labour of ten men
during the year, and therefore of equal value.
And his situation would *continue* unaltered.
Every year his machine would produce wages
for thirteen men, of whom seven must be employed in repairing and working it, and six
might, as before, be employed for the benefit of
the capitalist. But we have seen that, during
the year in which the machine was constructed,
only ten men were employed in producing wages
instead of twenty, and, consequently, that wages
were produced for only thirteen men instead of
for twenty-six. At the end of that year, therefore, the fund for the maintenance of labour
was diminished, and wages must, consequently,
have fallen. It is of great importance to recollect, that the only reason for this fall was the
diminution of the annual production. The
twenty men produced wages for twenty-six
men : the machine produces wages for only
thirteen. The vulgar error on this subject supposes the evil to arise, not from its true cause,
the expense of constructing the machine, but
from the productive powers of that machine.
So far is this from being true, that those productive powers are the specific benefit which

is to be set against the evil of its expensiveness. If, instead of wages for thirteen men, the machine could produce wages for thirty, its use, as soon as it came into operation, would have increased instead of diminishing the fund for the maintenance of labour. The same effect would have been produced, if the machine could have been obtained without expense; or, if the capitalist, instead of building it out of his capital, had built it out of his profits—if, instead of withdrawing ten men for a year from the production of wages, he had employed in its construction, during two years, five of the men whom he is supposed to have employed in producing commodities for his own use. In either case, the additional produce obtained from the machine would have been an additional fund for the maintenance of labour; and wages must, according to my elementary proposition, have risen *.

I have thought it necessary to state this possible evil as a part of the theory of machinery, but I am far from attaching any practical importance to it. I do not believe that there exists upon record a single instance in which the whole annual produce has been diminished by

* And yet it appears now to be thought, that wages may be *raised* by the destruction or (what is the same in immediate effect) the disuse of machines already constructed.

the use of *inanimate* machinery. Partly in consequence of the expense of constructing the greater part of machinery being defrayed out of profits or rent, and partly in consequence of the great proportion which the productive powers of machinery bear to the expense of its construction, its use is uniformly accompanied by an enormous *increase* of production. The annual consumption of cotton wool in this country, before the introduction of the spinning jenny, did not amount to 100,000 lbs.; it now amounts to 190,000,000. Since the power-loom came into use, the quantity of cotton cloth manufactured for home consumption has increased from 227,000,000 of yards (the average annual amount between the years 1816 and 1820), to 400,000,000 of yards (the annual average from 1824 to 1828 (Huskisson's Speech, 1830). The number of copies of books extant at any one period before the invention of the printing-press, was probably smaller than that which is now produced in a single day. Mr. Ricardo's proposition, therefore (Princ. 474), that the use of machinery frequently diminishes the quantity of the gross produce of a country, is erroneous, so far as it depends on the case which he has supposed, and of which I have stated the substance.

The other exception, that where the machine

itself consumes commodities which would otherwise have been consumed by labourers, and
that to a greater extent than it produces them,
applies only to the case of horses and working-
cattle, which may be termed animated machines. We will suppose a farmer to employ
on his farm twenty men, who produce annually
their own subsistence, and that of six other
men producing commodities for the use of their
master. If five horses, consuming, we will say,
as much as eight men, could do the work of
ten, it would be worth the farmer's while to
substitute them for eight of his men, as he
would be able to increase the number of persons who work for his own benefit from six to
eight. But after deducting the subsistence of
the horses, the fund for the maintenance of
labourers would be reduced from wages for
twenty-six men to wages for eighteen. I cannot
refuse to admit that such cases may exist, or
to deplore the misery that must accompany
them. They are, in fact, now occurring in
Ireland, and are occasioning much of the distress of that country. They seem, indeed, to
be the natural accompaniments of a certain
period in the progress of national improvement.
In the early stages of society, the rank and
even the safety of the landed proprietor is principally determined by the number of his de-

pendents. The best mode of increasing that
number is to allow the land, which he does not
occupy as his own demesne, to be subdivided
into small tenements, each cultivated by one
family, and just sufficient for their support.
Such tenants can of course pay little rent, but
they are enabled by their abundant leisure,
and forced by their absolute dependence, to
swell the retinue, and aid the political influence, of their landlord in peace, and to follow his banner in public and private war.
Cameron of Lochiel, whose rental did not
exceed 500*l*. a year, carried with him into the
rebellion of 1745, eight hundred men raised
from his own tenantry. But in the progress
of civilization, as wealth becomes the principal means of distinction and influence, landowners prefer rent to dependents. To obtain
rent, that process of cultivation must be employed which will give, not absolutely the
greatest amount of produce, but the greatest
after deducting the expenses. For this purpose a tract of five hundred acres, from which
fifty families produced their own subsistence,
and produced scarcely anything more, may be
converted into one farm, and with the labour of
ten families, and as many horses, may produce
the subsistence of only thirty families. Fortu-
nately, however, the period at which these alte-

rations take place is generally one of great social improvement; so that, after a short interval, the increased diligence and skill with which labour is applied, occasion an increase of even the gross produce. The fund for the maintenance of labourers now becomes increased from two different sources—partly from the increased efficiency of human labour when aided by that of horses and cattle, and partly from the results of a part of the human labour set free by the substitution of brutes. The ultimate consequences of such a change are always beneficial ; the change itself must, in general, be accompanied by distress.

But with the exception of these two cases, one of which produces only temporary effects, and the other, though apparently possible, seems never actually to occur, it appears to me clear that the use of machinery must either raise the general rate of wages, or leave it unaltered.

When machinery is applied to the production of commodities which are *not* intended, directly or indirectly, for the use of labourers, it occasions no alteration in the general rate of wages ;—I say the *general* rate of wages, because it may diminish the rate of wages in some employments,—a diminution always compensated by a corresponding increase in some

others. I was shown at Birmingham a small
screw, which, in the manufacture of corkscrews, performed the work of fifty-nine men ;
with its assistance one man could cut a spiral
groove in as many corkscrew shanks as sixty
men could have cut in the same time with the
tools previously in use. As the use of corkscrews is limited, it is not probable that the
demand for them has sufficiently increased to
enable the whole number of labourers previously employed in their manufacture, to
remain so employed after such an increase in
their productive power. Some of the cork-
screw-makers, therefore, must have been thrown
out of work, and the rate of wages in that trade
probably fell. But as the whole fund for the
maintenance of labourers, and the whole number of labourers to be maintained, remained unaltered, that fall must have been balanced by a
rise somewhere else—a rise which we may trace
to its proximate cause, by recollecting that the
fall in the price of corkscrews must have left
every purchaser of a corkscrew a fund for the
purchase of labour, rather larger than he
would have possessed if he had paid the former
price.

If, however, machinery be applied to the
production of any commodity used by the
labouring population, the general rate of wages

will *rise.* That it cannot fall is clear, on the grounds which I have just stated. If the improvement be great, and the commodity not subject to a corresponding increase of demand, some of the labourers formerly employed in its production will be thrown out of employment, and wages, in that trade, will fall—a fall which, as the whole fund for the maintenance of labour is not diminished, must be met by a corresponding rise in some other trade. But the fund *will be increased* by the additional quantity produced of the commodity to which the improvement has been applied : estimated in that commodity, therefore, the general rate of wages, or, in other words, the quantity of commodities obtained by the labouring population, will be increased by the introduction of machinery; estimated in all others, it will be stationary.

The example taken from the manufacture of corkscrews is as unfavourable to the effects of machinery as can be proposed ; for the use of the commodity is supposed to be unable to keep up with the increased production, and the whole number of labourers employed on it is, consequently, diminished. This, however, is a very rare occurrence. The usual effect of an increase in the facility of producing a commodity is so to increase its consumption as to occasion the employment of more, not less, labour than before.

I have already called your attention to the effects of machinery in the manufacture of cotton and in printing. Each of these trades probably employs ten times as many labourers as it would have employed if spinning-jennies and types had not been invented. Under such circumstances (and they are the usual ones), the benefits of machinery are not alloyed by even partial inconvenience.

*Fifthly.* Closely connected with this mistake, and occasioned by the same habit of attending only to what is temporary and partial, and neglecting what is permanent and general; of dwelling on the evil that is concentrated, and being insensible of the benefit that is diffused, is the common error of supposing that the general rate of wages can be reduced by the importation of foreign commodities. In fact the opening of a new market is precisely analogous to the introduction of a new machine, except that it is a machine which it costs nothing to construct or to keep up. If the foreign commodity be not consumed by the labouring population, its introduction leaves the general rate of wages unaffected; if it be used by them, their wages are raised as estimated in that commodity. If the absurd laws which favour the wines of Portugal to the exclusion of those of France were repealed, more labourers would be employed in producing commodities for the French market, and fewer for the Portuguese. Wages would temporarily fall in the one trade, and rise in the other. The clear benefit would be derived by the drinkers of wine, who, at the same expense, would obtain more and better wine. So if what are called the protecting duties on French silks were removed, fewer labourers would be employed in the direct production of silk, and more in its indirect production, by the production of the cottons, or hardware, with which it would be purchased. The wearers of silk would be the only class ultimately benefited ; and as the labouring population neither wear silk nor drink wine, the general rate of wages would, in both cases, remain unaltered. But if the laws which prohibit our obtaining on the most advantageous terms tea, and sugar, and corn, were altered, that portion of the fund for the maintenance of labour, which consists of corn, sugar, and tea, would be increased. And the general rate of wages, as estimated in the three most important articles of food, would be raised.

*Sixthly*. The views which I have been endeavouring to explain, are inconsistent with the

common opinion, that the unproductive consumption of landlords and capitalists is beneficial to the labouring classes, because it fur-
nishes them with *employment*. The maintainers
of this theory must forget that it is not employment, but food, clothing, shelter, and fuel—in
short, the materials of subsistence and comfort,
that the labouring classes require. The word
' employment' is merely a concise form of de-
signating toil, trouble, exposure, and fatigue.
All these, *per se*, are evils, and the less of them
that is required for obtaining a given amount
of subsistence and comfort,—or, in other words,
the greater the facility of obtaining that given
amount,—the better, *cæteris paribus*, will be the
condition of the labouring classes ; indeed, of
all classes in the community. What occasions
the prosperity of a colony ? Not the dearness
of subsistence, but its cheapness ; not the difficulty of obtaining food, clothing, shelter, and
fuel, but the facility. Now how can unproductive consumption increase this facility? How
can the fund from which all are to be maintained be augmented by the destruction of a
portion of it ? If the higher orders were to
return to the customs of a century ago, and
cover their coats with gold lace, they might
enjoy their own finery ; but how would that
benefit their inferiors ? The theory which I am
considering, replies that they would be bene-

fited by being *employed* in making the lace. It is true that a coat, instead of costing 5*l.*, would cost 55*l.* But what becomes *now* of the extra 50*l.*? for it cannot be said that because it is not spent on a laced coat, it does not exist. If a landlord with 10,000*l.* a year spends it unproductively, he pays it away to those who furnish the embellishments of his house and grounds, and supply his stable, his equipage, and his clothes. Suppose him now to abandon all unproductive expenditure, to confine himself to bare necessaries, and to earn them by his own labour, the first consequence would be, that those among whom he previously spent his 10,000*l.* a year would lose him as an employer; and beyond this the theory in question sees nothing. But what would he do with the 10,000*l.* which he would still annually receive? No one supposes that he would lock it up in a box, or bury it in his garden. Whether productively or unproductively, it still must be spent. If spent by himself, as by the supposition it would be spent productively, it must increase, and every year still further increase the whole fund applicable to the use of the rest of the community. If not spent by himself, it must be lent to some other person, and by that person it must be spent productively or unproductively. He might, perhaps, buy with it property in the

English funds ; but what becomes of it in the hands of the person who sells to him that funded property? He might buy with it French rentes ; but in what form would the price of those rentes go to Paris?—In the form, as we have seen, of manufactured commodities. *Quacunque via data*, every man must spend his income ; and the less he spends on himself, the more remains for the rest of the world.

The last theory, inconsistent with my own views, to which I shall call your attention, is that proposed by Mr. Ricardo in the following passage :—

' The labouring class have no small interest ' in the manner in which the net income of the ' country is expended, although it should, in ' all cases, be expended for the gratification and ' enjoyment of those who are fairly entitled to it.

' If a landlord, or a capitalist, expends his re- ' venue in the manner of an ancient baron, in ' the support of a great number of retainers or ' menial servants, he will give employment to ' much more labour than if he expended it on ' fine clothes or costly furniture.

' In both cases the net revenue would be the ' same, and so would be the gross revenue, but ' the former would be realized in different com- ' modities. If my revenue were 10,000*l.*, the

' same quantity nearly of productive labour
' would be employed, whether I realized it in
' fine clothes and costly furniture, &c. &c., or in
' a quantity of food and clothing of the same
' value. If, however, I realized my revenue in
' the first set of commodities, no more labour
' would be *consequently* employed : I should en-
' joy my furniture and my clothes, and there
' would be an end of them ; but if I realized my
' revenue in food and clothing, and my desire
' was to employ menial servants, all those whom
' I could so employ with my revenue of 10,000*l.*,
' or with the food and clothing which it would
' purchase, would be to be added to the former
' demand for labourers, and this addition would
' take place only because I chose this mode of ex-
' pending my revenue. As the labourers, then,
' are interested in the demand for labour, they
' must naturally desire that as much as possible
' should be diverted from expenditure on luxu-
' ries, to be expended in the support of menial
' servants.

' In the same manner a country engaged in
' war, and which is under the necessity of main-
' taining large fleets and armies, employs a great
' many more men than will be employed when
' the war terminates, and the annual expenses
' which it brings with it cease.

' If I were not called upon for a tax of 500*l.*

' during the war, which is expended on men in
' the situations of soldiers and sailors, I might
' probably spend that portion of my income on
' furniture, clothes, books, &c. &c., and whether
' it was expended in the one way or the other,
' there would be the same quantity of labour
' employed in production; for the food and
' clothing of the soldier and sailor would require
' the same amount of industry to produce them
' as the more luxurious commodities : but, in
' the case of war, there would be the additional
' demand for men as soldiers and sailors ; and,
' consequently, a war which is supported out of
' the revenue, and not from the capital of a
' country, is favourable to an increase of popu-
' lation.

' At the termination of the war, when part of
' my revenue reverts to me, and is employed as
' before in the purchase of wine, furniture, or
' other luxuries, the population which it before
' supported, and which the war called into ex-
' istence, will become redundant, and by its
' effect on the rest of the population, and its
' competition with it for employment, will sink
' the value of wages, and very materially dete-
' riorate the condition of the labouring classes.*'

Mr. Ricardo's theory is, that it is more beneficial to the labouring classes to be employed in

* Principles, &c., p. 475.

the production of services than in the production of commodities ; that it is better for them to be employed in standing behind chairs than in making chairs; as soldiers or sailors than as manufacturers. Now as it is clear that the whole quantity of commodities provided for the use of labourers is not increased by the conversion of an artisan into a footman or a soldier, either Mr. Ricardo must be wrong, or my elementary proposition is false.

Mr. Ricardo seems to have been led to his conclusions by observing that the wages of servants, sailors, and soldiers are principally paid in kind—those of artisans in money. He correctly states, that if a man with 10,000*l.* a-year spends his income in the purchase of commodities for his own use, he retains, after having made those purchases, no further fund for the maintenance of labour ; but that if he spends it in the purchase of commodities to be employed in maintaining menial servants, he has, in those purchased commodities, a new fund with which he can maintain a certain number of menial servants. It appeared to him, therefore, that the landlord would, in the latter case, be able to spend his income twice over ; to subsist twice as many persons as before. It did not occur to him that the landlord, by purchasing himself the subsistence of his servants, merely does

for them what they would be able to do better
for themselves; that, instead of spending his
own income twice over, he merely takes on himself the business of spending theirs for them *;
and that if he were to give to his servants the
value of their whole subsistence in money, the
whole body of labourers would be just as well
maintained as in the supposed case of his purchasing their subsistence, and then giving it to
them in exchange for their services. No one
would maintain that if it were the practice, in
this country, as it is in India, to give to servants
board wages, the demand for labour would be
lessened; or that if it were the practice, as it is
in semi-barbarous countries, to maintain servants to produce within their masters' walls the
commodities which we are accustomed to purchase from shops, the demand for labour would
be increased.    Still less could it be maintained,
that if those servants, instead of producing commodities, were employed in following their master's person, or mounting guard before his door,
such a change would create an additional demand for men, and be favourable to an increase
of population.

So far am I from concurring in Mr. Ricardo's

* He did not perceive that all that the landlord spends in purchasing
the subsistence and clothing of his servants is so much deducted from
what he would otherwise have to pay them in money.

opinion, that it is the interest of the labourers
that revenue should be spent rather on services
than on commodities, that I believe their interest to be precisely opposite. In the first
place, the labourer can generally manage better
his own income than it can be managed for him
by his master. If a domestic servant could earn
as wages the whole sum which he costs his
master, even if he were to spend it as he received it, he would probably spend it with more
enjoyment. Secondly, the income spent on services is spent in the purchase of what perishes
at the instant of its creation; that spent on
commodities often leaves results which, when
their first purchaser has done with them, are
serviceable to others. In this country the poor
are, to a great extent, clothed with garments
originally provided for their superiors. In all
the better class of cottages may be found articles of furniture which never could have been
made for their present possessors. A large portion of the commodities which now contribute
to the comfort of the labouring classes would
never have existed, if it had been the fashion in
this country, during the last fifty years, to prefer
retinue and attendance to durable commodities.
And, thirdly, the income employed on commodities is favourable to the creation of both material
and immaterial capital; that employed on ser-

vices is not. The duties of a servant are so easily
learned, that he can scarcely be termed a
skilled labourer; his accumulations are small
in amount, and seldom turned to much advantage. The artisan learns a trade, in which
every year adds to his skill, and is taught mechanical and chemical processes, often susceptible of indefinite improvement, and in which a
single invention may raise the author to wealth,
and diffuse prosperity over a whole district, or
even a whole nation. An industrious artisan
can often save a large portion of his income,
and invest it with great and immediate profit.
He purchases with his savings a small stock of
tools and materials, and by the vigilance and
activity which can be applied only to a small
capital, renders every portion of it efficient.
The ancestors, and not the remote ancestors, of
some of our richest and our proudest families,
the authors of some of our most valuable discoveries, were common mechanics. What menial servant has in this country, and in modern
times, been a public benefactor, or even raised
himself to affluence? Both history and observation show that those countries in which expenditure is chiefly employed in the purchase
of services are poor, and those in which it is
employed on commodities are rich.

Mr. Ricardo's theory as to the effects of war

is still more strikingly erroneous. It is, in the first place, open to all the objections which I have already opposed to his views respecting menial servants. The revenue which is employed in maintaining soldiers and sailors would, even if unproductively consumed, maintain at least an equal number of servants and artisans; and that portion of it which would have been employed in the maintenance of artisans would (as we have seen) have been far more beneficially employed. The demand for soldiers and sailors is not, as he terms it, an additional, it is merely a substituted demand. But a great part of that revenue would have been productively consumed. Instead of employing some labourers in converting suburbs into fortifications, and forests into navies, to perish by dry rot in harbour, or by exposure at sea, and others in walking the deck and parading on the rampart, it would have employed them in adding more and more every year to the fund from which their subsistence is derived. War is mischievous to every class in the community; but to none is it such a curse as to the labourers.

THE END.

# LETTERS

ON THE

# FACTORY ACT,

As it affects the Cotton Manufacture,

ADDRESSED TO

THE RIGHT HONOURABLE

THE PRESIDENT OF THE BOARD OF TRADE,

BY

NASSAU W. SENIOR, ESQ.

TO WHICH ARE APPENDED,

A LETTER TO MR. SENIOR FROM LEONARD HORNER, ESQ.

AND

MINUTES OF A CONVERSATION BETWEEN

MR. EDMUND ASHWORTH, MR. THOMSON AND MR. SENIOR.

LONDON:

B. FELLOWES, LUDGATE STREET.

1837.

LONDON:
R. CLAY, PRINTER, BREAD-STREET-HILL.

# ADVERTISEMENT.

THE following letters to the President of the Board of Trade, were written, as will appear from internal evidence, without any view to the press. A wish for their publication has, however, been expressed, with which I have reluctantly complied. My principal inducement has been Mr. Horner's permission to append to them his valuable commentary. As to those points in which we agree, I think that I can scarcely be wrong. As to those on which Mr. Horner's impressions differ from the representations that were made to me, I feel, of course, great diffidence. But it appears to me that the cause of truth will be best served by leaving the statements in my letters unaltered, so that the reader, with each side of the question before him, will be able to draw his own conclusions.

Now, it will be observed, that the statements which are confirmed by Mr. Horner, are of great practical importance. Mr. Horner agrees with me in thinking that a reduction of the hours of work in cotton factories, to ten hours a day, would be attended by the most fatal consequences, and that the evil would fall first on the working classes. He agrees with me, that the labour of children and young persons in factories, is comparatively light. He agrees with me,—and this is, perhaps, the most material point in the whole discussion,—that " on the subject of education, little has as yet been effected—that in nine cases out of ten, the instruction given is very little, and the incompetence of the teachers eminently conspicuous." He agrees with me as to the inconvenience of the present relation of the superintendent to the inspector. Indeed, he states, from his own experience, that until the inspector has a very different control over his assistants than he possesses at present, the public service must be expected to suffer. He agrees with me as to the hostility of the working classes to the present measure, and as to their hope, by making it intolerable, to pave the way to a ten-hours' bill; and on the necessity of destroying this hope, and the mischief which it produces, by a strong expression on the part of the legislature, of a determination not to interfere further with the labour of those who are past childhood. He agrees with me, that the machinery of the Factory Act creates both trouble and expense to the manufacturer. He compares it, indeed, to the code of excise regulations to which distillers, soap-boilers, and paper manufacturers are subjected—regulations which we know to be so mischievous as to render the manufacturers on whom they are inflicted, unable to encounter the competition of the foreign market. These are important admissions, and prove not only the absurdity of imposing any additional restrictions on the cotton trade, but the necessity, if we wish to render the Factory Act useful, or even tolerable, of amending some of its existing enactments.

The principal subjects on which my informants and Mr. Horner differ, appear to be these :—Mr. Horner believes the average annual rate of profit in the cotton trade, to exceed 10 per cent. He estimates it, indeed, on the facts stated to me, at 15 per cent., on the supposition that when my informants stated it at 10 per cent., they meant 10 per cent., with an additional 5 per cent. as interest. On the last point Mr. Horner is mistaken. Being aware that commercial men are in the habit of distinguishing between interest and profit, I always, in putting my questions, adverted to that distinction, and stated, that under the term profit I included interest. Many of the manufacturers on whose evidence I founded my statement, and many of those who have subsequently read the letters, remarked to me, that they themselves estimated their annual profits at 5 per cent., or even lower, as they thought that 5 per cent. for interest ought to be deducted from them; but only one has rated them higher. That one, a remarkably successful spinner and weaver, told me, that on examining his books for the whole period since he began the trade, he found that his profits (interest included,) had amounted annually to 11 per cent. But with this exception, 10 per cent. was the highest estimate given to me. The subject is certainly one of great obscurity. Scarcely any manufacturer knows what are his neighbour's profits, or can tell accurately what are his own. His own past profit he may indeed calculate, though even that calculation must admit many doubtful elements; such as the degree in which his buildings and machinery have been deteriorated by wear and tear, or by the invention of more advantageous processes. But the rate of his existing profits can never be more than a matter of rough guess. On the whole, therefore, in the absence of direct proof, I think myself justified in holding that 10 per cent., the rate fixed by the almost unanimous opinion of those whom I consulted, is at least as near an approximation to accuracy as can be expected.

Mr. Horner objects to my statement, " that the relay system appears on the whole, as far as the Manchester district is concerned, to have failed," and suggests that I should have spoken more correctly if I had said, that " the relay system, as far as that district is concerned, has not been much acted on." I fear that there is not much difference between these two statements; and I say so with great regret, as I fully concur with Mr. Horner in believing the relay system to be the best mode of reconciling the education of the children with the productive use of the fixed capital employed. This is one of my reasons for being anxious that the complaints of the manufacturers against the machinery of the Act, as distinguished from its substance, should be carefully considered, and, so far as they are well founded and remediable, be removed. They all stated

the machinery of the Act to be the great obstacle to the
relay system; they maintained, that with two sets of
children, coming and going at different periods, it was
absolutely impossible to comply with the clauses of the
Act, which respect the entries on the time books, the
certificates of school attendance, and the exclusion
from the mill of unemployed children.  And they also
stated to me that prosecution for mere formal offences
of this kind, was always hanging over their heads, and
from time to time actually occurring.  Mr. Horner de-
nies that any such prosecutions have taken place.  On
this matter of fact, my informants and Mr. Horner are
therefore directly at issue.  And I have not a shadow
of doubt, that each party believes his own statement to
be the correct one.

Perhaps the discrepancy may be accounted for,
partly by the circumstance that Mr. Horner can speak
only as to the year that has elapsed since he was transferred to the Manchester district, while my informants
refer to the whole of the three years that have passed
since the Act came into force; partly by the probability
that informations have been threatened which have not
been actually brought; and partly by the probability
that Mr. Horner does not know, or does not carry in
his recollection, all that his sub-inspectors have done.
The evidence of Mr. Edmund Ashworth, and of Mr.
Thomson, (pp. 40 and 41,) is important, as showing
the general opinion on this subject.*

* As this sheet was passing though the press, I received the
following letter from Mr. Edmund Ashworth :—

" *Egerton.*

The last point of difference, or rather of apparent difference, between Mr. Horner and my informants, to

---

"*Egerton, near Bolton, 6 mo. 5, 1837.*

"Respected Friend, N. W. Senior,

"On my return home I find that our establishment was last week visited by J. Heathcote, one of Leonard Horner's superintendents of factories, and we have now received notice of summons before the magistrates, to answer his charges.

"As these cases may serve to illustrate the subject we were speaking upon when I was in London, I take the liberty of stating them as briefly as possible.

"It is a well-known regulation, that no child under 13 years of age is allowed to work in a mill except it have a doctor's certificate of age, and also a schoolmaster's certificate of having attended school two hours each day. The doctor is appointed by the inspector. In this case he resides at Bolton, two and a half miles distant from us ; consequently, as it would be very inconvenient to send every child that distance to obtain a certificate previous to entering the mill, we entered into an arrangement with him to call at intervals of a few weeks, to certify all new comers ; he assured us no advantage should be taken, during these intervals, of children found in the mill on trial : of these we had four cases ; one had only worked two and a half days.

"It had been the practice of our book-keepers not to enter a child upon any of our various school and registry books, until it had obtained a doctor's certificate, viewing that as a preliminary to all other proceedings ; consequently we are charged with ten offences for these four children, namely : for each child not having a doctor's, and each a schoolmaster's certificate ; then for our registry under 13 years being erroneous, or false ; also for those names not being entered in our registry of all under 18 years of age.

"Although the circumstance of our being placed in this unpleasant situation has arisen from an arrangement made with us by a servant of the inspector's, for his own convenience, still we are liable, and, I believe, shall be convicted.

"There are one or two other cases charged against us ; as, for instance, the certificate of a child being lost, though passed by the doctor, &c., the particulars of all which, I trust, will be shown on the trial ; a newspaper report of which I will send when it occurs.

"The

which I need advert, respects the practicability of relieving the mill-owner from the prohibition of employing any child that does not produce proof of having attended school during the preceding week. I say apparent difference, because the plan which Mr. Horner appears to consider the alternative, namely, that the children should be excluded from factories until 11 years old, and then, if able to read and write, be admissible to work for 12 hours a day, is not the only alternative; and, in fact, is not the alternative proposed by the manufacturers. My disapprobation of such a plan as this is as strong as Mr. Horner's. No facts have been proved to me, and I do not believe that any exist, which show that it is proper to keep a child of 11 years old, for 12 hours a day, in attendance on the employment, however light, of a factory. The manufacturers all admitted to me that such a practice is inconsistent with real education. They do not wish to extend the present allowance of eight hours' employment. What they propose is, that education, during the time spent out of the factory, should be enforced, not by requiring a certificate of mere attendance at a place called, however undeserving the name, a school, but by proof of real proficiency. They believe

---

" The above will sufficiently confirm my previously expressed opinion, that we are every day liable to convictions from the errors or informalities of our clerks or schoolmasters, although we are at an expense of near 200*l.* a year to supply the needful means of observing this absurd and oppressive law.

" I remain, very respectfully, thy friend,

" EDMUND ASHWORTH."

that such a change will remove one of the principal obstacles to the relay system, will improve the schools, will stimulate the exertions of the children, and, what is perhaps the most important, will remove the indifference of the parents.

*Kensington, June 8, 1837.*

# LETTERS

York Hotel, Manchester, Tuesday, March 28, 1837.

My dear Sir,

We have now been for some time in the centre of the cotton district. Our principal objects of inquiry have been the effects of the Factory Regulation Act, as respects the cotton manufacture, and the consequences which may be expected from further legislative interference. And as Lord Ashley's motion is at hand, and will probably be disposed of before our return, I think you may not be unwilling to hear the results to which we have as yet come; although, in stating them, I have no doubt that I shall say much with which you are familiar.

I have always been struck by the difference between the hours of work usual over the whole world in cotton factories and in other employments; and did not, until now, perceive the reasons. It seems to arise from two causes: first, the great proportion of fixed to circulating capital, which makes long hours of work desirable; and, secondly, the extraordinary lightness of the labour, if labour it can be called, which renders them practicable. I will take them separately :—

I. I find the usual computation to be that the fixed capital is in the proportion of four to one to the circulating; so that if a manufacturer has 50,000*l.* to employ, he will expend 40,000*l.* in erecting his mill, and filling it with machinery, and devote only 10,000*l.* to the purchase of raw material (cotton, flour, and coals) and the payment of wages. I find also that the whole capital is supposed in general to be turned over (or, in other words, that goods are produced and sold representing the value of the whole capital, together with the manufacturer's profit) in about a year; in favourable times in rather less,— in others, such as the present, in rather more. I find also that the net profit annually derived may be estimated at ten per cent., some computations placing it as low as seven and a half, others as high as eleven; ten I believe to be about the average. But in order to realize this net profit, a gross profit of rather more than fifteen per cent. is necessary; for although the circulating capital, being continually restored to its original form of money, may be considered as indestructible, the fixed capital is subject to incessant deterioration, not only from wear and tear, but also from constant mechanical improvements, which in eight or nine years render obsolete, machinery which when first used was the best of its kind.

Under the present law, no mill in which persons under eighteen years of age are employed (and, therefore, scarcely any mill at all) can be worked more than eleven and a half hours a-day, that is, twelve hours for five days in the week and nine on Saturday.

Now, the following analysis will show that in a mill so worked, the whole net profit is derived *from the last hour*. I will suppose a manufacturer to invest 100,000*l.* :—80,000*l.* in his mill and machinery, and 20,000*l.* in raw material and wages. The annual return of that mill, supposing the capital to be turned once a-year, and gross profits to be fifteen per cent., ought to be goods worth 115,000*l.*, produced by the constant conversion and reconversion of the 20,000*l.* circulating capital, from money into goods and from goods into money, in periods of rather more than two months. Of this 115,000*l.* each of the twenty-three half hours of work produces 5-115ths, or one twenty-third. Of these 23-23ds, (constituting the whole 115,000*l.*) twenty, that is to say, 100,000*l.* out of the 115,000*l.*, simply re-place the capital—one twenty-third (or 5,000*l.* out of the 115,000*l.*), makes up for the deterioration of the mill and machinery. The remaining 2-23ds., that is, the last two of the twenty-three half hours of every day, produce the net profit of ten per cent. If, therefore, (prices re-maining the same,) the factory could be kept at work thir-teen hours instead of eleven and a half, by an addition of about 2,600*l.* to the circulating capital, the net profit would be more than doubled. On the other hand, if the hours of working were reduced by one hour per day (prices remaining the same), *net* profit would be de-stroyed—if they were reduced by an hour and a half, even *gross* profit would be destroyed. The circulating capital would be replaced, but there would be no fund to compensate the progressive deterioration of the fixed capital.

And it is to be remarked, that there are many causes now at work tending to increase the proportion of fixed to circulating capital. The principal, perhaps, is the tendency of mechanical improvement to throw on ma-chinery more and more of the work of production. The self-acting mule is a very expensive machine; but it dispenses with the services of the most highly paid operatives—the spinners. It has acquired, indeed, the *sobriquet* of " the Cast Iron Spinner." Though of re-cent introduction, we found it employed in a large pro-portion of the principal factories. At Orrell's splendid factory, we found a new blower enabling three persons to do the work of four. At Birley's, we found prepara-tion making for a newly invented process, by which the wool was to be conveyed direct from the willow to the blowing machine, without requiring, as it now does, a whole set of work-people for that purpose. At Bolling-ton, we found a new machine, which transfers the sliver direct from the cards to the drawing-frame, and thus dis-penses with another class of attendants. At another place, we found a weaving process, on a vast scale, differing from all others that we observed during our tour. And at Stayley Bridge we found a factory nearly finished, covering two acres and a half of ground, with buildings only one story high, (that is, ground floor and first floor,) —so that on each floor the whole operations will be carried on in one vast apartment or gallery, forming the four sides of a quadrangle, each side 450 feet long; thus saving all the labour employed in mounting or descending. Each of these five last improvements is recent,—so recent, indeed, as not to have been as yet copied by other establishments. One of them, the new weaving process, is still kept so secret, that we were allowed to visit it only as a special favour, and on the promise of not revealing its nature. And the effect of every one of them is to increase fixed, and diminish circulating capital.

Another circumstance, producing the same effect, is the improvement of the means of transport, and the consequent diminution of the stock of raw material in the manufacturer's hands waiting for use. Formerly, when coals and cotton came by water, the uncertainty and irregularity of supply forced him to keep on hand two or three months' consumption. Now, a railway brings it to him week by week, or rather day by day, from the port or the mine.

Under such circumstances, I fully anticipate that, in a very few years, the fixed capital, instead of its present proportion, will be as 6 or 7 or even 10 to 1 to the circulating; and, consequently, that the motives to long hours of work will become greater, as the only means by which a large proportion of fixed capital can be made profitable. " When a labourer," said Mr. Ashworth to me, "lays down his spade, he renders useless, for that period, a capital worth eighteen pence. When one of our people leaves the mill, he renders useless a capital that has cost 100*l.*"

2d. The exceeding easiness of cotton-factory labour renders long hours of work *practicable*. With the exception of the mule spinners, a very small portion of the operatives, probably not exceeding 12 or 15,000 in the whole kingdom, and constantly diminishing in number, the work is merely that of watching the machinery, and piecing the threads that break. I have seen the girls who thus attend standing with their arms folded during the whole time that I stayed in the room—others sewing a handkerchief or sitting down. The work, in fact, is scarcely equal to that of a shopman behind a counter in a frequented shop—mere confinement, attention, and attendance.

Under these circumstances, cotton factories have always been worked for very long hours. From thirteen to fifteen, or even sixteen hours, appear to be the usual hours per day abroad. Our own, at their commencement, were kept going the whole twenty-four hours. The difficulty of cleaning and repairing the machinery, and the divided responsibility—arising from the necessity of employing a double staff of overlookers, book-keepers, &c. have nearly put an end to this practice ; but until Hobhouse's Act reduced them to sixty-nine, our factories generally worked from seventy to eighty hours per week. Any plan, therefore, which should reduce the present comparatively short hours, must either destroy profit, or reduce wages to the Irish standard, or raise the price of the commodity, by an amount which it is not easy for me to estimate.

The estimate in the paper, signed by the principal fine spinners, is, that it would raise prices by 16 per cent. That the increase of price would be such as to occasion, even in the home market, a great diminution of consumption, I have no doubt ; and from all that I read and hear, on the subject of foreign competition, I believe that it would, in a great measure, exclude us from the foreign market, which now takes off three-fourths of our annual production.

It must never be forgotten, that in manufactures, with

every increase of the quantity produced, the relative expense of production is diminished—and, which is the same thing, that with every diminution of production, the relative expense of production is increased. If only ten watches were produced in a year, it is probable, that a watch would cost 100*l.* If there were an annual demand for 10,000,000 of watches, they would not, in all probability, cost a guinea a-piece. And this general law applies more and more forcibly, in proportion as the manufacture in question employs more expensive machinery and a greater division of labour : to the cotton manufacture, therefore, beyond all others. Up to the present time, production and cheapness have increased together. The yarn that cost forty shillings a pound when we consumed only 10,000,000 of pounds of cotton, now, when we consume 280,000,000, costs two shillings. Increase of price, and diminution of consumption, will therefore act and re-act on one another. Every increase of price will further diminish consumption ; and every further diminution of consumption will occasion an increased relative cost of production, and consequently a further increase of price. First will go the foreign market—already in a precarious state, and, once lost, irrecoverable ; since, according to the law to which I have referred, the more our rivals produce,—the wider the markets which are opened to their competition, in consequence of the rise of English prices,—the cheaper they will be able to produce. This again, by diminishing the quantity produced at home, will increase its relative cost of production ; and that again will increase prices, and diminish consumption ;—until I think I see, as in a map, the succession of causes which may render the cotton manufactures of England mere matter of history.

I have no doubt, therefore, that a ten hours' bill would be utterly ruinous. And I do not believe that any restriction whatever, of the present hours of work, could be safely made.

To-morrow, or the next day, I will endeavour to give you the result of our inquiries as to the working of the present Act.

Ever yours,

N. W. SENIOR.

*The Right Hon. Charles Poulett Thomson,*
*&c. &c. &c.*

---

York Hotel, Manchester, April 2, 1837.

MY DEAR SIR,

I NOW proceed to give you the result of our inquiries as to the operation of the Factory Act.

In considering that Act, care must be taken to distinguish between its *substance* and its *machinery*.

1st. The *substance* is, that, in factories, children under nine years of age shall not be employed at all, and those under thirteen not for more than eight hours a-day; and that they shall pass two hours a-day in school. The hours of working, except on Saturday, being twelve, it was supposed that by means of relays, the services of children might be obtained for the whole twelve hours.

2d. The *machinery* consists of enactments, that no child under thirteen shall be *allowed to remain* in a factory without a certificate of age from a surgeon, nor for more than eight hours a-day, nor without a certificate of its having attended school for twelve hours in the preceding week; and also in the appointment of inspectors, empowered to issue regulations and visit factories, and superintendents or sub-inspectors acting under their direction, and empowered to enter all school-rooms and counting-houses, but not those parts of a factory in which manufacturing processes are carried on.

The relay system appears on the whole, as far as this district is concerned, to have failed. Of the factories that we visited, only four employ it. Three of these are situated in country villages, and the number of children in the whole four is small, being only 243 out of 4,800 operatives, or about 1-20th. The objections urged were, in some places, the difficulty of obtaining children, and in all, the constant trouble and difficulty of making correct entries in the time-books, the exposure to disgrace and loss from the penalties inflicted for unavoidable errors, and the disturbance arising from a change of hands in the middle of work.

On the other hand, the fear that *all* the children under thirteen would be *everywhere* dismissed has proved vain. Of the factories that we have inspected, four only have adopted that course, the same number as that of those who employ relays.

The usual plan is to employ one set of children for the first eight hours of the day, and to get on as well as may be during the remaining four without them.

The consequences are—

1st. Loss to the parents who have children under thirteen, by the non-employment of those under nine, and by the reduced wages of those between ten and thirteen.

2d. Loss to the operatives who are the *direct* employers of the children as their assistants, first, by their having to employ more assistants above thirteen and at higher wages, and secondly, by their being able to get through less work after they lose the assistance of the younger children.

3d. Loss to the mill-owner, whose produce during the last four hours of each day is diminished in quantity, and deteriorated in quality, and who has sometimes to repay to his operatives a part of their loss.

The gainers are the children above thirteen, whose wages have risen, and the children under thirteen, so far as they are better educated and have less fatigue than before.

As to the value of this gain, however, as far as education is concerned, I am sceptical. If good schools and a good system of instruction were established, no doubt much could be learned in the two hours a-day of compulsory schooling.

But those portions of the bill which provided for the establishment of schools having been thrown out by the Lords, the school appears to be generally rather a place for detaining and annoying the children than of real instruction. Instead of the vast and airy apartments of a well-regulated factory, they are kept in a small, low, close room; and instead of the light work, or rather attendance, of a factory, which really is not more exercise than a child voluntarily takes, they have to sit on a form, supposed to be studying a spelling-book. We found a universal statement that the children could not be got into the school except by force; that they tried every means to remain in the factory, or, if excluded, to ramble over the fields or the streets.

It may easily be supposed that the *operatives* are outrageous against this state of things. Their original object was to raise the price of their *own* labour. For this purpose the spinners, who form, as I stated in my first letter, a very small (about 1-20th) but a powerful body among them, finding that they could not obtain a limitation of the hours of work to ten by combination, tried to effect it through the legislature. They knew that Parliament would not legislate for adults. They got up therefore a frightful, and (as far as we have heard and seen) an utterly unfounded picture of the ill treatment of the children, in the hope that the legislature would restrain all persons under 18 years old to ten hours, which they knew would, in fact, restrict the labour of adults to the same period. The Act having not only defeated this attempt, but absolutely turned it against them,—having, in fact, increased their labour and diminished their pay,—they are far more vehement for a ten hours' bill than before, and are endeavouring by every means to impede the working of the existing Act, and to render its enactments vexatious or nugatory. We hear everywhere of their conspiring to entrap the masters into penalties, by keeping the children too long in the mill, by keeping them from school, and by all the petty annoyances by which trouble can be created.

With respect to the *masters*, we have found them, with only two exceptions, favourable to the substance of the Act. They maintain, indeed, that the long hours of attendance did not injure the health of the children, provided the work-rooms were sufficiently ventilated : a thing which may be accomplished by the mere addition of a fan, worked by the engine with little trouble or expense, and, as we felt at Ashton's and Ashworth's, with perfect success. They maintain also that the factory children were not worse educated, indeed were better educated, than the children employed in other trades : and they complain that *they* alone are selected to be charged with the education of their dependants. But they admit that employment, however light, for twelve hours a-day, must prevent education. They are, as far as we have seen, without any exception, most earnest that their work-people should be educated ; and they are ready, for that purpose, to submit to their being restricted, while under thirteen, to eight hours a-day of employment; but they do complain most bitterly of the *machinery* of the Act.

1st. They complain of the clauses by which a master may be called before the magistrates, exposed, and fined, " for overworking a child," because a child has remained a minute too long within the walls of the mill from heedlessness, or from dislike of being turned out in the snow,— or perhaps as part of a conspiracy to make the act intolerable.

2d. They object to being liable to be accused, convicted, and fined, " for making false entries in the time-book," because one of 80 children has one day come at half-past eight and gone at half-past four, instead of coming at eight and going at four, the hours fixed for it; and entered in the time-book, on the supposition that they had been adhered to. It is to avoid this danger that the relay system has generally been unattempted or disused.

3d. They object to being convicted and fined "for neglecting the education of the children," because they have been unable to force a child to school, or have allowed one to work without a regular certificate of school attendance. They say that the children *will work*, and will *not go to school;* and that the mill-owner, whose time is filled with other things, cannot employ it in preventing eighty urchins from truancy.

Under such circumstances, we found, in some of the best regulated establishments, the forms of the Act in this last respect systematically disregarded ; the master, relying on his general high character, and not fearing to be suspected of having intentionally violated its substance. Others, however, were in constant anxiety lest it should be infringed ; and others we found in a state of absolute exasperation at the convictions which had been obtained against them while they were most diligently endeavouring to carry it into effect.

The same may be said as to the clauses which render the remaining of a child in a factory, without proof of its employment, conclusive evidence of its being over worked. In some mills, indeed in most, this is adhered to. The children are turned into the fields, or the streets, whatever be the weather, the instant the hour begins to strike. In others again it is systematically violated. Care is taken that they shall not work, but they are allowed to remain. But this again can be done with tolerable safety, only by a master who feels that he cannot be suspected of real misconduct, though he may be convicted and fined for noncompliance with forms.

4th. They complain of the power of the inspectors to issue regulations, which, after having been twice published in a county paper, become laws. They say, that regulations, minute and troublesome, are suddenly issued and suddenly altered or withdrawn; that they are not easily comprehended, and, by the time they have been understood, are revoked.

5th. They complain of the constant recurrence of Parliamentary interference. They are tired of having to come to town, canvass and expostulate every year, in order to keep off a ten hours' bill, or some other equally wild proposal. They say, that if they can once be sure that they shall have nothing worse than the present Act, they shall endeavour to work it, and believe that it may be made to work well; but that any further restrictions will be ruinous, and that even the fear of them is most mischievous.

It will appear from this statement, that the Government is not likely to be much troubled by demands from the manufacturers for improvements in the Factory Act. The manufacturer is tired of regulations—what he asks is tranquillity—*implora pace*. But, if alterations are to be made, the following are those which have been suggested to us :—

1st. That Government shall provide schools, and, at least, tolerable teachers. At present there seem to be none that deserve the name, except a few whom some opulent and enlightened mill-owners, such as the Gregs, Ashton, and Ashworth, have established themselves.

2d. That the duty of forcing the children to be educated, shall be transferred from the mill-owner to the parent; or (which they, with one exception, prefer) that education shall be enforced only by making a certain amount of it a preliminary to employment—by enacting, for instance, that after a given time no child shall be admitted to a factory till it can read, or be allowed to work full time until it can read and write fluently.

3d. That the mill-owner shall be punishable only for substantial, not for mere formal, violations of the law. That he shall no longer be liable to be fined and disgraced as a violator of the law, for an incorrect entry in a time-book, inadvertently made by his book-keeper, or because a child has stayed in the mill five minutes too long, in order to tie a shoe, or warm itself by the stove.

4th. That some control shall be exercised over the promulgation of rules by the inspectors; some appeal from their regulations, and some better mode of publishing them.

These seem to be all their wishes; and I must say, that they appear to me to be reasonable. The first.appears to be the most important; and I only repeat my own words on the Poor Law Report when I say, that the most pressing duty now incumbent on the Government is, to provide for the religious and moral education of the people. In fact, the Factory Act, by driving many children into other employments, makes the expediency of adopting a general system of education for all children even more urgent than it was before. " What are you doing here?" said Mr. Ashton to a little fellow, whom he found in one of his coal-mines. " Working in mine, till I am old enough to go into factory."

The general impression on us all as to the effects of factory labour has been unexpectedly favourable. The factory work-people in the country districts are the plumpest, best clothed, and healthiest looking persons of the labouring class that I have ever seen. The girls, especially, are far more good-looking (and good looks are fair evidence of health and spirits) than the daughters of agricultural labourers. The wages earned per family are more than double those of the south. We examined at Egerton three of the Bledlow pauper migrants. Being fresh to the trade, they cannot be very expert; yet one family earned 1l. 19s. 6d.; another, 2l. 13s. 6d.; and the other, 1l. 16s. per week. At Hyde we saw another. They had six children, under 13; and yet the earnings of the father and two elder children were 30s. a week. All these families live in houses, to which a Gloucestershire cottage would be a mere out-house. And not only are factory wages high, but, what is more important, the employment is constant. Nothing, in fact, except the strikes of the work-people themselves, seems to interrupt it. Even now, when the hand-loom weavers and lacemakers are discharged by thousands, the factory operatives are in full employ. This is one of the consequences of the great proportion of fixed capital, and the enormous loss which follows its standing idle for a single day. Nothing can exceed the absurdity of the lamentation over the children as " crowded in factories." Crowding in a factory is physically impossible. The machinery occupies the bulk of the space; the persons who have to attend to it are almost too distant to converse. Birley's weaving room, covering an acre of ground, had not space among the looms for more than 170 persons. Bailey's factory, covering two acres and a half, one story high, and therefore, taking together the ground-floor and first-floor, containing five acres of apartment, was to be worked by about 800 operatives, which gives more than 15 yards square to each. I only wish that my work-room in Southampton Buildings had as much space, in proportion to the people in it.

The difference in appearance when you come to the Manchester operatives is striking; they are sallow and thinner. But when I went through their habitations in Irish Town, and Ancoats, and Little Ireland, my only wonder was that tolerable health could be maintained by the inmates of such houses. These towns, for such they are in extent and population, have been erected by small speculators with an utter disregard to every thing except immediate profit. A carpenter and a bricklayer club to buy a patch of ground, and cover it with what they call houses. In one place we saw a whole street following the course of a ditch, in order to have deeper cellars (cellars for people, not for lumber) without the expense of excavation. Not a house in this street escaped cholera. And generally speaking throughout these suburbs the streets are unpaved, with a dunghill or a pond in the middle; the houses built back to back, without ventilation or drainage ; and whole families occupy each a corner of a cellar or of a garret. A good Building Act, strictly enforced, might give health not only to the factories but to the whole population. We tried, indeed, an experiment as to the comparative appearance of different classes of the Manchester population. We went last Sunday to the great Sunday-school in Bennett-street, where we found about 300 girls in one large room. We desired first all the carders to stand up alone, then all the piecers, then all the reelers, and so on through the various departments. Then we desired all those not employed in factories to stand up ; then all those employed in factories ; and on each of these trials not one of us could perceive the least difference between the apparent health of the different classes of factory children, or between the children employed in factories and those not so employed.

We inquired very sedulously as to the mode in which Mr. Horner has carried out the Act; and the testimony was generally, I may almost say unanimously, favourable. The mill-owners are angry, indeed, at his last report, and most vehemently opposed to his demand for further powers, and for authority to his superintendents to enter the mills ; but, notwithstanding this, they agree that he has performed his very difficult duties mildly and judiciously.                    Ever yours,

N. W. SENIOR.

P.S.—On looking back at this letter I see that I have omitted one point which was earnestly pressed on us,—namely, that the superintendents should be appointed by the inspector, and removable by him ; and the inspector made responsible for their conduct. Under the present system they may, and I believe often do, pull different ways.

*The Right Hon. Charles Poulett Thomson,*
*&c. &c. &c.*

York Hotel, Manchester, April 4, 1837,

My dear Sir,

I must own that I am somewhat alarmed at the rumours that the Government propose to render the Factory Act more stringent, in compliance with Mr. Horner's requisitions.

Those requisitions are two :—

1st. That magistrates who are mill-owners, or have some property in mills, or who are by trade or near relationship connected with factories, should not sit on the bench on prosecutions connected with offences under the Act.

2d. That the sub-inspectors or superintendents should have free access, without asking permission, to every part of a factory.

1st. The first of these proposed enactments would exclude from the bench on factory questions, all manufacturers or commercial men ; for who is there among them, in the manufacturing districts, who is not by trade or near relationship connected with factories ? It would therefore leave the enforcement of the Act to the clergy and country gentlemen,—classes generally opposed to the mill-owners in habits and politics, and without practical knowledge of the system in the working of which they would have to interfere. This might not, perhaps, be of great importance if the offences on which they would have to adjudicate were substantial offences. If *wilful* overworking a child, *wilful* false entries, or *wilful* obstructions of education were the punishable acts, the adjudication might, perhaps, be safely left with the country gentlemen ; but as the Act is worded, the offences may be mere formal ones. They may be the permitting a child to remain too long in a mill, or an inadvertent error in one among 1000 entries ; or non-compliance with the education clauses, with which Mr. Horner himself declares that " in many cases strict compliance is nearly impracticable." If for such offences as these the judge is to be a person without sympathy for the accused, or knowledge of the difficulty, I fear that provisions now severely vexatious may become almost intolerable.

2d. The free admission of the sub-inspectors would, however, be still more opposed. The "personel" of a large factory is a machine as complicated as its "materiel," and is, I think, on the whole, the great triumph of Sir R. Arkwright's genius. In such an establishment from 700 to 1400 persons, of all ages and both sexes, almost all working by the piece, and earning wages of every amount between two shillings and forty shillings a-week, are engaged in producing one ultimate effect, which is dependent on their combined exertions. Any stoppage, even any irregularity in one department, deranges the whole. A strict and almost superstitious discipline is necessary to keep this vast instrument going for a single day. Now how, ask the mill-owners, could this discipline be kept up, if the sub-inspectors were at liberty to walk over our establishments at all hours; listen to the complaints and jealousies of all our servants, and at their instigation summon us as criminals before the magistrates? Could the discipline, they ask, of a regiment or of a ship be carried on, if we had sub-inspectors of regiments, with power to ask all the privates for grievances, and summon their officers for penalties?

I firmly believe that if this enactment is carried, the following will be the consequences:—

1st. That a considerable number of the educated and intelligent mill-owners, that is, of those who have the sensibilities of gentlemen, will cease to follow their occupation within the British Islands.

We have already found one who is preparing, if such a clause is passed, to form an establishment in the Tyrol; and others have told us that they shall resist it by main force. This was probably an idle menace; but it shows the degree of irritation that the mere proposal has excited.

2d. That from a large proportion of the Mills, the children under thirteen will be excluded, and forced, therefore, into other employments, unprotected by any regulations whatever.

I mentioned in my former letter, that this has already been done to some extent. And it is remarkable, that of the four establishments seen by us, which have adopted this manner of escaping from the Act, three,—that is to say, Lambert Hoole and Jackson's, Cheetham's new mill, and Orrell's,—are of first-rate magnitude. A very slight additional pressure, occurring too at a time of diminished manufacturing activity, would render it prevalent.—Mr. Horner disbelieves the probability of such an event, because " it cuts off the future sup-" ply of useful hands ; as children, to be profitable to " their employer, must begin to learn their trade at a " much earlier age than thirteen." I agree as to this fact,—but not as to the inference. A manufacturer who excludes children under thirteen, may still carry on his business with work-people who acquired their skill under the old regulations, or with a supply from other mills. Some years hence, the evil may be great, and may be irremediable ;—but, by that time, the manufacturer in question may have quitted business.

3d. I fear a very dangerous state of feeling among the work-people. I need not tell *you*, that we are approaching a season of great difficulty. Excessive shipments have injured the Asiatic market,—internal supply, the continental,—and financial embarrassment, the American. Already the manufacturers complain of diminished or suspended demands, are holding stocks, and talking of working short time. If the dense and ignorant population of the manufacturing districts, trained in combinations, and accustomed to high wages, is partly thrown out of work, and the remainder reduced in income, scenes of violence may follow, which may frighten away capital, already having a tendency to emigrate.

On the whole, the result of my tour has been a mixture of pain and pleasure. I have seen a vast, well paid, thriving, and apparently happy population. But I see, impending over that population, calamities which may be, and I hope will be averted—but which will inevitably fall on them, if the suggestions of those who call themselves their friends are even partially followed.

To enforce ventilation and drainage, and give means and motives to education, seems to me all that can be done by positive enactment.

Ever yours,

N. W. SENIOR.

*The Right Hon. Charles Poulett Thomson,*
*&c. &c. &c.*

# LETTER

## FROM MR. HORNER TO MR. SENIOR.

---

Leeds, May 23, 1837.

MY DEAR SIR,

I AM very much obliged to you for allowing me to see your letters to Mr. Thomson, on the Factory Act; and as you bid me criticise them freely and fully, I will avail myself of the privilege, because I think you have come to some wrong conclusions; and if I succeed in convincing you that they are so, an important step will be gained in the right consideration of the Factory question.

I concur in all you say, as to the importance of interfering as little as possible with the productive powers of the fixed capital; you have placed that in a very clear point of view. Every minute of the twenty-four hours that it stands idle, beyond the time required to repair and keep the machinery in efficient working state, is obviously so much dead loss, and by so much increases the cost of production; nothing, therefore, can justify legislative interference, except an overruling necessity connected with the welfare of the living beings who work the machinery. That necessity, so far as regards *children*, was, to my mind, clearly established by the Factory Inquiry; for it was proved beyond dispute, that a large number of children, not free agents, but compelled to work as their parents, who had the disposal of their labour, chose to agree to, were employed for a greater number of hours in the day, than was consistent either with their having a fair chance of growing up in full health and strength,—the working man's capital,—or with an opportunity of receiving a suitable education. The latter disadvantage is so clear, that no one who has fairly considered the subject now hesitates to admit it. Independently of all higher considerations, and to put the necessity of properly educating the children of the working classes on its lowest footing, it is loudly called for, as a matter of police, to prevent a multitude of immoral and vicious beings, the offspring of ignorance, from growing up around us, to be a pest and nuisance to society; it is necessary, in order to render the great body of the working classes governable by reason; and it is prudent to educate them, for the purpose of developing and cultivating their natural faculties, and of thereby adding to the productive powers of the country.

But no education that will have much influence on the moral character can be got without a long continued attendance at school, and at that time of the day when the mind of the child is fresh, and not fatigued by previous confinement and labour; for otherwise good habits will not be fixed : therefore the hours of work of children in factories ought not to exceed eight daily; and I do not think that the moral training of the child can be rightly accomplished, unless it continues to attend a well-taught school until it has attained its thirteenth year. Length of attendance at school is the more necessary for the children of the lower orders, because they are cut off from those opportunities of moral and intellectual cultivation, which the children of the more wealthy classes enjoy, from the conversation of educated persons around them. But this principle is applicable not to factories only, but to all trades in which infant labour is resorted to ; and it ought to be applied in every case where the children's labour can be regulated by a law which, with reasonable pains, can be carried into effect.

I agree with you in thinking that a limitation of the hours of labour of persons above the age of childhood, to any thing less than twelve hours a day, is uncalled for, they being free agents ; and that a reduction of the hours of work in Cotton Factories to ten hours a day, would be attended with the most fatal consequences; and which would first be felt by the working classes.

I admit that the labour of children and young persons in Cotton Factories is comparatively light, in so far as muscular exertions are concerned ; but there cannot be a question that, on the average, children who work eight hours only, and get fresh air and exercise for two hours daily, *and in day-light*, must grow up more healthy and strong than those confined to the factory for twelve hours ; and who, for a great part of the year, go to and leave the mill in the dark.

I am not clear as to the accuracy of your statement on the rate of profit in the cotton trade. It is very possible that, at the particular time of your inquiry, ten per cent. may have been the average net profit, on spinning, coarse and fine, and power-loom weaving; but the vast fortunes which have been made in the course of a few years, and in so great a number of instances, in all parts of the country where the cotton manufacture is carried on to any extent, by men who began without a shilling, and entirely on borrowed capital, for which they had to pay a heavy interest, prove to my mind that the average rate of net profit, *in any period of five years* since the cotton trade rose into consequence, must have greatly exceeded ten per cent. in well-managed factories. The statements of people engaged in trade, as to their profits, especially where a complicated process of manufacture makes it difficult for us to verify them, must be received with great caution: their object always is to show for how little they work. They take a large margin, in their estimates of the cost of production, for tear and wear, of machinery, &c. bad debts, and sundry possible contingencies; and they prudently take care to keep themselves *quite safe* in their calculations. Besides, in the cotton manufacture, five per cent. for interest on outlay is, I believe, invariably added as a part of the cost of production, before they speak of profit; and therefore that source of income is over and above the ten per cent. you state, unless I am greatly mistaken.

### *Factory Act.*

I regret that your opportunities of inquiry as to the working of the Act were not more extensive; because, if they had been so, I am firmly persuaded that you would have come to conclusions in several respects different from those you have formed. I know some of the persons from whom you derived your information, and I trace their opinions in your letters, because they have been again and again expressed to myself. It was very natural that you should be disposed to listen with attention to their statements, for they are able, good, and benevolent men; and they have done much to improve the moral condition and add to the comforts of their work-people. But you were not sufficiently well prepared to cross-examine them, and to test the soundness of their reasoning, by an acquaintance with the internal economy of mills, and by an appeal to facts at variance with their opinions, of which I could produce many. Some of them, at least, I know to be men of a warm temperament and of a proud spirit, who wish to have their own way of doing good, and who kick against any attempt to force them to do good in any other way. Some were sore from having been fined: they were proceeded against, not for acts of inadvertence, but for doing that which their neighbours did not do, and which they might easily have avoided, if they had taken a little pains, and had been actuated by a disposition somewhat more submissive to a law, which they knew the inspector had received strict orders to enforce; full warning having been given to them by public advertisement, and by direct communication from myself. I allude to some for whom you know me to entertain great respect, and of whose benevolent exertions for their people I have spoken to you and others with the highest praise. The statements of these gentlemen are to be received, therefore, with an allowance: the most honest men sometimes view things through a medium which distorts the truth.

Another circumstance does not appear to have been sufficiently considered by you. The law was not passed for such mills as those of Messrs. Greg and Co., at Bollington, Messrs. Ashworths, at Turton, and Mr. Thomas Ashton, at Hyde: had all factories been conducted as theirs are, and as many others I could name are, there would probably have been no legislative interference at any time. But there are very many mill-owners whose standard of morality is low, whose feelings are very obtuse, whose governing principle is to make money, and who care not a straw for the children, so as they turn them well to money account. These men cannot be controlled by any other force than the strong arm of the law; and the Gregs, and Ashworths, and Ashtons, and others like them, must consider that the Act, and the rules and regulations issued under its authority, have been framed to check the evil practices of those who have brought discredit upon the trade; and they must submit to some inconveniences in order that their less scrupulous neighbours may be controlled. If these gentlemen were distillers, or soap-boilers, or paper-makers, they would not, I am very sure, knowingly rob the revenue of a shilling; but would they, on account of their high character, be listened to for a moment, if they were to complain of the trouble of keeping books, and observing regulations ordered by the commissioners of excise, or were to demonstrate against being subjected to the indignity of a public officer entering their premises without their leave? And if such restraints are indispensable for the sake of the revenue, ought they not to be submitted to with cheerfulness when the sole object of the interference is to improve the condition of thousands of children, and therefore ultimately, that of the whole factory population of the United Kingdom? If the restrictions do cause a reduction in some degree of present profit, by raising the wages of children, is there not the most well-grounded reason to expect that that outlay will, in the end, return with interest, by their having a more moral and intelligent set of work-people, who will be more regular in their attendance, will take better care of the machinery, and be less apt to be misled into *strikes;* and that thus there will be less interruption to the productive powers of the fixed capital, the great point to be aimed at, as you so clearly demonstrate?

You state, that " the relay system appears on the whole, as far as this district is concerned, to have failed." If you had said that it has not been much acted upon, as far as that district is concerned, the statement would not have been liable to be misunderstood, as it is in the way you put it; for, in so far as the *practicability* of the system is concerned, the experiment has not only not failed, but has, in my opinion, succeeded beyond what its most sanguine advocates could have anticipated, considering the many obstacles it has had to contend with. It was to be expected that, for a time at least, a system which at first occasions some trouble, would not be adopted unless from necessity; and up to the present day, in such populous places as Manchester, Stockport, Ashton, and Staly Bridge, there has been comparatively little scarcity of children *certified to be* 13 years of age. From the great imperfection of the Act, in all that relates to the enactments for the determination of the ages of the children, it is impossible for the inspector to check the most palpable frauds, and to prevent the admission of children to work full time, long before they are 13 years of age. I have tried various checks, but with very partial success; and I am persuaded that fully one-half of the children now working under surgeons' certificates of thirteen, are in fact not more than twelve, many not more than eleven years of age. Until this defect in the fundamental part of the Act be remedied, the object of the law will, to a great extent, be defeated. Had it not been for this facility of finding children *nominally* of thirteen years of age in the above named places, I have little doubt that the relay system would have been much more extensively in operation. In every instance which has come to my knowledge, *where it has been fairly tried,* it has succeeded. But I have entered so fully into this subject in my Reports, that I cannot do better than refer you to them; and I rest the proof of what I assert, upon what I have there stated, and on the special return I made to the House of Commons on the 6th of the present month. I shall quote a few passages from those Reports.

"The factory where the relay system is in operation on the largest scale in my district, is at the cotton works of Messrs. Finlay and Co., at Deanston, near Doune, in Perthshire. This factory is on a great scale, the water power being equal to 300 horses, and 800 persons being employed, of whom 442 are under eighteen years of age. Mr. Smith, the able and enlightened resident partner of the establishment, is a zealous advocate for the limitation of the hours of the children, and for the enforcement of their attendance on school; and immediately upon the Act coming into operation, he adopted the relay system. He has now 106 children under eleven years of age working upon that plan, and attending school for at least two hours a day for six days out of the seven in each week. I visited the works on the 18th of June, and conversed with Mr. Smith, and with two of his overseers, in order to ascertain how the plan was working after a four months' trial. The account I received was, that at first there was some awkwardness, but that the difficulties were overcome, and the plan was going on smoothly, without inconvenience of any sort to the business of the factory."—*Report of 21st July,* 1824, p. 11.

I saw Mr. Smith in London a month ago, when he informed me that the relay system has been going on at their factory uninterruptedly since he began it, more than three years ago, and that he is more and more convinced of its practicability and advantages.

"The prejudices that exist against the system of so working with relays of children are, however, beginning to give way : and the assurances which I have been able to give of the success of that plan, in every instance where it has been fairly tried, have overcome the reluctance to adopt it in many cases. There are now sixty-five mills in my district, where it is in operation; some upon an extensive, but in general upon a small scale : the total number of children so working by relays being 776, by my last returns. More would have adopted the system, but for a strong expectation that the law is to be altered, and that it would therefore be better to wait for some time before they make the change in their works, and incur any expense about schools."—*Report 24th of February,* 1836, p. 13.

"These arguments in favour of the relay system are not theoretical speculations, but the results of experiments fairly made. In my reports from my former districts I stated several instances where this plan of employing children had been extensively acted upon with complete success; and I am happy to say that I have already found several mills in my new district where it is adopted. I have seen it in operation in 30 factories, under various modifications, some employing double sets, but more generally three children are engaged to work eight hours for two who used to work 12. I found the plan more general in the West Riding of Yorkshire than in the other parts of my district which I visited; and Mr. Baker mentions 14 mills where he found it in operation in August. Mr. Marshall, of Leeds, has long acted upon it in his extensive works, indeed for nearly two years before the passing of the present Act; and his sons, who take an active part in the direction of the mills, informed me that they find no difficulty in it. I found it in full operation with 300 children in the admirable establishment of Messrs. Wood and Walker, at Bradford ; and Mr. Walker, in a conversation I had with him on this point, bore equally decided testimony to its practicability, and he also can speak from the experience of several years. Messrs. Hives, Atkinson, and Co., of Leeds, who have more recently adopted it in their large factory, and under an excellent arrangement, told me that they even preferred it to employing the children full time, finding them more cheerful and alert, and that consequently they got their work better done. Were it necessary, I could mention other instances of the plan working successfully; and the testimony of those who have fairly tried it is so strong in its favour as to warrant the expectation that many, ere long, will become converts to it, even among those who most decidedly pronounced it, before trial, to be impracticable."—*Report of 12th October,* 1836, p. 9.

" In my last report I mentioned a great number of instances where this system had been adopted ; and within the last three months a great increase has taken place, especially in the West Riding of Yorkshire. Mr. Baker has just sent me a report, from which it appears that, in the town and neighbourhood of Halifax alone, there are forty factories where there are 635 children working by relays, and regularly attending school. I have seen it in operation in large mills and in small mills, in towns and in country situations, and all I have seen has confirmed the opinions I have expressed in former reports, formed upon experience in my last district, that this mode of working children is not only perfectly practicable, but attended with very little difficulty after it has been but a short time in operation. Masters, managers, and operatives, have, in numerous instances in the last three months, expressed the same thing to me."— *Report of 18th January, 1837, p. 45.*

In my report of the 12th of October, I mention, that Messrs. Hives, Atkinsons, and Co., of Leeds, are acting upon this plan ; and when I visited their factory ten days ago, they expressed their unqualified approbation of it ; the best proof of which is, that, while on my inspection of their mill on the 9th of December last, I found 65 children so employed ; on my visit to it on the 15th instant, I found 123.

The following are extracts from my journal of inspection at Manchester:—28th of October, 1836.—" Visited the mill of Mr. Bazley, New Bridge Mill, in Water Street. Here I found the relay system in full operation. I did not see Mr. B., but John Powdrell, the manager. They have at present twenty-eight children on half time, and would have double the number, but the children leave them for mills where P. said they still get full-time employment. They work by a double set. P. said that he is very friendly to the short-time, mainly for the sake of the education ; and when I said to him that I saw no impracticability in the working by relays, he replied, that there is none—' Where there is a will, there is a way.' "

5th of November.—" I visited the mill of J. Pooley and Sons, at Hulme. It was in excellent order in all respects ; I have seen none better, and few so good, if any, in Manchester. They employ about fifty children by relays of three for two, and send them to the National School, which is near at hand, and to the Sunday Schools of different sects. Mr. Pooley, jun., said, that the men who employ the children did not like the plan at first, but now that they have got used to it, and that they know that their masters desire it, it goes on very well."

On the 6th of the present month, I made a return to the House of Commons of the number of mills in my district that are acting upon the relay system ; and if you refer to it you will find that 524 out of 1289 factories are working upon that plan.

I have cotton mills, woollen mills, and flax mills, working on this plan, in large towns, small towns, and country situations; and I think you will admit that I am justified in maintaining that its *practicability* has been abundantly established.

With regard to the losses stated by you to be consequent upon the restriction of the labour of children to eight hours a day, I have to observe, that, where the relay system is adopted, the mill-owner pays, at least, the same gross amount of wages, and generally more ; so that the working classes receive as much or more than they did before the interference of the law. A man with three sons, who formerly sent two of eleven and twelve years of age to the factory, and received six shillings a week for their labour, now sends the little fellow of nine years old, who was not employed at all, because twelve hours a day were too much for him, and he still· receives his six shillings; with the advantage that the two elder boys have now time for their education, which they had not before, and have a game at football in the green fields besides. It seems to me perfectly reasonable that a man who receives two shillings a week by the labour of his child—and few receive less for the eight hours' work—should be obliged to spend one-twelfth part of it, two-pence a week, for the education of that child.

On the subject of education, I agree with you that little has yet been effected. Except in those cases where good schools are attached to the mills, or in their immediate vicinity,—and these are comparatively rare,—little more can be said to have been hitherto accomplished, than the establishment of the principle, that attendance at a factory for a part of the day and at a school for another part, are two things perfectly compatible ; but that is no inconsiderable step in our progress to a better state of things. In nine cases out of ten, the instruction given is very little, and the incompetence of the teachers is eminently conspicuous. If we stop where we are, we shall be far short of what ought to be done for the benefit of the factory children, because the necessity of interference for the sake of their bodily health was trifling in comparison of that called for by their destitution as regards moral training. The country insists, and most happy I am that it does insist, that the factory children shall be educated ; but the order cannot be complied with, unless schools and teachers be provided, where the children may be able *to purchase* that commodity with which they are required to supply themselves. I hail the Factory Act as the first legislative step in this country towards that to which, under some modification or other, we must sooner or later come—a compulsory education for 'all classes. Among the more wealthy classes, shame of exposure would compel a man to educate his children if he were unwilling to do his duty to them ; but there are many ignorant uneducated parents among the working classes who cannot perceive the advantages of sending their children to school, and nothing short of compulsion will induce them to spend a portion of their earnings for that purpose.

As to what you say of the difficulty of getting the children to go to school, the representations made to you have been greatly exaggerated. They are true, I have no doubt, in many cases, where no pains have been bestowed to impress upon the children and their parents ; that attendance at school must be as regular as attendance at the mill ;—but I have made particular inquiry upon this point, and the certificates show, in a great many cases, as regular an attendance as you would find in most schools. Since I have had some parents punished, under the 29th section, for neglecting to send their children to school, the attendance has been better. I have recommended the masters to fine the children for playing truant ; to make the master or an overlooker the treasurer, in order to avoid all suspicion of the fines going into his own pocket, and to distribute the sum collected periodically, in the form of rewards in the school. By contrivances of various kinds, the difficulty will soon be got the better of; if we had good schools, where the children were evidently deriving useful instruction, a large proportion of parents would set a just value upon the opportunity, and look after the attendance of their children.

What you say of many of the operatives being hostile to the Act, accords with my experience, as I have stated in my Report of the 18th of January, 1837, page 46. But this applies chiefly to the Ten-hour Bill men, and those under their influence. When all hope of the limitation of the labour of adults is set at rest by some strong expression in Parliament, the opposition will greatly diminish. Operatives in numerous instances have expressed to me their approval of the Act, and particularly of that part of it by which their children " get a bit of schooling."

The masters maintained to you, that factory children are better educated than the children employed in other trades; so have mill-owners maintained to me, but they failed in giving any evidence of the assertion. For proofs of the deplorable ignorance of factory children in the cotton trade, I beg to refer you to my Report of the 12th of October, 1836, (p. 10,) and to that of the 18th of January, 1837 (p. 47,) where you will find that out of 2000, of 13 and 14 years of age, who were individually examined, 1067 could not read. I say *cotton*, because your inquiries were restricted to that branch; but it is no better in the woollen and flax mills; and, by an extraordinary inconsistency, children in silk mills are not required to attend school by the present Act ; an absurdity which I hope to see corrected in the proposed amending act.

The masters complain bitterly, you say, of the machinery of

the Act. They know perfectly well that without other machinery than what is contained in the Act itself, the law could not be enforced; and so, doubtless, parliament was aware, and they gave the inspectors the power of making such regulations as, in the working of the Act, might be proved to be necessary; a power which has been represented as novel, and as being unknown to the constitution; whereas there are precedents without number. The principle upon which the inspectors have all along acted has been, to endeavour to discover in what way the law could be carried into effect with the least possible inconvenience to the mill-owner or his work-people. To those mill-owners who have complained of the machinery, I have said again and again—" You see what the law requires as well as I do; and if you will point out a mode by which it can be carried into execution, with less trouble to you than attends compliance with our regulations, we shall give it our best attention, and will gladly adopt it if we can." *Nothing practicable has been suggested.* Objections have been made in abundance by some mill-owners; but they have proposed no substitute;—the demand is, " Do away with your troublesome machinery;" which is another way of saying, " Do not put the law in force."

The inspectors could not stir a step without some regulations; and we framed, at first, such as appeared to us to be necessary. After these had been put to the test of practical application, some were found unnecessary, others unreasonably troublesome; and we found too that some additional regulations were called for, in order to check frequent and gross evasions of the law. We, therefore, set earnestly to work last October, and issued a new code, which had previously received the sanction of the Secretary of State, by which the labour of the mill-owner is greatly diminished from what it was under the former regulations. This proceeding has been represented to you as if we had been capriciously and arbitrarily using vexatious rules, " not easily comprehended, and, by the time they have been understood, revoked." No rule or regulation has been issued without a copy having been sent, free of expense and postage, to every mill-occupier; and there was also an advertisement in the county newspaper twice, in addition to that delivery of notice. No rule or regulation has been attempted to be enforced by legal steps, until a considerable time had elapsed after the delivery of such notice, and after such advertisement.

With regard to the complaints stated at pages 20 and 21, under the heads 1, 2, and 3, I may challenge the complainants to bring forward a single instance of a mill-owner having been proceeded against for any such frivolous cause. They have been prosecuted for allowing a child to remain in the factory longer than the law allows; not because they were humanely protecting the child from the inclemency of the weather, but because they were employing it to *clean the machinery*, while the adult was at his dinner, or after the mill stopped at night; a practice which would be very common, if it had not been enacted that the child must not remain in the mill longer than the hours specified; because, cleaning machinery not being one of the enumerated processes in the 1st section, they could not otherwise be prevented from working the children any number of hours at other things than the processes so enumerated. No mill-owner has been prosecuted for making a false entry, " because one of 80 children has one day come at half-past 8," &c.; but because he was working the 80 children 12 hours a day, and falsely stating in his Time Register that they worked only eight hours. No mill-owner has been prosecuted " because he has been unable to force a child to school," but because he has for weeks and months paid no attention to the enactment requiring school attendance.

I shall next notice the suggestions stated at p. 12:—

1. I have already said that, to be consistent, Parliament must do something to provide schools and teachers where none already exist.

2. I do not see how the mill-owner can be relieved from the obligation now imposed upon him, viz. that he must not employ any child that does not produce proof of having attended school during the preceding week. *The impossibility of getting work*, unless the school be regularly attended, is the grand compelling power both over the parent and the child. It has been suggested by some, that children should be excluded from factories until they are 11 years of age ; when, if they could read and write, they should be admissible to work 12 hours a day. There are strong objections to this. It is a great injustice to the parents ; because children, by the time they are eight or nine years of age, can, with perfect safety to their health, be employed in a factory for eight hours in the day, and thus earn a large proportion of the sum necessary for their maintenance and education: by coming into the mill they acquire habits of regularity and industry,—no unimportant part of their education; and they are in a warm, dry place, generally far more healthy than the dwellings of their parents. Besides, if they were to be examined as to their education before getting work, it could only be as to the mechanical power of reading and writing,—the mere initiatory step in that process which alone is entitled to be called education. There is, moreover, the great objection that they would not be long enough at school for the formation of habits.

3. If the mill-owner were not punishable for mere *formal* violations of the law, he would very soon contrive to escape from all punishment for *substantial* violations. Any public officer who should prosecute for such informalities as are here stated must be a fool, and would be unfit for his situation;

but if the mill-owner will not observe the *forms* by which the inspector can alone judge whether the law has been *substantially* obeyed, he surely deserves punishment. But the punishment ought to be very different for neglecting to obey a regulation and for overworking a child. As bringing a mill-owner into court is a very serious, and to many the most serious punishment, it is worthy of consideration whether it would be safe, or sound in principle, to authorize the inspector summarily, and without bringing the party into court, to impose a fine not exceeding a small sum, for all such minor offences, giving the party the option to pay the fine, or to be proceeded against by information in the usual way.

4. To a control by government over the promulgation of rules and regulations by the inspectors, I see no objection, but, on the contrary, should rejoice to see it established. The inspectors, however, ought to have a full opportunity of stating to the controlling party why they consider the rules they have proposed necessary. As to an appeal, that is more questionable, and, with the supposed control, hardly necessary. What better mode of publication could be devised than that now practised, I am at a loss to conjecture. We could not employ any more expensive messenger than the postman; and the transmission of a copy, free of charge, to every mill-occupier, and two advertisements in the county paper, appear to me to be very full notice of what mill-owners are required to attend to.

You make me assume a tone of decision, which I am not conscious of having employed, when in your third letter you speak of my making "requisitions." On the subject of magistrates, who are themselves mill-owners, or nearly connected with them, sitting on factory cases, all I have said is contained in the following paragraph in my Report of the 12th of October, 1836:— "It is, in my opinion, a matter very much to be regretted, that magistrates, who are themselves mill-owners, or who have property in mills, or who are by trade or near relationship connected with factories, should sit on the bench in cases of prosecution for offences against this Act. They must often, unconsciously to themselves, have a bias in favour of such offenders; and, at all events, this serious evil will arise,—that, however uprightly they may act, their motives for leniency will always be liable to misconstruction, and a doubt will be thrown on the purity of the administration of the law." I have also joined with my colleagues in recommending that the disqualifying clause in Sir John Hobhouse's Act, 1 and 2 Wm. IV. c. 39, sect. 10, should be introduced into the proposed amending Act.

When I tell you that I have had mill-occupiers trying cases against other mill-occupiers living in the same town, upon several occasions;—a mill-owner, sitting as a single magistrate upon an information against *his own sons* the tenants of his mill; a mill-occupier deciding upon an information laid against

*his own brother*; and all these giving, in every instance, the
lowest penalty which they had power to award in the case of a
conviction, in some cases for a second and even a third offence,
I think I was bound to bring the subject before the Secretary of
State. Whether it be practicable to have the law administered
in such cases by magistrates who are not interested parties,
Parliament is best able to decide.

If you will examine the return of convictions laid before the
House of Commons in the present session, and printed, No. 97,
you will find that the prosecutions have not been for mere formal
offences, but for grave violations of the great enactments in the
statute, or wilful neglect of regulations without the obser-
vance of which the law would speedily become a dead letter; as
its predecessors became, for want of a proper machinery to
enforce obedience to them.

I have recommended that, in place of the superintendent
getting admission to the interior of the factory by sufferance,
he should be able to go there as a matter of right; because, at
present, it is in the power of a mill-owner, by excluding him,
to set the law at defiance so long as he is out of the immediate
reach of the inspector. I remain of the opinion, that such a
right is wanting for the due enforcement of the law. If a
power were given to the inspector to issue a warrant to the
superintendent to enter the interior of a mill upon his declaration in writing that he has good reason to believe that the law is
violated there, the evil perhaps might be remedied to a great
extent, without conferring the right upon the superintendent to
go at pleasure into the factory. Two of the mill-owners whom
you saw, and whom I met with in London at the beginning of
this month, and who spoke to me on this point, stated to me
that their objection to the admission of the superintendent
would be very much diminished if he were more under the
control of the inspector than he is at present, by holding his
appointment from him; and if thus the inspector were made
responsible for the good conduct of his deputy. Upon this last
subject you agree, I know, with these gentlemen; and you
have adverted to it shortly in the postscript to your second
letter. There are few things less to be envied than the possession of patronage when it is to be exercised in the selection of
a proper man for such an office; but I am satisfied (and I speak
from experience) that, until the inspector has a very different
control over his assistants than he possesses at present, the public service will be exposed to suffer from collisions between them.

I am, my dear Sir,

Yours, very faithfully,

LEONARD HORNER.

N. W. SENIOR, Esq.

MINUTES *of a Conversation on Friday, the 22th of May, 1837, between Mr. Thompson, Mr. Edmund Ashworth, and Mr. Senior.\**

THE following paper was read by Mr. Thomson:—

A belief that whatever regulations are permanently established by the legislature for cotton-mills, will sooner or later be imposed on calico printers, has made me watch with interest the operation of the present enactments. The calico printers are, in fact, much more obnoxious to reproach than the spinners, for they now employ children at a much earlier age, work them harder, and work them longer. An ordinary day's work in a print ground is 10 hours of actual labour; but at the busy season, in spring and autumn, or during the shipping months, the hours of actual labour are extended to 12 or 14, and sometimes (with a relay) through the night. If the law interfered to prevent this, it would not be a question of profit to the manufacturer, but of employment for the people. Time is an element in the calculations of a manufacture, dependent on season, taste, and fashion. That which one month fetches a high profit, in the next is sold for none at all, and, in the following, to a heavy loss. A calico printer cannot work to a stock as a spinner or weaver, whose production being the same from year to year, is saleable some time or other. The consequence is, that the printer is often idle for weeks, and often again has double the work he can perform in the ordinary hours of labour. It is the same in all countries,—France, Switzerland, Germany, and the north of Europe. It is irremediable: and the law that imposed restrictions on the hours of labour in calico printing would destroy the trade, and involve masters and labourers in common ruin.

The factory system of education is wholly inapplicable to calico printing. The child is actually a part of a machine, like a lynch pin; and just as when the pin is out, the wheel comes off, so a tier-boy absent stops his master. I once proposed to try the experiment. In order to educate 300 children, I intended to form them into classes of 30 each, and place each class for one hour under a schoolmaster; and thus, in 10 hours per day, to give to the whole number one hour's education per day. The schoolmaster's salary would have been 12*s.* per week; the wages, at 2*s.* 6*d.* each per week, of 30 supernumeraries, to replace the class, would have been 4*l.* 7*s.*; but I abandoned it, on finding that the only result would be the giving an inadequate, and, in fact, almost useless education, at the expense of

* Mr. Thomson's print-works, at Primrose, near Clithero, are among the most extensive in the kingdom.

about 250*l.* a year. To have doubled the time would have doubled the expense.

A more grave objection than the expense was, that the children would have been sent into school dirty from their employment, their minds unprepared, or ill-prepared, for a sudden transition from mere animal labour to mental, and for a short period only, and then back to work again. The relay system would require a doubling of the hands, which, in very few situations, are to be had.

Having abandoned this project, I adopted with success a system, which throws on the parents the *onus* of attending to the education of their children, and secures it by making it their interest. Apprenticeships in the various branches of calico printing, viz. pattern drawing, engraving, block cutting, block printing, are eagerly sought after by parents for their children, as leading to high wages. I have made the ability to read and write at 14 years of age an indispensable qualification. The effect of this is strikingly shown in the demand for teaching which it has produced. The Sunday schools of the Established Church not teaching writing, as being a secular employment, were deserted for those of the Methodists and Catholics. The children have been allured back to the Establishment by gratuitous night schools twice a week, when writing and arithmetic are taught. Such apprentices as are already indentured, though not qualified, have received notice, that if they are not able to pass an examination at the expiration of their apprenticeships, they will not be employed as journeymen. Lastly, notice has been given, that after the 1st of July, 1838, no child, whatever its age, will be received into the manufactory who cannot read; and it forms a part of my plan, considerably to extend the qualification for apprenticeships as soon as certain arrangements regarding the schools of the neighbourhood, now in contemplation, are carried into effect.

*Mr. Ashworth.*—We have found so much advantage from our people being able to read and write, that, although opposed in feeling to the compulsory education forced upon us by the present Factory Law, we are anxious to see a law of the nation, a general law, enforcing education on all trades, by making it unlawful for any child, unable to read and write, to be found working out of its parent's house.

*Q.* Have you any, and what objection to a law forbidding a parent to obtain profit from the labour of his child, until that child had made a certain proficiency in reading and writing?

*A.* Except within its own parent's house, under his own roof. I suggest this limitation, on the ground that it would be too much an infringement upon domestic society, to interfere with the parent's arrangements in his own house. I never expect a law to be well observed, unless obedience is made the interest of those affected by it. The regulation which I propose by holding out education as the condition for a parent's receiving a lucrative return for his children's labour out of the house, would effectually induce him to see to their attaining it. But at the same time, there must be the facility of obtaining that education. There must be both the motive and the means—the means must be provided by Government. At present such means do not exist.

Q. Do you see no objection to the Legislature imposing a condition on parents whose children work from home, and none on those whose children work at home?

A. I do not see any: There are few families in which the children can permanently obtain their livelihood in their parents' house; sooner or later they all quit it.

Q. Supposing there were an indisposition to promote this education, on the part of the parents, or a total indifference to it, would not the proposed law occasion a preference of domestic employment to that which would lead the children abroad; of hand-loom weaving, for instance, to factory work?

A. I think not; parents may be, and unhappily often are, indifferent to the education of their children, but not to their getting good wages, or to their advancement in the world; and those objects are best obtained by sending them from home. A child can be earlier and more effectually profitable to his parent, by attending a factory than a hand-loom. Children cannot become weavers till the age of ten, eleven, or twelve; they are admitted to the factories at nine, and generally they are able to get more in a factory at eleven, than they would in their father's house at eleven. Again, hand-loom weaving is a declining trade; mill occupations are an increasing and improving trade.

Q. (To Mr. Thomson.)—What amount of education would you consider sufficient for the children in your employ?

A. Constant attendance at the Sunday school, morning and afternoon, and attendance at the night school twice a week for two hours each night.

Q. That would be,—how many hours on Sunday?

A. On Sunday that would be six hours.

Q. Six hours in school?

A. Three hours in the morning, and three hours in the afternoon.

Q. With the attendance at church, that would make from eight to nine hours a-day, on Sunday?

A. Generally, young children who attend Sunday schools, do not attend the church service—at least, not regularly, but in sections, as there may be accommodation.

Q. The whole time given to education would be ten hours per week?

A. It would.

*Q.* But in your paper, you described one hour a day on the week days, which, with the 6 hours on Sunday, makes 12 hours a-week, as inadequate?

*A.* Two hours of continued attention are much more than twice as efficient as a single hour. The first quarter of an hour and the last are generally wasted: I think the two hours would be usefully employed.

In fact, however, I was assuming the adoption of the proposal, that no child unable to read, or perhaps to write, should be admitted into a factory. The ten hours a week, therefore, which I have just mentioned, would be employed only in keeping up and extending an education of which the foundation had been previously laid.

*Mr. Ashworth.*—If a national course of education were enforced, and children received in Infant Schools up to seven years of age, and in the National School from seven to ten years of age, they would then, nine-tenths of them, have sufficient education for the general profession of artisans.

*Mr. Thomson.*—On such a plan I am now proceeding at Clithero. Two schools, an infant, and a British or National school, are now in a course of erection ; the operation of which will render unnecessary the present restrictions.

*Q.* What restrictions?

*A.* I speak of my own regulations with regard to the non-admission of apprentices who cannot read and write.

*Q.* You think, that if your regulations were applied to the cotton manufacture, the education clauses of the Factory Act would be unnecessary?

*A.* I do.

*Q.* What effect did your plan produce on the desire and means of procuring education in your neighbourhood ?

*A.* It produced a great desire on the part of the parents to have their children taught reading and writing, when they found that without these qualifications they were refused apprenticeships, and admission into situations that were eagerly sought after. The new demand in the town for education was so considerable, that new schools, both day and night schools, were formed by private schoolmasters. There are now three schools more than there were before this regulation ; and, as I mentioned before, those who have the management of the Church of England Sunday school, have found it necessary to open schools for reading, writing, and arithmetic, two nights in the week, to prevent the children from being drawn off to the schools of the Methodists and Catholics, where writing is taught on the Sunday.

*Q.* Had you any difficulty in obtaining schoolmasters?

*A.* No difficulty in obtaining schoolmasters to teach reading, nor indeed to teach writing ; but great difficulty in obtaining masters with higher qualifications. In the lower classes, when a man can do nothing else for his livelihood, he becomes a schoolmaster; men whose failure in life is often to be attributed to their own improvident and vicious habits.

*Mr. Ashworth.*—In reference to the practicability of applying national education, I would say that I have been lately engaged in taking, or rather in having taken for me, the statistics of education of the borough of Bolton, containing about 54,000 inhabitants. There were 61 schools; and of the 61 schoolmasters there were only 13 who had been educated for the profession; 25 had taken it up from poverty, and the remainder for a livelihood. With such masters little can be done ; but with able teachers great progress might be made, at little expense. We have lately established a school in Bolton, under the title of "The Bolton British School," on the "London British and Foreign School" system, where we educate 500 children, at the cost of twopence each per week. They consider three years a sufficient length of time to teach them reading, writing, and arithmetic, and some acquaintance with mechanical drawing. Such an education can be given between the ages of seven and ten.

*Q. (To Mr. Thomson.)*—Do you think that those whom you have admitted to apprenticeships, as capable of reading and writing, can read so as to amuse themselves ?

*A.* They cannot all read fluently ; some do : but if we had exacted too much at first, we should have had no hands. We found that the parents cared little or nothing about their children's education, for its own sake; mere exhortations would have driven them away ; it was only by making it decidedly their interest, that I could do any thing. It was this that led me to adopt the plan detailed in my paper. I found from experience, that the parents themselves would never do any thing for the education of their children ; that even where schools exist, as they do in our neighbourhood, they never enforced the attendance of the children, and never took any pains to procure education for them ; so that it was necessary not only to explain to them that it was their duty, but to make it their immediate and direct interest.

*Q.* In many cases, are not the parents jealous of their children being better educated than themselves? Do they not dislike it ?

*A.* I have never seen that feeling.

*Mr. Ashworth.*—And I have never seen it.

*Q.* Then it is indifference on their parts, not dislike?

*A.* Indifference, rather than dislike.

*Mr. Thomson.*—The lower classes are not sensible of the advantages of education.

*Mr. Ashworth.*—I have generally found them so ignorant, as not to know the disadvantages they laboured under. It is to be observed, that when a case does occur that an individual can both read and write, and becomes more successful in his business, the rest of the community seldom refer his success to his education, but to some other cause, such as superior conduct ; and very often attribute the whole of it to what they call a gift of intellect. The great objection which I have to the mode in which education is now provided in the manufacturing districts, is that it is given on Sundays. Too many of the young people are brought up with the feeling, that they have performed their duties by simply attending a school, and not a place of worship, on the Sabbath day ; and at a great number of those schools, but little of real religious instruction is given. None but the Church teaches religion ; the Church does teach the fundamental principles of religion; but you cannot find any others that do so. I feel it to be lamentable, that the Sabbath should be the only day in the week devoted to receiving instruction—that we rob the Sabbath of its peculiar service, in order that we may devote the whole of the working days to work. At the same time, the instruction to which the appropriate duties of the Sabbath are sacrificed, is not such as best fits the child for its employment during the week. The result is, that the children receive neither good social, nor good religious instruction.

What I wish would be, that sufficient secular instruction should be given in the working days, and that such instruction should be given to them on the Sabbath as might be peculiar to their religious profession.

I have seen the evil, in many cases, of persons growing up to manhood, and feeling satisfied in their moral duty by simply attending at a Sunday school, and not attaching themselves to any religious body or profession. I speak of this now, not from any isolated case, but generally as an evil growing up to be combated in a succeeding generation.

*Q.* I think the chapel connected with your school is Independent ?

*A.* We have three. I speak now looking at Bolton, where there are 9000 children educated out of a population of 54,000 ; and, as Mr. Thomson has previously said, the schools where writing is taught are much followed : on the other hand, some of the promoters of such schools, joining with me in opinion that the Sabbath day is too much devoted to secular education, have shown a wish to abolish writing in their schools, and those schools have consequently sunk in the estimation of the scholars.

*Q.* Would you yourself consider writing as too secular ?

*Mr. Ashworth.*—I should decidedly say, too secular for Sunday. At the same time, my religious profession have no Sunday schools.* They hold that the Sabbath should be wholly devoted to its peculiar service.

---

\* Mr. Ashworth is a member of the Society of Friends.

*Mr. Thomson.*—If the schools of the Established Church would dispense with a peculiar test as to their weekly schools, that is, would admit the children of other denominations, without compelling them to learn the Catechism,—and their own Sunday schools, and the Sunday schools of each sect of Christians were made schools for religious instruction,—it would be a great improvement.

*Q.* But according to your scheme of an evening school for only two hours on two days in the week, would it be possible to give a sufficient quantity of mere intellectual instruction, if the Sunday were wholly devoted to religious and moral instruction?

*Mr. Thomson.*—This is leaving out my proposal of the children going till seven years of age to an infant school, and for three years afterwards to a national or British school.

*Mr. Ashworth.*—I may further say, I have tried most perseveringly evening schools, and so long as I attended them personally, success resulted; but when it was left to the inclination of the parents and the children, without my almost compulsory superintendence, it fell away.

*Q.* I was told at Manchester, that the children in the cotton factories were, on the whole, better educated than the children of the same class in other employments: do you think that it is so?

*Mr. Ashworth.*—As respects the children of English parents, the children in cotton factories are not better educated than those in other factory employments in Lancashire; because the education which they receive is not peculiar to the cotton manufacture. But as far as my own experience goes, I should say, that the factory children are better educated than children in other parts of the country; certainly better than the children of the agricultural labourers. The manufacturing parents are, as I have already stated, indifferent to the education of their children. The agricultural parents are often positively hostile. In a part of the south, which I have frequently visited, parents have often asked, "Will my boys be any better ploughmen or spade-labourers for learning to read and write?" A school which was established there by a near connexion of my own, on his own estate, and at his own expense, was very unwillingly attended, and only in obedience to his express desire; and so unpopular was education in the neighbourhood, that a clergyman used his influence to prevent the attendance of the children at the school, although no sectarian religious instruction was given to the children; and there was no Sunday school. The clergyman and his wife actually went from door to door, to forbid their going. There is a feeling in that district, that education would spoil the labouring classes. We cannot combat this prejudice throughout the whole country, without the aid of the Legislature.

*Q.* There is another subject upon which I wish for Mr. Ashworth's and Mr. Thomson's opinions. I have stated in my letters to Mr. Poulett Thomson, that it was represented to us that a great number of prosecutions had been brought under the Factory Act, for mere formal offences. I have stated that the manufacturers complained to us that a master may be called before a magistrate, exposed, and fined, for overworking a child, because a child has remained a minute too long within the walls of the mill, from heedlessness, or from dislike of being turned out in the snow, or, perhaps, as part of a conspiracy to make the Act intolerable. I have also said, that they object to being liable to be accused, convicted, and fined, for making false entries in the time-book, because one of 80 children has one day come at half-past eight, and gone at half-past four, instead of coming at eight and going at four, the hours fixed for it, and entered in the time-book on the supposition that they had been adhered to; and that it is to avoid this danger that the relay system had been generally unattempted or disused. I have also said, that the manufacturers have objected to being convicted and fined for neglecting the education of the children, because they had been unable to force a child to school, or have allowed one to work without a regular certificate of school attendance; that they say the children will work, and will not go to school; and that the mill-owner, whose time is filled with other things, cannot employ it in preventing 80 urchins from truancy. In a letter which I had the day before yesterday from Mr. Horner, he states his disbelief that any mill-occupier has ever been fined for such offences as the two first, and his conviction that no punishment had been inflicted except for wilful violations of the substance of the law. What is your opinion on these statements?

*Mr. Ashworth.*—I do not personally know of any cases of such convictions; but we conceive ourselves liable to them, inasmuch as we are obliged to keep an account at the mill of the time of the children coming and going,—neglect of which subjects us to a penalty. Again, we send the children to a school at about ten minutes' distance; the schoolmaster gives a certificate of the attendance of those children at the school: if we have not that certificate we are liable to a penalty; and again, we are liable to a penalty if a child has been only an hour, or an hour and a half, at school, instead of two hours.

*Q.* But do you employ the children without a certificate?

*A. We do employ them without a certificate, when they are not possessed of one, otherwise the machinery must remain idle.* It is utterly impossible for any manufacturer to employ a moderate number of hands without being liable to a penalty every day.

*Q.* What proportion do you suppose of your hands, speaking generally, have certificates?

*A.* 10 per cent. require certificates.

*Q.* Are you able to comply with the requisitions of the Act, as to the entries in the time-book ?

*A.* Of the time of their coming in the morning, and our driving them away, we are; but as respects the intermediate time of their going out of the mill to the school, and their return from the school to the mill, we are not able to control their attendance.

*Q.* Therefore, in point of fact, you are liable to prosecution, from some source or another, for almost all the children you employ.

*A.* Yes; as to the fifty that go in and out of our mill, we are liable every day to penalties, which might be enforced against us, on proofs derived from our own records. This plan gives the superintendents great power of annoyance, if we were to thwart them; and although I do not know of any particular cases of conviction, for mere formal offences, still the general opinion is, that it is within the power of *any* superintendent to obtain a conviction from *any* manufacturer. It is the general feeling, that we are entirely in the hands of the superintendent, by his having so very many points upon which he can enforce a penalty under regulations made by his superior, which it is almost imposssible literally to observe; and although I do not know personally of any such convictions, it is the general opinion that such convictions have taken place.

*Mr. Thomson.*—I know that the masters complain, that convictions have taken place upon the most frivolous accusations.

*Q.* Do you think that the substitution of a test for education, instead of the education clauses, would effect the object, without the inconvenience?

*A. Mr. Ashworth.*—I think that it would be, inasmuch as it would then become the interest of the parents to see to the education of their children; at present they feel averse to the small degree of compulsion which is now exercised over them. The answers of many of our men, when reproved for the irregular attendance of their children at school, have been to that effect.

*Q.* Would it be an improvement if the master were altogether exonerated, and the parent only fined.

*Mr. Ashworth.*—In such cases the school, and the schoolmaster, would have to be provided by some other authority; at present, the responsibility as to providing a school rests in effect with the master. The present law enforces the attendance of the scholars, but not their proficiency; and I know many cases where the attendance is merely nominal, and little or no education is attempted to be enforced.

*Q.* Your school appeared to me, when I visited it, to be conducted by an excellent master, and to be efficient; do you find that the goodness of the education thus supplied, increases, or rather creates a wish in the children to attend it, and in the parents to send them ?

*A.* The system we have adopted, which is that of the British and Foreign School Society, renders the studies of the children much less irksome ; and when the attendance is entire, not mixed with mill labour, the children attend very cheerfully, but those who belong to the mills, go for short periods, are compelled to wash, and clean themselves previous to entering the school, and then immediately enter their classes, and attend to rather a laborious mental duty for two hours, therefore feel averse to it ; we have more truants from those who come from the mill, than from all our other scholars put together, although the number from the mill is only one-fourth of the whole.

THE END.

R. CLAY, PRINTER, BREAD-STREET-HILL.

# Grounds and Objects
of the Budget

*Edinburgh Review* (July 1841)

THE history and the prospects of the manufacturing industry
of Great Britain, have long excited mixed feelings of
pleasure and of pain, of pride and of regret, of satisfaction and
of uneasiness, in all thinking minds. We have raised the value
of. British industry far beyond the value of that of any other

European community. We have accumulated a capital far exceeding, both positively and in relation to our population, that of any other existing nation, or indeed of any nation whose history is known. Though struggling with a bad climate and a moderately fertile soil, that industry and that capital have made our land more valuable than any other country of equal extent. In no portion of Europe does the whole amount of wages bear so large a proportion to the whole number of labourers; or the whole amount of profit to the whole number of inhabitants; or the whole amount of rent to the whole cultivable area. So far as wealth has been our object, we have been successful beyond the dreams of avarice. And our success has not been obtained by the sacrifice of present enjoyment. We have not grown rich by parsimony. Whatever may be thought of some portions of our own countrymen, the English, and they form the bulk of the population of Britain, are not a saving people. In every occupation and in every rank—among labourers, mechanics, shopkeepers, capitalists, and proprietors—there is a tendency to the display and the consumption of wealth little known on the Continent. The Government has been still more extravagant than its subjects; so that we have exhibited the strange spectacle of a nation rising rapidly to enormous wealth in the midst of profuse public and private expenditure.

But sacrifices we have made, and they are very serious ones, both as they affect our present happiness, and as they endanger, at no remote period, our future welfare; and we have diminished the advantages of our position, aggravated the difficulties which are necessarily incidental to it, and multiplied tenfold its dangers, by legislative errors which we are now beginning, we trust not too late, to rectify.

Some dangers, some difficulties, are, as we have said, incidental to our position. What they are, will be best seen by comparing the state of our labouring population with that of the nations which surround us.

In every other portion of Europe, indeed in every other portion of the civilized world, the bulk of the free population are occupiers or proprietors of Land; employing themselves partly in raising food for their own consumption, and partly in rough manufactures for their own use. The cottage of the French *Paysan* or of the German *Bauer,* is a much worse habitation than that of the English labourer—but it is his own. He feeds on the inferior vegetables, or on a bread which would be rejected by an English beggar—but they come from his own garden or his own field. His dress is coarse and ill-made— but his linen has perhaps been grown, spun, and woven in

his own house; and his woollen garments are often the produce of his own sheep. He is not a diligent workman—but
he is almost always working. He does nothing well—but a
great many things tolerably. Both his labour and his skill are
diffused, instead of being, like the Englishman's, concentrated.
Such a population may be ill-fed, ill-clothed, and ill-lodged; but
it is at least secure of employment. The only accidents to which
it is subject, are the accidents of the seasons. Such a population necessarily acquires habits of economy and prudence. Every
head of a family is to a certain degree a capitalist. He is accustomed to make present sacrifices for future objects; to reserve a
portion of his crop for seed ; and to proportion the daily consumption of the remainder to the number of days that must elapse
before the harvest recurs. The greatest of all improvidences,
improvident marriage, is repressed, partly by the comparative
unproductiveness of the labour of women and children—partly
by the difficulty of procuring a house and land for a new family,
except on the death of a previous occupant—partly by legal restrictions—and still more effectually by the customs which these
different causes have produced.

Such a population has almost always a deep respect for property and for authority. Every man values highly his own
small possessions, and reverences the law which protects them.
And even if the law become oppressive instead of protective,
a scattered peasantry have neither the knowledge, the habits,
nor the opportunities, which would enable them to combine in
resisting it. A tranquil, unadvancing, indolent, but frugal and
contented poverty, with little to hope, but still less to fear, is the
state of the great mass of the inhabitants of continental Europe.

On the other hand, in Britain, particularly in England,
the very large majority of the population consists of labourers
hired by the week or by the day, dependent for subsistence
solely on their wages, and for their wages solely on the will of
their master. Both the skill and the diligence of the British
workman are unrivalled ; hence, when these admirable qualities
are well directed, the high value of his labour, and the large
amount of his wages. But the skill and diligence of each individual can be applied to only a few purposes, and are useful only
under numerous and complicated conditions. The continental
workman may in general be compared to the tools which he
uses—his axe or his spade,—an instrument of no great efficiency,
but always fit for independent use. The British workmen, and
more especially the most numerous classes, those employed in
manufactures, resemble the component parts of the vast machines
which they direct. Separately taken, they are as useless as a

single wheel or a single roller. Combined with many hundreds or many thousands of others, each helpless when alone, a hundred families can produce results which could not have been obtained by the individual labour of a thousand. But the instant the moving power that animates one of these great bodies ceases to act—the instant the engine ceases to be supplied with water, or the factory with capital—the component parts lose their mutual support, and, with that support, their value. The engine becomes old iron, the spinners and weavers become paupers.

It might be supposed, that classes exposed to such contingencies, would save in their prosperity a fund to support them in adversity. But such is not the habit of the English. They have not been accustomed, like their continental rivals, to treat their earnings as the means of further production, or even of future support. When wages are high, they work fewer hours and inhabit better houses; and, if there still remain a superfluity, the women and girls waste it in dress, and the men in drink or luxurious living. When wages fall, they endeavour to increase their earnings by more assiduous labour, and to economize, first in house-rent, then in dress, then in fuel, and ultimately in food. When their earnings become insufficient for a maintenance, they throw themselves on the parish. The virtue which they possess the least is providence.

We have already remarked, that the greatest of all improvidences is improvident marriage. But among many classes, perhaps among most classes, of mere labourers, although it may be clear that the usual period of marriage is far too early, and that the welfare of the whole body would be much promoted if that period were generally retarded, it is difficult to say that any given marriage is improvident. The great object of machinery is to supply strength and skill; its great triumph is to render the labour of women and children as efficient as that of men; and in many extensive branches of manufacture this has been effected. A girl of eighteen can attend to a power-loom as well as a full grown man; a child of thirteen is more valuable as a piecer than an adult—its touch is more sensitive, and its sight is more acute. A factory lad of eighteen who marries a factory girl of the same age, finds himself immediately richer; and although he may be pinched during some of the following years, yet as each child attains the age of nine years it can earn more than its support; and the earnings of three children between the ages of nine and sixteen can, in prosperous times, support the whole family. It was under the influence of this enormous stimulus, with some assistance from immigration, that the population of our manufacturing districts increased during the thirty years that elapsed between

1801 and 1831—the last period for which the returns are published—at a rate equalled only in some portions of America. During the ten years between 1801 to 1811, the population of Lancashire increased at the rate of 23 per cent; during the next ten years at the rate of 27 per cent; and during the last ten years also at the rate of 27 per cent. That of Lanark increased at the rate of 31 per cent in the first period; of 27 per cent in the second; and of 30 per cent in the third. At the beginning of that period, in 1801 the two most populous counties in Scotland were Lanark and Perth; the former containing 146,000 inhabitants, the latter 126,000. At the end of the period, in 1831, Lanark contained 316,000, and Perth only 142,000. While the population of the manufacturing county increased at the rate of more than 100 per cent, that of the agricultural district increased at the rate of less than 14 per cent. During the same period, the population of the North Riding of Yorkshire, a district chiefly agricultural, rose from 158,000 to 190,000; that of the West Riding, a manufacturing district, from 565,000 to 976,000.

It is scarcely necessary to remark how much the habits which we have described, must aggravate the sufferings incident to any serious interruption of our manufactures. The millions whom we have crowded into densely-peopled districts, are accustomed not merely to prosperity, but to constantly advancing prosperity. All their calculations assume a constantly increasing demand for labour—a demand which shall absorb a supply quite unrestrained by any prudential checks. A painful question follows, as to the temper and the conduct which may be expected from them under a reversed state of circumstances. If the demand for British manufactures, instead of increasing, should diminish ; if the new swarm of candidates which every year throws into the labour-market should be rejected; if the employment of all should become precarious; if many establishments should be discontinued, and others give work only for three or four days a-week ; if the wages for this diminished and irregular work should themselves be diminished ; if a family, accustomed to earn forty shillings a-week, and to a proportionate expenditure, should fall to an income of nine or ten shillings, and no prospect of improvement were afforded—what, we repeat, is the temper and the conduct to be expected from the sufferers ? Are they likely to treat these evils as mere calamities, or as injuries ? If as injuries, are their habits likely to induce them to patience, or to attempts at redress, or resistance ? If patience is not to be expected from them, are their struggles likely to be formidable ?

We fear that, to every one of these questions, we must give an alarming answer.

If the commercial policy of the British legislature had been prudent, or barely impartial; if our rulers had been wise enough to know, that in a state of freedom industry will spontaneously take the most productive course; or just enough to feel, that interference in favour of one class of producers, or one class of proprietors, to the injury of any other class, or of the community in general, is injustice, even if it be not folly ; if, in pursuance of these principles, they had allowed every man to exert himself in the mode which he thought most advantageous, the Government might have to deplore the misfortunes of trade, but could not be held responsible for them.   Or if it had been guilty of interference, but had interfered only from ignorance ; if errors of judgment had been the only errors of which it could be accused ; if the members of the legislature could not be charged with direct selfishness ; if they could not be accused of legislating, at the expense of the public, for the benefit, or supposed benefit, of the class to which they belong, though the detection of their mistakes might lower them in public estimation, it would not occasion public resentment.

It is scarcely necessary to state at length how far each of these assumptions is from the truth.

For centuries, the Government has laboured to fetter and misdirect the industry of the people.  Instead of confining itself to its true task of defending its subjects from foreign and domestic violence and fraud, it has taken on itself the task of rendering them, or of rendering certain classes of them, rich.  It has dictated to them what they shall produce, and to whom they shall sell, and what they shall purchase, and to what markets they shall resort.  It has considered the whole body of consumers as a prey to be sacrificed to any class, or to any section of a class, that chose to ask for a monopoly.  And when one class has complained of the privileges granted to another, it has bribed it into acquiescence by allowing it to inflict a further injustice on the public.  In order to benefit the class engaged in exporting supplies to the colonies, it prohibits or restricts the direct trade between the colonies and foreign countries.  In order to induce the colonies to submit to these prohibitions and restrictions, it prohibits or restricts the importation into the British islands of foreign colonial commodities, the public suffering by each set of rules; first, by being confined to the market of the British colonies ; and secondly, by those colonies being stunted, and that market rendered still more unfavourable by the restrictions laid on the colonies.  To benefit the lumberers of Canada, and the owners of some old vessels fit only for the American timber trade, it imposes duties from 500 to 100 per cent on the

best timber, because it is the cheapest; duties not only not productive, but positively injurious to the revenue. To reconcile
the shipowners to the additional expense of about 15 per cent
thus imposed on British ship-building, it imposes higher duties
on the same commodities when imported in a foreign than in a
British ship. To benefit the British tanner, it subjects foreign
tanned leather to a prohibitory duty ; and it purchases the silence
of the manufacturers who use leather for their material, by imposing prohibitory duties on almost every foreign commodity, of
which leather forms a part. The favourites, of course, of the
legislature, have been the landowners, the class to which they
themselves belong. The importation of cattle, sheep, swine,
beef, lamb, mutton, and pork, they absolutely prohibit; and
on grain, they impose duties which, on an average, raise the price
of bread 20 per cent;—which cramp our trade, which convert our
customers into our rivals, which lower wages, and, what is perhaps a still greater evil in a society constituted as ours is, render
employment uncertain.

If this has been the conduct of the rulers of this country, we
repeat the question, what is likely to be the conduct of their
subjects if such a reverse as we have alluded to should occur?
When they are told, and told with truth, that the government
has ventured to assume the direction of manufactures and trade ;
when they are told, and truly told, that it has used this monstrous usurpation for the benefit, or the supposed benefit, not of
the many, but of the few ; when they find, that of all the monopolies which it has conferred, that which it enforces most rigidly,
and maintains most pertinaciously, is the monopoly of food; when
they find, that this is the monopoly which inflicts on them the
most suffering, and gives, or is intended to give, to the governing class the greatest immediate profit—are they likely to endure it as a misfortune or to resent it as an injury? If they resent it, we repeat, what form is their resentment likely to take—
sulky submission, or fierce struggles for redress ? and, in the latter alternative, to what degree are they formidable?

These questions scarcely require an answer. The manufacturing
population of Great Britain consists of many millions of persons
concentrated in towns, or in districts as populous as towns, accustomed to political discussion ; with their own leaders and their own
press ; organized in combinations, with executive, deliberative,
and corresponding officers ; with funds for the separate purposes
of each distinct society, and for the general purposes of the
united societies ; and trained, by a long and successful contest
against the combination laws, to elude or to defy the authority of
the state. Such a population is formidable even in prosperity ;

it would become doubly formidable in adversity, even though that adversity arose from causes involving no blame to the government. But if it were miserable, and could trace its misery directly to the legislature; if it could accuse the governing body, not of error, but of oppression and robbery; if it felt itself sacrificed to the rents of landlords, and to the profits of sugar planters and timber merchants—what limits can we assign to its passions or to its violence? Are we sure that our wealth, our political greatness, or even our constitution, would come out safely from such a struggle?

We are grieved to come forward as alarmists. We deplore the necessity, and do not much like the character; but we believe that the dangers which we have hypothetically suggested are really imminent; and we feel it to be a duty to state to the public the grounds of our conviction.

At the conclusion of the war, we possessed a commercial and manufacturing supremacy which no other nation has ever attained. Positively, indeed, neither our trade nor our industry were nearly as extensive as they are now; nor was it possible that they should be so when our population did not exceed two-thirds of its present amount. But relatively to other nations they were much greater. We had enjoyed internal peace while every country in Europe had been laid waste by war, and every capital had been held by an enemy. We had become the workshop of the world, and the rest of the world seemed willing to continue a relation from which it benefited as much as ourselves. But for this purpose our own consent was necessary. If we wished to sell, we must buy; if we wished to increase our sales in proportion to our increasing population, we must increase our purchases in the same proportion. Our first act was to establish a corn law. We say to *establish* a corn law; for that which previously existed had, from the altered value of money, become nominal. By the memorable law of 1815, the law to which our subsequent calamities and our present dangers may be traced, the importation of wheat was absolutely prohibited when it was under the famine price of 80s. a quarter. Butcher's meat we absolutely prohibited, whatever might be its price. Next to meat and bread—indeed, in as far as the majority of our population is concerned, next to bread—the most important article of food is sugar. We imposed on all foreign sugar prohibitory duties. The north of Europe, then the great market for our manufactures, and within a week's sail from our shores, sold to us the best timber and at the cheapest rate; the Canadas, a distant, thinly-peopled country, offered us timber almost worthless for building purposes, and at a much higher price. By imposing differential duties, rising from 100 to 500 per cent, we forced the community to resort to the bad customer instead of the good one—to use the distant market instead of the near one—to take the inferior instead of the superior commodity, and to pay for it a larger price. We repealed in words most of our prohibitions, except where food was concerned; but still subjected foreign manufactures to duties scarcely ever falling below 20 per cent on their value—that is, on their value here; all expenses of commission and conveyance being added to their original cost, and generally rising above that extravagant rate.

It is difficult to say what would have been the whole effects of these regulations, if foreign nations had submitted to them. That they must have been highly mischievous, is indeed obvious. As every regular trade is a trade of barter—as every thing that we regularly import is, in fact, received in exchange for British manufactures which we export—every obstacle to importation must be an obstacle to exportation. Every diminution of demand for foreign commodities, must be a diminution of demand for the British commodities with which the foreign commodities would have been purchased. They must therefore, under any circumstances, have retarded the growth of our manufactures and commerce. Still, if we had been able to force foreign nations to take our commodities, and to pay for them in the forms which we chose to approve, our condition, though far less favourable than it would have been under a system of free trade, would still have been safe. But for this purpose we must have been able to apply to them the treatment which drove our North American colonies to resistance and separation. We must have been able to prohibit them from manufacturing for themselves, or from trading with any manufacturing country except ourselves. To do this was quite in the spirit of our commercial policy; but, luckily for the rest of the world, we had not the power. The agriculturists whose produce we rejected, of course turned their surplus labour and their surplus capital towards manufactures. 'You taxed us,' said a New-Englander, 'into independence, you fought us into a maritime power, and 'you now enact that we shall be manufacturers.'

The new interests which our folly had created, followed our example where we were wrong more eagerly than where we were right. They saw that our industry had flourished in the midst of prohibitions and restrictions, and they believed that it had flourished in consequence of them. To these fetters they gave the name of protection, and called on their governments to impose them. Their governments, with the instinctive love of regulation and restraint by which every government is infested, were ready enough to answer the call. In one country indeed, whose staple produce, since it interfered with no class interest of our own, we freely admitted, those who benefited by our commerce resisted the alteration. The southern Anglo-American states, whose cotton and tobacco we consent to receive, would have separated from the Union if the Anti-British tariff of 1828 had been persisted in ; and if we had continued to receive the flour of the northern states, that tariff would never have been imposed. But we deserved no such support from any European people. Foreign legislatures could lay no duties on our products, they could impose no restrictions on our commerce, which they could not justify, and more than justify, by our own example. A network of tariffs is gradually excluding us from our nearest and natural customers—our European neighbours ; and confining us to our own colonies and dependencies—to the semi-barbarians of Africa and Asia, and to the young communities of America. We cannot illustrate this part of our subject more effectually, than by the following extract from the truly admirable and statesmanlike speech of Lord Palmerston, mentioned at the head of this article—

‘ Protection is a game that two can play at. It is impossible that a great country like England can go on protecting, as it is called, its various interests, and that other countries should not follow the example. Can we tell other countries that they ought to diminish the duties of their tariff ; that competition is the very life of trade ; that emulation inspires activity and enterprize; and that without enterprize and activity commerce can never flourish, nor be beneficial to those who carry it on ? can we hold these doctrines to other nations, and at the same time persist in our own restrictive system ? When we propound these civil principles to foreign governments, they listen to our arguments with incredulity; they appeal from our doctrines to our practice ; they point to our own tariff, and tell us in diplomatic paraphrase, “ when you alter your own commercial system ; when you bring down to a moderate amount your excessive import duties, we may become converts to your doctrines, and shall be ready to talk with you about a revision of our own tariff.”

‘ I have had to discuss these matters with most of the foreign states with which we have commercial relations, and they are all in the same story. They invariably give us to understand, that when we ask them to permit a more liberal admission of our manufactured goods into their markets, we ought to set them the example by allowing a more liberal admission of their produce into our market. Commerce, they observe, is a system of barter; and if we exclude from our ports their corn, their timber, their sugar, their coffee, every great article, in short, of their produce, which they could offer us in exchange for our commodities, how can we suppose that they can carry on trade with us ?

‘ I have said that one great evil of our restrictive system is, that it

induces other states to fancy that it is the secret of our prosperity, and
that it sets them to imitate our example. Is this an imaginary evil?
far from it. In proportion as the increase of communication between
countries in time of peace has enabled every country to be better informed as to what is going on elsewhere, other nations have seen more
deeply into the details of our restrictive system, and have been tempted,
some by ignorance, some by prejudice, some from a spirit of retaliation,
to imitate our example.

'First, there is the Prussian Commercial Union, which has spread
itself over almost all of the central and northern states of Germany.
That league has just renewed itself by treaty for twelve years from 1842.
Next year their deputies will meet for the purpose of revising their
tariff; and this House and the country deceive themselves greatly, if they
imagine that a perseverance in our restrictive system, and in our prohibiting duties, will not induce the German League to continue their
present high duties upon our manufactures, and perhaps to increase those
duties in such a manner as to shut our commodities out from the whole
of that part of the market of Europe. Russia and Sweden prohibit a
great number of our manufactures; and when we ask them to relax
their tariff, they say, take our corn and timber, and then we will talk
with you about admitting your manufactures into our ports. About two
years ago, Sweden sent over here a nobleman of high distinction, and of
great influence in his own country, for the purpose of endeavouring to come
to some agreement with us for a mutual modification of the tariffs of the
two countries; but timber was our stumbling-block; and we had no hope
at that time of being able to carry through Parliament any arrangement of
our timber duties, that would have met the views of the Swedish government; we had had a mortifying experience, but a short time before, of the
manner in which any proposition of that kind was likely to be dealt with in
this House. France, which ought to be a great market for our commodities;
France, a country so near to us, producing many things which we want,
and wanting many things which we produce; France has a tariff which
excludes many of our principal manufactures. But France will not alter
her tariff unless we alter ours. As an instance of the extent to which
this mania of protection rages, France, not content with prohibiting our
cotton goods, and excluding by high duties our iron, has lately descended
to a minuteness of protection which would be ludicrous, if it were not an
indication of the force of existing prejudices on these matters. France
has lately laid an excluding duty upon our needles and fish-hooks, for
the purpose of protecting that important branch of her own national
industry! The Belgians, too, are running wild with the notion of
protection, and are for excluding, by protecting duties, almost every
thing which the industry of man can make.

'When you preach to these foreign nations the absurdity of such practices, they reply:—It is all very well; but we observe that England has
grown wealthy and great by these means, and it is only now, when other
nations are following her example, that she has discovered that this system is a bad one: when we shall have attained the same pitch of commercial prosperity which England has reached, it will then be time enough

for us to a abandon a system which perhaps may then no longer be necessary.  It is in vain we tell these people that England has grown great and
prosperous, not by means of this fallacious and mischievous system, but
in spite of it.  It is in vain we tell them that this protective system has
checked our growth, and has prevented the full development of our
national resources.  Until we prove by our practice that we are sincere
in our doctrines, neither France, nor Belgium, nor Germany, nor
Russia, nor Sweden, nor any other country in either hemisphere, will be
induced to relax their own restrictive and prohibitory laws.

    ' The United States of America have imitated our example, and have
established a protecting tariff.  The ill effects of this tariff upon the
commerce between these two countries, has been mitigated by the circumstance that the Southern States are chiefly agricultural, and have
few or no manufactures to protect; and that thus the protecting tariff of
the north cannot prevent a great trade between the two countries—the
result of which is to send over to us vast quantities of that slave labour
cotton, which all parties have acknowledged is so essential for us to
have, and which it would be impossible for us to do without.  Yet no
man can doubt that, if England and the United States were mutually to
revise their scales of import duties, the commerce between the two
countries would greatly increase.  But are the United States the only
country in America where this vicious system has taken root?
Mexico is following the example—and who, does the House think,
are the parties who have petitioned the Mexican government for
protection against the importation of British manufactures into
Mexico?  Why, some renegade sons of England, who have established
manufactories in Mexico, and who are endeavouring to prevail upon
the Mexican government to exclude, by high protecting duties,
British manufactures of the same kind as those which they are
themselves making.  Such is the course which our restrictive system
induces other countries to take.

    ' And what, then, is the state of our trade generally with other coun-
tries?  It is quite true, as stated by the right hon. bart. the member
for Tamworth, that there is nothing in the condition of our foreign
trade to inspire despondency; I trust that the resources of the country
are too deeply rooted to be withered even by this vicious system, though
it prevents their full growth and development.  But if you examine
and analyse our foreign trade, you will trace in it remarkable proofs of
the injurious effects of this system.  You will see how these protecting
laws cramp the industry of the country.  Every year a smaller and
smaller portion of the manufactures which we export, consists of articles
in the making of which much labour and skill are employed.  Every
year a greater portion of our exports consists of articles of an elementary
nature, which are not destined for use and consumption, but are to serve
as materials which are to afford employment to the foreign manufacturers.  For instance, the exportation of cotton goods does not increase
in the same proportion as the exportation of yarn.  Then, again, look to
our artisan and capitalist.  Both of them are leaving the country.  The
capitalist goes elsewhere, with the notion of finding cheaper labour : the
artisan with the hope of obtaining better remuneration for his industry.

Every year our protecting system is raising up against us, in other parts of the world, manufacturing competitors ; and every year British skill, British industry, and British capital, are transferring themselves abroad, to render the competition of foreign countries more and more formidable. We are thus ourselves assisting to exclude our own commerce from the markets of other countries. If this system is persevered in, we shall at last come down to that spendthrift industry, which is to consist in exporting machinery as well as the elements of manufactures ; and when our exports consist of capital, skill, industry, machinery, and materials, we shall no doubt wonder how it happens that our finished manufactures are no longer able to compete with those of other countries in the markets of the world.'

We are induced to add another extract from a different production ; because it shows that, even without the interference of foreign governments, our own Commercial Code is enough to destroy our commerce. It forms part of a letter from Mr Muller of Lubeck, inserted by Mr Hickson in his Report to the Hand-Loom Commissioners.

'Although our agricultural neighbours in Mecklenburg and Holstein complain much about the present system of corn laws in England, yet all our manufacturers are happy to see them continued. They hope soon to be able to push the English entirely out of foreign markets, and to furnish themselves all the articles we still import from England. If your corn laws remain *in statu quo,* it may be taken for granted that in ten or fifteen years there will be very little demand for English manufactures on the Continent. If a free trade, as formerly, could be re-established in corn, the landowners would soon augment their wheat fields, secure to themselves by it a constant revenue, and be able to purchase and consume a great deal of British manufactures of all kinds. Mecklenburg and Holstein alone, with 1,000,000 inhabitants, would become important customers of England.

'I cannot understand the policy of your government, by which, while you ruin us, you injure yourselves at the same time. England is essentially a manufacturing country ; we were agricultural, and were content to pay you with our corn for your manufactures ; now you refuse to take our corn, and, as we have nothing else with which to buy, you compel us to manufacture for ourselves. The policy you are pursuing, is making the whole German people your rivals instead of your customers. Cloth manufactories, hemp and flax spinning-works, iron founderies, and hardware manufacture, are increasing rapidly among us, and your cotton trade must expect to compete more and more with continental establishments. Every year adds to the number of steam-mills in Germany ; and every acre laid down in pasture transfers some of our cheap labour, by which you might be fed, to manufactures, which, ultimately driving yours out of the market, will cause a large portion of your industrial population to starve.

'To your corn laws must be attributed the Prussian League, by which your manufactures are already excluded the greater portion of the German States. By-and-by, you will not have a market left in Europe. At present, however, not only the Hanse Towns of Hamburg, Lubeck, and Bremen, but the large provinces of Holstein, Mecklenburg, and Lauenburg, admit all British manufactures free of duty. But of what avail is it that we are ready to receive your manufactures, when our farmers and peasants have nothing to buy them with but the produce of the soil? Receive our corn, and we will in a year or two receive thrice the quantity of goods we do at present. Besides coal, slates, salt, cutlery, earthenware, for which we have always a ready market, there are many articles we should be glad to purchase with corn from Great Britain and Ireland, which we can obtain from other countries only for gold.'

' Perhaps the most formidable competition we have to anticipate,' adds Mr Hickson, ' is from the United States of America. By diverting their attention from agriculture, we have made a manufacturing and commercial nation of a people of the same habits of industry, the same spirit of enterprise, with ourselves. Already has their progress been so great, that the export trade of America is increasing in a ratio four times greater than our own. I see nothing to prevent their foreign commerce exceeding that of the United Kingdom within less than another twenty years. With the great advantage of cheap food, the current of emigration will constantly be directed thither. America is regarded by many of our artisans as their second home. There many of their friends are settled, and our best workmen are at all times much more easily induced to follow a capitalist to America, where their own language is spoken, than to France or Germany. High wages in the United States, it is supposed, will be an obstacle to manufacturing progress; but this is really a very slight impediment where machinery is employed in manufactures. Nor is the difference between the wages of skilled artisans here and in America very great; they are high in both countries. The difference in America is less in favour of the mechanic than of the day-labourer ; and for working cotton-spinning and power-loom machinery physical strength is not required, and the labour of women and children can be obtained as cheaply in America as in Lancashire. Miss Martineau states, that in Boston the earnings of young women, at needlework, are but 9d. per day.

' The progress already made in power-loom weaving in the United States, proves that, in this respect, they have encountered no difficulties which cannot be overcome. Mr Galbreath, of the firm of Johnstone and Galbreath, Glasgow, told me that he was informed, upon authority upon which he could depend, that already there were at Lowel 4800 powerlooms in full operation. Mr Galbreath had been led to enquire into the subject, finding American cotton cloth competing with his own at Canton; and at Valparaiso, monopolizing nearly the whole of the trade. He was in the habit of exporting largely, but foreign competition was fast gaining upon him in every third or neutral market.'

We repeat that we are sorry to appear as alarmists ; but do not the foregoing statements justify alarm ? Who can read them and doubt, that, on the event of the contest now raging between the principles of Monoply and Freedom, not merely the immediate prosperity of the country—not merely the question, whether the labouring population shall or shall not consume sugar, or shall or shall not be taxed 20 per cent on their bread, or whether the higher classes shall submit to an income-tax in peace—but the extension, and even the maintenance of our manufactures and commerce; and with those manufactures and commerce, the permanence of our welfare, of our institutions, we might almost say of our civilization, essentially depends.

The early progress of any nation that attempts to rival us in manufactures, must be slow. It has to contend with our vast capital, our mineral wealth, our traditionary skill, our almost infinite division of labour, our long-established perseverance, energy, and enterprise, our knowledge of markets, and with the habits of those who have been bred up to be our customers. There is no reason to believe that, in the absence of disturbing causes, we should ever have lost a market that we once possessed, or should ever lose one which we now enjoy. In the absence of disturbing causes, we might for centuries have preserved the superiority which we possessed twenty years ago, and might even now look forward for centuries to come to an export trade, not merely undiminishing, but increasing with the general increase of wealth and population in the civilized world. But if the products of a rival once meet us in any third market upon an equality, it is a proof that all these difficulties have been surmounted. If they shall once have obtained a superiority, that market, so far at least as respects the commodity in which we find ourselves undersold, is gone for ever. 'We find by 'experience,' said Mr Gardner, (a very intelligent manufacturer, examined by the Committee of the House of Commons on Hand-Loom Weavers in 1835,) 'that if we lose a market one year, 'we lose it altogether. It is not well to trifle with trade : by 'trying experiments for only one year, we might shut ourselves 'out. Once in possession of the market, they would keep 'it.' The explanation is to be found in the well known law of manufacturing industry, that, *cæteris paribus*, with every increase of the quantity produced the relative cost of production is diminished; and, what is the same in different words, that with every diminution of the quantity produced the relative cost of production is increased. The larger the production the greater is the division of labour, and consequently the skill of the workman, the smaller the expense of superintendence, the more extensive the use of machinery; in short, every element of production becomes relatively more efficient, and every source of expense is relatively diminished. Hence it is that the price of a manufactured commodity falls as the consumption of it extends. Hence also the difference between the sum at which a large contract can be made, and that which must be paid on a small one. A single pin could not be made for a shilling—when they are made by millions, a shilling can purchase them by hundreds.

' The instant, therefore, that any given class of manufacturers
' begin to feel that their competitors are outstripping them—
' the instant they find that commodities similar to their own
' meet them in the market at a lower price—that instant they
' ought to know that they are engaged in a contest which, if its ele-
' ments continue the same, must terminate ruinously. If they can
' change those elements, they may perhaps regain their ground.
' But, if they are unable to do so, their relative inferiority must
' become more striking every year. The less they produce the
' greater will be the relative cost of the produce; while the more
' their rivals produce, the less will be their relative cost of pro-
' duction. First comes a fall of profits, next a reduction of
' wages, then irregular employment even at reduced wages,
' until the capitalist is ruined, or forced to change his business
' or the seat of his manufacture, and the workman must follow
' his example, or be supported by charity.'*

' As soon as I hear that a bale of my goods,' said an eminent manufacturer to us some four years ago, ' is met in the markets of
' China or Peru by a similar article from Germany at a lower
' price, that instant I remove my establishment to the Tyrol :
' for I shall know well what is to follow.' The warning was given, and our informant acted on it; and his skill and his capital are now using the fine water powers of the Voralberg, to aid the competition which he did not choose to encounter even when it was weaker. The contest indeed, in some respects, resembles a civil war : the force that was to-day on one side, may to-morrow, if the chances of success appear to have altered, be found on the other. The capital which to-day employs hundreds or thousands of British workmen, may to-morrow not merely leave them unemployed, but actually be on its way to set to work hundreds or thousands of their continental rivals.

It is obvious that, under such circumstances, not merely years, but even months become important. The evils, the dangers, are not only progressive, but progressive in an accelerated ratio. The cloud which long remained a mere speck on the horizon, has now rapidly dilated, and may break while we are calculating the rate of its approach.

It is with deep alarm, therefore, that we have observed the sluggishness of public opinion on this subject. The manufac-

---

* Report of the Commissioners on Hand-Loom Weavers.

turing districts, notwithstanding their vast population, are of comparatively small extent, and lie at a distance from the metropolis.
Until the Reform Act they were almost totally unrepresented,
and even now they possess a representation grossly inadequate.
The receivers of rents, tithes, dividends and salaries, are scattered throughout the country : they form, with colonial proprietors, professional men, and the more opulent merchants and
bankers, almost the whole educated society of Britain and Ireland. In that society the manufacturers do not mix. They
must reside among their works and their work-people, in neigh-
bourhoods from which coal-mines and steam-engines have banish-
ed all whom business does not detain. Of their situation, their
wants, their feelings, or their sufferings, little is known in one
House of Parliament, and nothing in the other, and scarcely any
thing by the community at large. The consequence has been,
that the dangers which we have described can hardly be said to
have attracted public attention. The great majority of the
higher classes have never heard of them. Others, and we lament
to find Sir Robert Peel among the number, disbelieve, or affect
to disbelieve, their existence ; and of those who know that there
is peril, very few appear to be aware of its magnitude or its im-
minence. It seemed probable, therefore, that on this occasion,
as it has often happened before while escape was possible, the
danger would not be known or appreciated ; and that, as we
repealed the Stamp Act after the North American colonies were
lost—as we emancipated the Catholics after the affection of
Ireland was forfeited—so we should liberalize our Commercial
Code when the preservation of our trade had become impossible.
Then, indeed, when half our mills are stopped, and the others
are working short time—when the ruin which has fallen on the
hand-loom weavers shall have spread to the spinners, the power-
loom weavers, the shipbuilders, and the numberless trades that
depend on our exports for their existence—when Manchester and
Birmingham have to pray for rates in aid from the surrounding
parishes, and can justify their application by showing their absolute inability to support their own poor—then, the voice of
starving millions will be heard. Corn laws, and timber laws,
and sugar laws, and differential duties, and sliding scales, will
be swept away. But would these be the only sacrifices ? Are
we sure that the Peerage, or the Church, or even the Monarchy,
could resist the storm ? Even if the worst extremities should be
avoided, still the mischiefs of a sudden and total change, effected
by such means, would be unutterable ; and, in all probability,
they would be endured in vain. Commerce and manufactures
fly from the seat of a revolution : they languish under the mere
fears of a revolution. In agricultural countries, like Spain or

France, revolution, though it destroys the happiness and the morals of the existing generation, yet, in as far at least as the educated classes are concerned, it may leave the elements of future prosperity unimpaired. For Great Britain there are no such hopes; with her capital frightened away, and her fixed machinery destroyed, the value of her labour would sink at least to the general level of Europe. She might open her ports to corn, but she would be unable to purchase it; she might repeal her timber duties, but she would cease to be a great maritime power; she would become the abode of a potatoe-eating population, dense and miserable, and therefore formidable to its governors, but defenceless against exterior aggression. Under such circumstances could we retain our colonies? could we retain our Indian Empire? could we retain the union with Ireland? could we keep faith with the public creditor? could we preserve the resemblance of our present power, or of our present prosperity?

Under the influence of such apprehensions, we saw with little regret the continuing deficiency in the revenue. It afforded means of forcing the public to look at the state of our trade, and at the monstrous code by which it is fettered. And, what is of far more practical importance, it afforded the means of saying to classes, and even to individuals—' Unless you will consent to ' allow us to increase the revenue by diminishing duties, we ' must tax you. If you wish sugar to continue at 8d, a pound, ' or bread at 9d. a loaf, you must pay for those blessings by a ' tax of L.50 on your house, or perhaps L.500 on your income.'

Lord John Russell, in the remarkable speech mentioned at the head of this article, stated, that to meet the deficiency of L.2,400,000 in the income of the present year, the Government had only four courses to pursue,—1. By petty taxation to make up a part of the deficiency, providing, of course, for the remainder By the issue of Exchequer bills—that is, by borrowing.    2d, To raise the whole by a loan. 3dly, To add greatly to the direct taxation of the country ; and 4thly, By diminishing prohibitory import duties, at one and the same time to increase the revenue, and increase the comforts of the people. In fact, however, these four expedients are reducible to two—increased taxation and improved taxation; for borrowing is merely taxation deferred, to fall, when it does come, with the severity of compound interest. If we meet this year's deficit of L.2,400,000 by borrowing at 4 per cent, the deficit next year will be L.2,496,000 ; being the deficit of the year and the interest of the loan—and that L.96,000 will be a burden imposed on the country for ever. A loan, therefore, this year, if the events of the last two months should occasion the adoption of such a course, will render it necessary to raise next year, and indeed for an indefinite period, L.2,496,000 a-year by taxation, either increased or improved, instead of L.2,400,000. The delay of a single year will cost the country, for ever, more than three times as much as the annual grant for the purposes of Education; and nearly twice as much as the annual expense of the Poor-Law Commission—an expense which has been the pretext for so many petitions.

Many circumstances concurred to render more than usually perceptible the advantage of adopting improved instead of increased taxation. A series of crops, all rather inferior to the usual average in amount, and some in quality, had materially raised the price of wheat, particularly of good wheat. A diminished supply of sugar from our own possessions—the supply to which our present tariff confines us—had increased, in a still greater proportion, the price of sugar. Commercial difficulties, arising in a great measure from the irregular importation of corn, occasioned by the fluctuating duty, aided by the tendency of a high price of provisions to produce a low rate of wages, had occasioned distress so extensive as almost to deserve to be called universal among the largest body of our labourers—those engaged in manufactures. Their employment had become irregular, and their wages, when employed, had fallen; while the prices of the commodities on which their wages are chiefly expended, had risen. The Report and the Evidence of the Committee of the House of Commons on ' Import Duties,' had produced a deep and wide impression. Although the worst effects of the protective system—the growing danger to which it exposes our export trade—was little understood—we believe, indeed, that it is little understood even now; yet the immediate effects of that system on the price of the principal articles of consumption, and on the revenue, began to be perceived. The public began to see, that, as to many of those articles, the best market was absolutely barred against them; and that, as to many others, it was mischievously confined. They began to perceive that they were suffering under an oppressive *taxation*, not merely without benefit to the revenue, but to its loss. Whatever may be the burdens imposed on the inhabitants of the British empire for the purposes of external security, or for those of internal tranquillity and improvement, or of fidelity to our engagements, they will be cheerfully submitted to. Nothing will be grudged for the maintenance of the public faith, or for the keeping up our military and naval establishments; for the proper splendour of the monarchy; for the support of the ministers of religion and justice; or for the extension of education. The sacrifices necessary for these purposes will be readily undergone. But men became indignant when they found that the taxation under which they were labouring, instead of increasing the revenue devoted to these great objects, actually diminished it; when they found that a loss of twenty or thirty millions to the consumer, produced a further loss of five or six millions to the exchequer.

The feeling which, in this country, is a necessary precursor to any great change—the feeling that that change was necessary and inevitable—began to prevail. And its extension was most powerfully assisted by the consideration which forced itself even on the most careless minds—what must be the alternative while that change was deferred. The deficit existed and was increasing. An income tax, a duty on the devolution of land, a house tax, an increased window tax, further duties on horses, servants, and carriages—such were the expedients which, though they might be delayed by loans, only to be aggravated, must be ultimately resorted to. At length it seemed probable that the cause of that helpless body, the great mass of her Majesty's subjects, might be taken up with some prospect of success. At length it seemed probable, that a Budget which would relieve our financial difficulties by adding to our comforts—which would benefit the Exchequer by benefiting the consumer—might be accepted for the sake of its immediate and palpable effects; although its still greater but more remote advantages—the security which it would give to our existing commerce, and the avenues which it would open to the extension of our trade—might be unperceived or undervalued. And while these circumstances rendered the late Session an eminently favourable opportunity for proposing such a Budget, there were others which rendered its early adoption peculiarly important. Our commercial treaty with Brazil was entered into for fifteen years; expiring in 1842, on two years' notice. Under the provisions of that treaty, they admit our commodities at a duty not exceeding fifteen per cent *ad valorem.* It contains no stipulation as to the amount of duty to which we may subject theirs; and on their staple, sugar, we impose one of 300 per cent. They have testified their disapprobation, by giving the earliest possible notice for the termination of the treaty. In 1842, also, the United States of America must reconsider their tariff. The admission of their grain would secure the votes of the corn-growing states, and prevent any alteration unfavourable to us; as it would have prevented, according to the opinion of our minister, Mr Addington, the original enactment of its objectionable parts. Our commercial relations with these great countries—the best foreign markets left to us—

cannot remain stationary. We stand in the remarkable position of being able to make to them concessions, as they are called, which will be still more beneficial to ourselves; and to ask from them concessions by which they will be gainers. Such a favourable field for commercial diplomacy was never opened before. Another ground for immediate action was the state of feeling in Northern Germany. The states forming the north-western German Commercial League—a league adopting the tariff which, next to that of Switzerland, is the most liberal in Europe—were at the beginning of the Session proposing the prolongation of the league. The following extract from the Report of the Commissioners on Hand-Loom Weavers, shows the use which might be made of this state of things :—

'The treaty is not yet complete, and we are strongly of opinion that a favourable opportunity now exists for an arrangement between your Majesty's Government and the countries constituting the North-Western League, which would be beneficial in its immediate results, and still more so by the example which its benefits would in time hold out to the rest of Germany. A very few concessions on our part, and still fewer, if indeed any be required, on theirs, would produce an increase of commerce between the two countries, which would be useful to us, but of course much more so, from the proportion it would bear to the rest of their commerce, to the countries constituting the North-Western League. To the influence of such an example we attach great importance. The questions whether freedom of commerce is or is not a public benefit—whether what is called protection is or not a public mischief—are no longer considered in Germany by those alone who make political science their study. They are canvassed by merchants, manufacturers, and, what is still more important, by consumers. In every part of Germany in which the individual interests of local manufacturers do not prevail, not merely a belief in the superior advantages of free trade, but an earnest desire for it, is extending. This is particularly the case in the smaller states constituting the North-Western League, in the Hans Towns, and the Grand Duchies of Mecklenburg, and in the vast regions forming the Austrian empire. In general, it will be found that the benefits of commerce are best understood in the smaller states: because the less the state the greater is the proportion which its foreign commerce is likely to bear to its home trade, and also, because in a small community the effect of every institution is more obvious. Russia, France, and England, all without doubt suffer from their restrictive systems, and all would be benefited by a change; but among the many causes which affect the prosperity of such vast and complicated bodies, the effect of any single one is not easily ascertained or easily demonstrated. In the simply constituted communities of the Hans Towns, or the Duchies of Mecklenburg, or even of Hanover, the influence of a single change becomes immediately perceptible. On the other hand, in the greater part of the Austrian empire there is as yet no manufacturing interest which can ask for protection at the public expense. She cannot supply her own actual consumption of manufactured goods, much less could she supply those which she would be desirous and able to consume, if a more extensive export of the produce of her own fields, pastures, forests, and mines, afforded to her the means of purchasing them.

' If the result of a negotiation with the North-Western League were a freer intercourse between the two countries, and if the benefits derived by the people constituting that league were, as we have no doubt they would be, obvious and notorious, we are firmly convinced that there would arise, throughout the vast and productive dominions of Austria, a desire for an increased intercourse with this country, which the Austrian government would not be able, and we think would not be desirous, to oppose.'

It was obvious, however, that to propose such a Budget, was to place at the mercy of the opposition the ministerial majority in the existing House of Commons. If the opposition chose to resist it as a body, it was certain that they would be joined by ministerialists—fearing inconvenience to themselves or to their constituents from some portion of the scheme—sufficient in number to place the government in a minority. And it was probable that the opposition would be reinforced by the whimsical, irresolute individuals—the pest of a balanced state of parties, some voting without assignable motives, and others on motives that will not bear exposure—who, in a crisis, almost always assist the party which they profess most to disapprove.

There were however grounds, and strong grounds, for hoping that the opposition would refuse the party triumph which would be placed within their grasp. No man had denounced more firmly than their great leader the ruinous expedient of loans in time of peace; and it was not likely that he would be willing to incur the risk of having to signalize his resumption of office by severe additional taxation. He is known to be a friend of commercial freedom. What man of any intellectual eminence is not so? And he had not distinctly avowed that preference of a fluctuating to a fixed corn duty, to which he has since most unfortunately pledged himself. It was probable, therefore, that if he could restrain the ignorant and unscrupulous members of his party, he would follow the example set by the Whigs, when Mr Wallace and Mr Huskisson introduced reforms, which, without detracting from their great merit, were far less useful and less urgent than those in contemplation. We feel sure that Sir Robert Peel wanted the power, not the will, to act thus. The Cabinet seem to have thought it probable, or at least possible, that he had both the power and the will. Had they thought otherwise, it appears clear that they would have brought forward their Budget at an earlier period of the Session, when preparation could have been made for a dissolution before the Easter recess. But though they did not despair of success, they must have felt that, as a party measure, it was a most dangerous one. The event depended on the patriotism of Sir Robert Peel and the discipline of his followers;—followers who despise him for his defects, and hate him for his merits. But, to use the words of Lord John Russell, they did not shrink from the resolution, when once its advantage to the country was agreed upon.

The first indication given to the public of the plan resolved on by the government, was the proposal for the revision of the customs in the West Indian and North American colonies, brought forward by Mr Labouchere on the 12th of March. Under the existing law, beef, pork, fish, coffee, cocoa-nuts, tea, raw sugar, molasses, and rum, when imported into those colonies from any foreign country, are still absolutely prohibited;—the commodities selected for exclusion being, as usual, the principal articles of food. On flour, timber, and lumber, duties are imposed varying from 20 per cent *ad valorem* to 40. On another class of commodities, few of which seem to deserve enumeration, an *ad valorem* duty of L.7, 10s. per cent is imposed; on glass, soap, refined sugar, tobacco, and cotton manufactures, a duty of 20 per cent; on clocks and watches, leather manufactures, linen, musical instruments, wires, books, papers, and silken manufactures, a duty of L.30 per cent; and on unenumerated manufactures a duty of 15 per cent.

In the room of this oppressive and anomalous tariff, Mr Labouchere proposed to give to the British colonies a freer trade than is enjoyed by any European nation, except Switzerland; indeed, practically, a much freer trade than that of Switzerland: for the Swiss trade is fettered by the transit duties imposed by the countries among which it has the misfortune to be imprisoned. The British colonies have for their neighbour, the sea. It would have placed them in the situation in which they themselves have proclaimed, that they can compete with the slave labour of the whole world.*

We have said that Mr Labouchere's proposals were an indication of the intentions of the government. The short conversation which followed their introduction, shows that those interested in monopolies took the alarm. Mr Palmer, the member for Essex, complained that these propositions carried out to its full extent the system of free trade—that every petition which fostered or supported free trade had the protection of the Secre-

* See Mr Burnley's speech in the *Trinidad Gazette* of the 11th Feb. 1841.

tary for the Colonies ; and declared, with an almost ludicrous mis-
use of the word *protection*, that every class had the same right to
be protected by the State against the competition of foreigners,
which a child had to be protected by its parents, (we presume
against violence.)   Mr White, the member for Sunderland, rose
in defence of the shipping interests, and claimed protection for
them ; because, to use his own words, ' the British cannot, *owing*
' *to the timber duties, build their ships so cheaply, nor, with*
' *our present corn laws, can they victual them so cheaply* as fo-
' reigners, and therefore they cannot compete with foreigners.'
And when they came again before the House, on the 5th of
April, the apprehensions of the enemies of commercial freedom,
that they formed only part of an extensive scheme of reform, became apparent.   Mr Goulburn thought it very desirable that
some information should be given to the House, as to the
extent to which the principle of the resolutions was to be
carried out.   He thought that the inhabitants of the North
American colonies might apprehend, that a similar change
would be· carried into effect with respect to the timber imported from those colonies into Great Britain.   He was anxious
to know whether this was not only one of a series of measures ?   Mr Palmer's fears had now ripened into a belief that,
if these Resolutions were carried, they would be followed by
an attack on the corn laws ; and certainly Lord John Russell's
answer was not calculated to allay these fears.   ' The principle,'
said Lord John Russell, ' on which the right hon. gentleman
' (Mr Goulburn) seemed to proceed was, that you must give
' advantages to the British manufacturers against the colonies.
' The colonies must take *their* silk, leather, cotton, &c.   Then
' the people of the colonies say, we feel ourselves aggrieved by
' this restriction.   Then to satisfy *them* you say, they shall have
' advantages against the farmer and the labourer of the United
' Kingdom.   Then the farmer and the labourer complain, and
' you, to satisfy *them*, give them advantages against the manu-
' facturer—and so you go on in this vicious circle of constantly
' endeavouring· to do something for the advantage of a particular
' class, instead of looking to the benefit of the whole community.'
    When the leader of the ministeralists denounced so unreservedly
the folly and the mischief of the protective system, it was clear
that the Cabinet had resolved to attempt its reform.   On the 30th
of last April—a day which will long be memorable in English
history—the long-expected Budget was brought forward.   It
turned, as all those who believed that the Ministers would do their
duty had fully expected, on TIMBER, SUGAR, and CORN.   With

respect to timber, the Chancellor of the Exchequer proposed to diminish the enormous difference between the duty imposed on colonial and Baltic timber, by raising the duty on the former from 10s. a load to 20s., and reducing that on the latter from 55s. to 50s. From this change, which would still give to colonial timber an advantage of 150 per cent, he expected an increase of revenue of L.600,000 a-year. The duty on colonial sugar being 24s. per hundred-weight, and that on foreign sugar 60s., he proposed to leave the former duty unaltered, but to lower the latter to 36s. per hundred-weight—still leaving to colonial sugar an advantage of 50 per cent. From this change he calculated on an increased revenue of L.700,000 a-year. The remainder of the deficit was to be raised by an alteration of the corn laws; by substituting for the present fluctuating scale, which oscillates between freedom and prohibition—which seems intended to give the least possible advantage to the Exchequer in proportion to the suffering which it inflicts on the people—a fixed duty, producing a regular trade, and a revenue that may be relied upon. The amount of the proposed duty was not stated on the 30th of April; but was afterwards announced to be 8s. a quarter on wheat, 4s. 6d. on barley, 3s. 4d. on oats, and 5s. each on rye, peas, and beans.

The language of the leaders of the opposition left their future treatment of this memorable Budget doubtful. Mr Goulburn and Mr Herries asked time for consideration. Sir Robert Peel refused to express any opinion, ‘as he felt deeply the magnitude of the in- ‘ terests involved, and wished to pause before he pronounced an ‘ irrevocable judgment.’ But the temper manifested by the subordinate members of the opposition, led to no hope that the wiser views of their chiefs would control them. All the buzz and whisper- ing on their benches, all that the French call *la physiognomie de la chambre,* indicated the determination of those who think they pro- fit by the great monopoly of corn, to come forward to the rescue of all their brother monopolists, and to collect into one phalanx every defender of every abuse. And the leaders of the small section of mischief-makers, who promote evil because it is evil, and obstruct improvement, not because they think it may inter- fere with their interests, but because it is good—because it may promote a state of prosperity fatal to their influence—laboured to impute to the authors of the measure every dishonourable mo- tive; and, while they did not venture to object to the proposal, endeavoured to arm and excite against it the prejudices and the fears of every separate class of the community—commercial, manufacturing, and agricultural.

A very few days showed the mistake of the Government, in pla*
cing any reliance on the public spirit, or at least on the power,
of their principal opponents. Lord Sandon, the member for
Liverpool, with the concurrence of the heads of his party, moved
as an amendment to the motion for the House going into Com*
mittee on the sugar duties—' That, considering the efforts and
' sacrifices which Parliament and the country have made for the
' abolition of the slave trade and slavery, with the earnest hope
' that their exertions and example might lead to the mitigation
' and final extinction of these evils in other countries, this House
' is not prepared (especially with the present prospects of the
' supply of sugar from British possessions) to adopt the measure
' proposed by her Majesty's Government for the reduction of
' the duty on foreign sugar.' It is scarcely necessary to state
that this resolution was carried by a majority of 36 ; and that a
subsequent resolution moved by Sir Robert Peel—' That her
' Majesty's Ministers do not sufficiently possess the confidence of
' the House of Commons to enable them to carry through the
' House, measures which they deem of essential importance to
' the public welfare, and that their continuance in office, under
' such circumstances, is at variance with the spirit of the con-
' stitution,'—a motion made avowedly for the purpose of prevent-'
ing the discussion of the proposed alteration on the corn-laws—
was carried by a majority of one.

The Budget therefore, as a whole, has never been considered by
the House. One portion of it, providing for the relaxation of the
prohibitory duties on sugar, it has rejected; the others it has re*
fused even to discuss. We regret that our limits force us to follow
its example in this particular, and to confine our attention to the
Sugar Resolutions; leaving timber and corn to a future opportunity.

The proposed alteration in the sugar duties, the only subject on
which the House pronounced an opinion, was debated, as far as the
leader of the opposition was concerned, on the narrowest possible
grounds. Sir Robert Peel denied that there existed ' any over*
' whelming moral obligation, in compliance with which we were
' bound to abstain from the consumption of sugar as the produce of
' slave labour, or that supporting the Government plan involved
' any charge of violating conscientious principles. He had on for-
' mer occasions voted in favour of great and important relaxations
' in the duties and imposts affecting various commodities, the pro-
' duce of slave labour. With respect to cotton he had so voted. He
' had supported the proposition with respect to the consumption of
' coffee, the produce of Brazil or Venezuela. It was not *his* opposition
' which led to the abandonment of that plan ; he repeated, there-

' fore, that he did not oppose the present motion on the ground
' of any overwhelming moral obligation.   Nor would he ask the
' continued exclusion of foreign sugars on account of the interests
' of the West Indian proprietors ; for to them the liberality of
' this country had been so great that, if the present question in-
' volved merely their interests, the country had a right to call on
' them to make a considerable sacrifice to the public advantage.' On
what grounds, then, did Sir Robert Peel rest his vote against
permitting even the detailed consideration of the proposed Resolutions—against merely allowing the House to go into committee
upon them ?   On two grounds, and on two grounds only.  First,
that the adoption of the Government plan would have the effect
of deciding, that sugar could not be produced by free labour in
the West Indies.   And that the result, according to the report
of his speech in the *Times*, in all the West Indian colonies, or, according to the corrected speech, the result in Jamaica, would be
the total expulsion of the white population ; and the occupation of
the soil by a population of negroes, content with the mere necessaries of life, without producing any exportable commodity whatever, and with no trade with England or with any other country.
Secondly, that ' the amount of remittances made from India
' was about L.3,200,000 for the purposes of Government annu-
' ally, and there were private remittances made to the amount of
' half a million.  There was no mode of making these remittances
' except by the medium of these sugars.'  And he drew a painful
picture of the distress to which portions of the inhabitants of that
vast country are occasionally subject—distress which is always
incidental to a dense population subsisting on the cheapest of the
articles of human food, rice, and therefore without a substitute
when the crop is deficient.  ' These were the grounds on which
' he should, for the purpose of presenting to the world the ex-
' ample that free labour in the West Indies could succeed, and
' for the purpose of giving encouragement to the productions of
' the East Indies, give his vote in favour of the proposition of the
' member for Liverpool.'

The first of the two grounds assigned by Sir Robert Peel may be
easily disposed of.  The total exports from Bengal during the year
1837-1838, the last for which we have a return, amounted in value
to 75,544,884 rupees.   Those from Bombay were 44,604,168.*
The return from Madras for that year has not been published.
We will assume, however, that it did not materially vary from that
of the previous year, which amounted to 27,854,757 rupees ;†

---

* Porter's Tables, Part ix. p. 137.        † Ibid. Part viii. p. 31.

making, including the exports from Bengal and Bombay, a total of 146,001,806 rupees; or, taking the rupee at its average value of two shillings, L.14,600,180 sterling. Of this amount, only 46,044,085 rupees, or L.4,604,608 sterling, not 30 per cent of the whole, was exported to the United Kingdom. The export of sugar to the United Kingdom during that year was 443,353 cwts., worth in bond in London, after all expenses were paid, less than L.700,000. What becomes, then, of Sir Robert Peel's statement, that sugar affords the only mode by which India can make her remittances to England? or what becomes of the necessity of excluding foreign sugars for the sake of the agricultural population of the Peninsula? Can it be supposed that the trade of India depends on a commodity which does not form one twentieth part of her annual exports?—a commodity, too, which till within the last five or six years she never has exported? Could the welfare of eighty millions of people be seriously affected, even if our admission of foreign sugar should totally exclude Indian sugar from our market? Why, if the whole L.700,000 which their sugar was worth had been pure gain to them—if the sugar, instead of costing them, as we know it must have done, four-fifths of its value in the expense of production and carriage, had been miraculously supplied to them at the shipping ports, and had been worth there the L.700,000 which it was worth in London, that sum divided among the population would not have given them twopence a-head. One-fifth of this sum, that is to say L.140,000, or less than a farthing and a half a-head, was the utmost benefit that they actually received. We are most anxious to promote the welfare of our Indian fellow-subjects, and to give encouragement to their productions; but we do not think that they themselves would ask us to submit to the loss of *millions* in order to give them *thousands*—we do not believe that they would ask that every man, woman, and child in the British islands should pay a *shilling*, in order to give every inhabitant of British India a *halfpenny*. It has been said that no avarice is so unblushing, because none is so tolerated, as that of a monopolist claiming a vested interest in a public injury; but this is a claim which even avarice would not venture to maintain.

The only other ground on which Sir Robert Peel rested his opposition—namely, that the adoption of the Government plan must necessarily lead to the expulsion of all the whites from the West Indian colonies, or at least from Jamaica, and the total occupation of the soil by the negroes—will sink as rapidly and as easily under a short statement of facts. All the facts that are necessary are contained in the following Table; which we extract from a

pamphlet, entitled ' Common Sense View of the Sugar Ques-
' tion :'—

| Years | Population. | British Sugar. | | Foreign Sugar. | | Total Annual Consumption per Individual. | |
|---|---|---|---|---|---|---|---|
| | | Price. | Entered for Consumption. | Price. | Entd. for Consump. | | |
| | | s.   d. | cwts. | s.   d. | cwts. | lbs. | parts. |
| 1831 | 24,356,719 | 23   8 | 4,364,243 | 17   11 | 79 | 20 | 11-100 |
| 1832 | 24,719,080 | 27   8 | 4,187,135 | 21   5 | 605 | 19 | |
| 1833 | 25,077,441 | 29   8 | 4,021,595 | 22   5 | 71 | 17 | 99-100 |
| 1834 | 25,437,802 | 29   5 | 4,154,411 | 23   3 | 50 | 18 | 31-100 |
| 1835 | 25,798,163 | 33   5 | 4,421,145 | 27   5 | 31 | 19 | 21-100 |
| 1836 | 26,158,524 | 40   10 | 3,922,901 | 27   11 | 33 | 16 | 58-100 |
| 1837 | 26,518,885 | 34   7 | 4,349,053 | 21   3 | 43 | 18 | 28-100 |
| 1838 | 26,879,246 | 33   8 | 4,418,334 | 21   3 | 65 | 18 | 42-100 |
| 1839 | 27,239,607 | 39   2 | 4,171,938 | 22   1 | 49 | 17 | 16-100 |
| 1840 | 27,599,968 | 49   1 | 3,764,710 | 21   6 | 2,316 | 15 | 28-100 |

It appears from this table, that the average price in bond of
British sugar, during the four years that preceded the abolition of
slavery, was 27s. 7¼d. per cent. For the four years which immediately succeeded, 35s. 7¼d; and for the last two years, 44s. 1½d; the
average of the whole ten years being 37s. 3d. That the price in
bond of foreign sugars, during the first of those periods, was 21s. 3d.;
during the second, 24s.5½d.; and during the last two years, 21s.9½d.;
the average of the whole ten years being 22s. 6d.; and it appears
also that the foreign price has a slight tendency to rise—owing,
without doubt, to the increased demand of the civilized world,
increasing, as it is, in population and wealth. The price for the
first five years having been somewhat under 22s. 6d. per cwt., and
during the last five years rather above 22s. 9½d., a new demand for
the internal consumption of the British islands will, of course,
have a tendency to create a rise in the foreign sugar market;
under that general law affecting the cost of the production of all
agricultural produce—namely, that with every increase of demand,
the relative cost of production, and consequently the price, rises,
just as, with every diminution of demand, the cost of production,
and consequently the price, falls. But the British demand bears
so small a proportion to that of the whole world, that this rise is
not likely to be permanent; and we will assume the fact most favourable to Sir Robert Peel's argument, or rather to his statement—for he has not supported it by any argument—that foreign
sugar will continue to be supplied to us at its average price for the
last ten years, namely, 22s. 6d. per cwt. To this price the Government Budget proposed to add a differential duty of 12s. per cwt.
making 34s. 6d. per cwt., the price with which the British planter
would have to contend.

We request our readers to pause, and to reconsider this state-ment, and the calculations on which it is founded, and to ask themselves whether there is any rational ground whatever for believing that foreign sugar can be supplied at a price less than 34s. 6d. per cwt.—original price and differential duty included? And we request them to ask themselves whether there is any rational ground for believing that a price of 34s. 6d. per cwt.—a price greatly exceeding the average price before the abolition of slavery, and nearly equalling the average price of four out of the six years that have elapsed since that period—is a price so ruinously low, that it must, in the words of Sir Robert Peel, ne-cessarily lead to the expulsion of all the whites from the West Indies, or from Jamaica alone, and to the total occupation of the land by the negroes?

But in stating the question thus, we have omitted one of its main elements.

The Plan of the government must be considered as a whole ; it must not be separated from the Resolutions of the 12th of March for the remission of colonial taxation. 'I found,' said Mr Labouchere when he moved these Resolutions, ' that the du-' ties imposed upon wheat flour, upon salted pork and beef, upon ' shingles, upon oak staves, upon lumber, varied from twenty to ' forty per cent *ad valorem.* Now, when he considered that ' these were either articles which constituted the food of the ' people, and necessary for them to procure from foreigners, ' or articles absolutely required for the cultivation of the soil, ' and for the sole manufacture that was carried on in these ' islands, he thought that such a range of duties was per-' fectly immoderate and excessive. He therefore proposed to ' reduce all these special duties considerably. He believed that ' the duties which he proposed to substitute for the old duties, ' would amount to twelve or fifteen per cent *ad valorem.* The ' following were the present duties, and those which he proposed ' to substitute :—

| ' Articles. | Present Specific Duties. | | | Proposed Specific Duties. | | |
|---|---|---|---|---|---|---|
| | £ | *s.* | *d.* | £ | *s.* | *d.* |
| ' Wheat flour (except into Canada, which is free,) | | | | | | |
| ' the barrel, . . . . . | 0 | 5 | 0 | 0 | 2 | 0 |
| ' Beef and pork, salted, the cwt., . . | 0 | 12 | 0 | 0 | 4 | 0 |
| ' Shingles, the 1000, of 12 inches, . . | 0 | 7 | 0 | | | |
| ' ———————— above 12 do., . . | 0 | 14 | 0 | 0 | 3 | 6 |
| ' Oak staves and headings } Red, . | 0 | 15 | 0 | | | |
| ' the 1000, . } White, . | 0 | 12 | 6 | 0 | 7 | 0 |
| ' Wood hoops, the 1000, . . . | 0 | 5 | 3 | 0 | 2 | 6 |
| ' Pitch, pine, and other lumber (one inch thick,) ' the 1000 feet, . . . . | 1 | 1 | 0 | 0 | 10 | 6 |

' He came now to an article which was of the utmost importance
' to the support of the West Indies, and which was absolutely
' prohibited ; he meant fish, the produce of foreign fisheries. He
' meant to do away with this prohibition. He was no friend to
' prohibitions in general. He wished for all commercial pur-
' poses that the word were erased from the statute-book, or that
' it should not be acted upon as a general principle; but very
' sparingly used under any special circumstances, though he could
' not see any that would well justify it. Recollecting that fish
' constituted the principal food of the West Indies, it was most
' unjust to limit those colonies to a single and often a very nar-
' row supply. The duty which he proposed to put upon fish,
' would be equal to an *ad valorem* duty of 25 per cent. The
' duty would be for fish, dried or salted, not the produce of Bri-
' tish fisheries, by the cwt. 2s. 6d., and for pickled fish by the
' barrel, 5s.'

To these important relaxations he added the reduction of
the 30 per cent, 20 per cent, and 15 per cent *ad valorem* duties,
to one uniform duty of 7 per cent. The restrictions thus proposed to be relaxed, were estimated by the witnesses examined
before the Committee of the House of Commons which sat in
1832 on West Indian affairs, as adding 5s. 6d. per cwt. to the
cost of production of sugar. That this is not an extravagant
estimate, may be considered from the following official statement
of the average prices of produce and merchandize in Jamaica, for
the year 1836, the last of which the returns are published.*

*Average Prices of Produce and Merchandize.*

|  |  | Sterling Money. |
|---|---|---|
| Sheep, | . . . . | £3 0 0 |
| Goats, | . . . . | 2 0 0 |
| Swine, | . . . . | 2 0 0 |
| Milk, per quart, | . . . | 0 1 3 |
| Butter, Salt, per lb. | . . . | 0 2 6 |
| Cheese, per lb. | . . . | 0 1 8 |
| Wheaten Bread, per 17 oz. | . . | 0 0 7½ |
| Beef, per lb. | . . . . | 0 0 10 |
| Mutton, per lb. | . . . | 0 2 1 |
| Pork, per lb. | . . . | 0 1 0 |
| Rice, per quart, | . . . | 0 0 10 |
| Coffee, per quart, | . . . | 0 1 8 |
| Sugar, per lb. | . . . | 0 0 10 |
| Salt, | . . . . | 0 0 5 |

|  |  | Wages of Labour. |
|---|---|---|
| Domestic, per week, | . | £0 16 8 |
| Predial, per day, | . . | 0 2 6 and 3s. 4d. |
| Trades, | . . . | 0 5 0 |

* Porter's Tables, Appendix to Part vii. p. 41.

The prices stated in this paper are so extravagant that we doubted its accuracy; and obtained from the Board of Trade the following return—the last which that Department possesses —of the prices in the market at Kingston, Jamaica, in 1837, 1838, and 1839. These prices are generally somewhat lower; but they correspond with the return of 1836 sufficiently to show its general correctness.

*Average Prices of Produce and Provisions at the Kingston Market, Jamaica,* 1837-39.

|  | | 1837. | 1838. | 1839. |
|---|---|---|---|---|
| Sheep, . . . each | | £2  5  0 | £1 16  0 | £2  0  0 |
| Goats, . . . „ | | 1 10  0 | 1  0  0 | 0  8  0 |
| Swine, . . . „ | | 2  5  0 | 1 15  0 | 12s. to 40s. |
| Milk, . . per quart | | 0  0 10 | 0  0 10 | 0  0  7½ |
| Butter, Fresh . per lb. | | 0  3  0 | None sold. | None sold. |
| „  Salt . „ | | 0  1  3 | 0  1  0 | 0  1  3 |
| Cheese, . . . „ | | 0  1  6 | 0  1  0 | 0  1  6 |
| Bread, Wheaten „ | | 0  0  4 | per 10 oz. 3d. | per lb. 5d. |
| Beef, . . . . „ | | 0  0  7½ | 0  0  6 | 0  0  6 |
| Mutton, . . . „ | | 0  1  3 | 0  1  0 | 0  1  3 |
| Pork, . . . . „ | | 0  0  7 | 0  0  7½ | 0  0  9 |
| Rice, . . . . „ | | 0  0  4½ | 0  0  3½ | 0  0  9 |
| Coffee, . . . „ | | 0  1  0 | 0  0  7½ | 0  1  6 |
| Tea, . . . . „ | | 0  7  0 | 0  0  0 | 0  8  0 |

The prices of fish, timber, and manufactured commodities, are not given; but if they bear any proportion to those of the enumerated articles, it follows that the restrictions imposed by our present colonial policy on Jamaica, render it one of the most expensive residences in the world. Almost every commodity that is mentioned, is at nearly double the English price; and many exceed it by 200 per cent. The adoption of Mr Labouchere's Resolutions would render it one of the cheapest. If the reductions which he proposes in timber, lumber, and the other articles used in the cultivation and manufacture of sugar, should reduce the existing burdens on the production of that article from 5s. 6d. to 1s. 6d. per cwt.—and we are inclined to think that they would be reduced still lower—this would amount to rather more than the difference between the present price of British sugar, 38s. per cwt., and the lowest price at which foreign sugar can, under the plan of the Government, be obtained—namely, 34s. 6d. per cwt. We have seen that, during four out of the seven years that have passed since the abolition of

slavery, our colonies supplied us with sugar at 35s. 7¼d. per cwt.,
and they did so with profit to themselves.  But 31s. 7¼d., if Mr
Labouchere's Resolutions had become law, would have paid them
as well as 35s. 7¼d. did before.  And yet Sir Robert Peel ventured
to state, that the admission of foreign sugar at 34s. 6d. per cwt.
would decide that sugar could not be produced by free labour
in Jamaica.    He ventured even to call Mr Burnley as his
witness.   Mr Burnley stated, and with truth, that if a monopoly
of the labour market were continued to the negroes, they would,
like all monopolists, continue to abuse it, and the cultivation of
the colonies would be ruined.  Sir Robert Peel first assumes, that
the admission of foreign sugar will destroy the cultivation of
sugar in Jamaica ; and, that in consequence of the cultivation of
sugar having been destroyed, the immigration of labourers into
Jamaica will be stopped.    And then he says, Mr Burnley's prediction will be accomplished, and the cultivation of the colony be
destroyed.  According to Sir Robert Peel's reasoning, the means
by which the prediction is to be accomplished, is, its having been
previously accomplished.   The ruin of the sugar cultivation is
to stop the immigration of labourers, and stopping the immigration of labourers is then to produce the ruin of the sugar cultivation ! It would be difficult to cull out for a new treatise upon Logic,
a more apt exemplification of what is called reasoning in a circle.
    What Mr Burnley said was, that if they had freedom of trade,
and no obstructions were placed in the way of their obtaining
labour, they wanted no protection or monopoly.
    ' The removal of these restrictions once effected,' said Mr
Burnley,  ' I shall hail with pleasure the day when every mono-
' poly is done away with.  Thank God ! we are now emancipated
' as well as our labourers, and we can walk abroad bold and
' erect, and claim the benefit of the freest principles ; and if we
' are honestly and fairly allowed to trade with all the world with-
' out restriction, we fear no competition from any quarter in the
' colonial market of the mother-country : and when that is
' effected, the agriculture of Trinidad will successfully compete
' with that of every country depending upon slave-labour.   I
' firmly believe that the most advantageous mode of proceeding
' would be, to tear up all our treaties for the suppression of
' the slave-trade, withdraw our cruisers from the coast of Africa,
' and allow all who pleased to procure labourers to work in Cuba,
' the Brazils, and elsewhere, under the influence of the whip ;
' and, in the British colonies, from the higher motive of personal
' benefit.' *

---

* *Trinidad Gazette,* 11th February 1841.

These were the words of one of the largest proprietors in Trinidad, where he presided at a meeting of merchants and planters, every one of whom would certainly have contradicted him, had contradiction been possible. And yet Mr Burnley is the witness, and the only witness, on whom Sir Robert Peel relies to prove that the admission of foreign sugar at a differential duty of fifty per cent, will decide that sugar cannot be raised in the West Indies by free labour !

We believe that we are as anxious to promote the success of the great experiment of negro emancipation as Sir Robert Peel can be. The Whig party has been the steady friends of that noble cause : the Tories have been its steady enemies. After Mr Wilberforce, supported by no party except the Whigs, and with the despotic Tory premier as his impotent associate, had for twenty long years proposed the abolition of the slave trade, and been every year defeated—after the struggle had continued, and hopelessly continued, through three Tory administrations—the Whigs were one year in office, and in that year they carried it against a Tory opposition, headed by Sir Robert Peel's future colleagues,— Lord Castlereagh in the Commons, and Lord Westmoreland, Lord Sidmouth, Lord Liverpool, (then Lord Hawkesbury,) and Lord Eldon in the Lords. From 1806 to 1830 was another period of Tory rule, and though the British slave-trade had ceased, British slavery continued, with slight mitigations forced from the planters, and from their friends the Tories, by the Whigs. At the end of 1830 the Whigs were again in power, and on the 1st day of August 1834, slavery had ceased within the British colonies. Every concession to the negro race has been extorted from the Tories. They fought for the slave-trade and they fought for slavery. From 1796 to 1806, they pretended that if the slave-trade were discontinued, the cultivation of sugar must be abandoned. From 1806 to 1833, they predicted ruin if slavery were touched; and they now predict that the cultivation of sugar by free labour must utterly cease, and Jamaica sink to the condition of Haiti, if it be protected only by the low differential duty of fifty per cent!

Sir Robert Peel, with Lord Stanley by his side, cannot decently avoid admitting that the emancipation has succeeded; but by holding that a differential duty of 150 per cent on slave sugar is necessary, in order to render free sugar worth raising, he has in fact destroyed the value of that admission. We are told, and with truth, that foreign nations are watching the progress of our great experiment. We are told, that on its success depends its imitation by France, by Denmark, by Holland, and by Spain. If we admit that the experiment, so far as respects the production of exportable commodities has failed—if we admit that free-grown sugar cannot compete with slave-grown sugar, even at a protection of 50 per cent—if we tell foreign nations, that after they have set their negroes free, they must, not merely for the first few years, but for an indefinite period, submit to pay 37s. for every hundred-weight of sugar that they consume instead of 22s.—what rational hope can we entertain that they will follow our example? We commenced emancipation by an act great and magnanimous, but yet liable to throw a serious obstacle in the way of all our neighbours. We purchased the right to give liberty, by paying L.25 a-head for every individual on whom we bestowed it. It will be difficult for any other nation to disregard this precedent, and may be still more difficult to follow it. The British Parliament is so accustomed to deal with millions; and British taxation, it must frankly be admitted, from our peculiar arrangements, falls so much more lightly on the governing class than on their inferiors, that the extent of the price which we were to pay was not very anxiously estimated. The crimes of ages were to be atoned for; 800,000 of our fellow-subjects were to be raised from mere articles of property into beings with legal rights and defined responsibilities; a stain was to be wiped from our national character; and the capital sum which was to be the price of this great and memorable act, was, after all, to be paid by posterity. We became responsible only for the interest; and that interest, we repeat, from the mode in which our taxes are imposed, falls principally on the unrepresented classes. No other nation could borrow the necessary principal so readily, or pay the interest with so small a pressure on its aristocracy. This evil, however, whatever be its amount, has been incurred. No nation will find it easy, in future, to emancipate its slaves without purchasing the right from the proprietors. But if we seriously wish our example to be followed, let us beware how we increase the amount of the purchase money. Let us beware of showing that the compensation to be paid at the outset is the least onerous part of the bargain. The immediate and direct payment may be severe: let us prove, and we firmly believe that we have the means of proving, that the immediate and direct payment is all that is necessary; and that if a colony in which the negroes have been freed be not pauperized by protection and monopoly, it can, in a very few years, supply sugar as cheaply after emancipation as before.

But we can show this only by retracing our steps. The losses which emancipation, as we have managed it up to the present time, have inflicted on us, are such as no other nation will be willing or able to undergo. The following table, extracted from the Pamphlet on 'The Common Sense View of the Sugar Question,' shows that the sums which we have indirectly paid for emancipation already equal its original price :—

| Years. | Quantity Consumed. | Difference of Price. | | | Amount of tax or Premium to West India interest. |
|---|---|---|---|---|---|
| | | L. | s. | d. | £ |
| *1834 | 4,154,411 | 0 | 6 | 2 | 1,280,943 |
| 1835 | 4,421,154 | 0 | 6 | 0 | 1,326,343 |
| 1836 | 3,992,901 | 0 | 13 | 0 | 2,549,885 |
| 1837 | 4,349,053 | 0 | 13 | 4 | 2,679,934 |
| 1838 | 4,418,334 | 0 | 12 | 5 | 2,743,048 |
| 1839 | 4,171,938 | 0 | 17 | 1 | 3,471,151 |
| 1840 | 3,764,710 | 1 | 7 | 7 | 5,192,161 |
| Total tax since abolition, | | | | . | 19,243,465 |

Now, we are confident that in this instance, as it almost always happens in such cases, the indirect payment, while it has been far more oppressive to the contributor than the direct payment, has been far less beneficial to the receiver. The direct payment went straight and net to the claimants. Whatever we lost, the compensated proprietors received. But of the indirect payment they have received only a fraction. While we gave them a monopoly against ourselves, the negroes established a monopoly against them. Their labour became negligent and irregular. At certain periods of the crop they combined to refuse all work whatever, unless bribed by extravagant wages. And they used those wages, not so much for the purpose of obtaining increased comforts, as future indolence. They required a dollar for a day's work, and dawdled away the next three days in idleness. Of the millions which seven years of colonial monopoly have cost us, we firmly believe that not one-tenth has benefited either the proprietor or the negro. The remainder has been paid for idleness and extortion. The planter knows that we must have sugar, and can have it only from him. He cares little, therefore, what is the current payment for labour, since he knows that we must repay him. The negro finds that he can get what-

* The crop of the year 1834 was produced before the emancipation; and therefore that year ought to be left out. But if the loss which occurred in the present year be added, the total will much exceed the sum mentioned in the table.

ever he and his companions agree to ask ; and, in a country where
no settled price of labour has previously existed, his demands and
his expectations are unreasonable.  And having been trained to
consider field labour as an evil and a degradation, high wages do
not lead him, as they would in a community of long-established
freedom, to continual toil, but to inconstant exertion, with frequent intervals of sloth or dissipation.

How, then, are we to retrace our steps ?  How are we to
escape from a state of things injurious to the health and comfort
of the British people, injurious to the revenue, and very doubt-
fully beneficial to the planter or to the negro ?  How are we to
show to foreign nations what Sir Robert Peel declares it essential
to show to them, that sugar can be advantageously produced by
free labour within the Tropics ?  By the mode pointed out by
Sir Robert Peel's own witness, Mr Burnley.  By removing the
double bondage of monopolies with which the cultivation of
sugar has been fettered.  By giving to the colonist, what Mr
Labouchere's Resolutions would have conferred on him—free
commerce in all commodities with all the world ; and by depriving
him, in return, of the monopoly which experience has shown to
be injurious both to the economy and to the extent of his
cultivation.  By forcing him, under the strong stimulus of competition, to exact from his labourers regular and diligent work at
moderate wages.

We may be told that these premises lead to a system of
perfect impartiality ;—a system which would admit foreign and
colonial sugars at the same duties.  This is true, and this is the
system which we should prefer.  It obviously would be the best
for the consumer, and for the revenue.  The consumer, not being
confined by fixed regulations in the choice of his market, would
obtain the largest quantity at the cheapest price.  The duty, not
being affected by partial considerations, would be fixed at the
point which would afford the greatest revenue.  Differential
duties must necessarily be injurious to the revenue.  The duties
on the favoured and disfavoured commodity may be both too
low, or both too high ; or one may be too high and the other too
low ; or one may be of the proper amount, and the other above
or below it ; but they cannot both be right.  It is impossible that
different duties on commodities, the same in kind, can each be
assessed at the rate which would produce the greatest amount of
revenue.

We further believe that a system of perfect impartiality, coupled
with the freedom of trade which, we repeat, is a part, and an essential part, of the measure, would be the best for the colonies.  We

have already alluded to the evils which their reliance on the monopoly of this country inflicts on both the planters and the negroes—on the waste which it produces, of capital on the one side, and of time on the other. And we have shown the enormous burdens inflicted on them by the restrictions to which we subject their commerce. But set free their commerce, and then throw them on their own resources ; let both parties know that their success depends on economy and industry, and all experience shows that industry and economy will be the result. They are now treated as the English labourer was treated under the abuses of the unamended poor law : their gains do not depend on their exertions. As the consumption of sugar by the higher classes of this country is uninfluenced by its price, the price has risen more than in proportion to the diminution of supply : 3,442,812 cwt., the colonial importation of 1840, at 49s. per cwt. produced a larger return than 4,421,000 cwt., the great exportation of 1835, gave at 33s. per cwt. They have actually gained by the deficiency of their production. This certainly is no school of improvement. That, under such circumstances, free labour shall be found more expensive than slave labour, is not merely probable, but necessary. But put them on an equality ; let each class of producers be subjected to the same motives, and we firmly believe with Mr Burnley, that the free labourer will be found within the Tropics, as he has been found in every other portion of the world, a cheaper productive instrument than the slave.

In fact, the experiment has been tried, and tried for a considerable time, and on an extensive scale, in Porto Rico. That flourishing colony is situated in the same latitude as Jamaica, is nearly of the same size, though rather smaller, and contained in 1835 nearly the same population—that is to say, 319,161 persons, of whom only 34,336 were slaves.[*] Its chief exports consist, like those of Jamaica, of coffee, sugar, and rum. We possess a detailed account of its state up to the year 1833, from Colonel Flinter, who was for many years a resident proprietor. Colonel Flinter was not a political economist, or even, in political matters, an instructed man. His opinions on protecting duties, on the colonial system, and on the independence of its neighbours, which he thinks every country ought to maintain, are worthy of the darkest ages of Toryism. But notwithstanding his ignorance and his presumption in political speculation, he was a man of intelligence and observation, and, as far as can be in-

* Turnbull, *Travels in the West,* p. 555.

ferred from his book, of perfect good faith.   He states the object
of his work on Porto Rico to be—' To make known the im-
' portance of the Spanish colonies, to suggest plans for their
' improvement, to explain the merits of the Spanish colonial go-
' vernment, to point out the beneficent operation of the Spanish
' slave code in protecting the bondman, and in preparing him for
' emancipation ; and to demonstrate, by unanswerable facts, the
' mighty advantages of free over slave labour, in security, in
' economy, and in productiveness.' *

  ' It must be peculiarly gratifying,' he adds, ' to those who
' advocate the emancipation of the slaves on sound and salutary
' principles, to discover, by the facts which I present for their
' consideration, that free labour on a large scale, and attended
' by the most beneficial consequences, has for some years been
' in practical operation in the island of Puerto Rico, and that
' the free black and the slave work together in the same field
' with the white man.' †

  Our limits force us merely to refer the reader to the facts and
calculations from which he infers that three-fourths of the produce exported from the island, or consumed in it, is the produce
of free labour ; and to those from which he deduces that in every
sort of cultivation—in those kinds even which are the most laborious and the most unhealthy, in sugar and indigo, as well as
in coffee—cultivation by free men is the cheapest.‡   ' I believe,'
he says, ' that there is not a single estate on the island which
' cultivates sugar only by slaves, that can pay one shilling of
' interest on the capital.   The proof of this is, that all the large
' sugar establishments on the south coast, which are worked
' exclusively by slaves, are involved in debt and difficulty; while
' those on the north coast, where there is a mixture of free
' labour, unless in particular cases where there has been great
' mismanagement, are free from debt.   It is evident that the
' slave costs more as a labourer, and works less than the free
' labourer.'§

  Colonel Flinter's testimony is confirmed by Mr Turnbull,
who appears to have visited the island in 1838.   He states, as
the most remarkable fact connected with Porto Rico, that the
fields are cultivated and sugar manufactured by the hands of
white men under a tropical sun.   He states that he has seen

---

* Flinter's *Porto Rico* Preface, p. 5.          † Preface, p. 7.
‡ P. 266.                                        § P. 280.

white men acting as hired labourers, even in the severest labour exacted from negroes—digging cane holes, and working without a murmur or a sense of degradation, in the same field with free coloured men, free negroes, and slaves.* If the free grown sugar of Porto Rico, unaided by differential duties, can compete with the slave grown sugar of Cuba, what is there to prevent that of Jamaica from doing the same?

This, it may be said, is a triumphant refutation of Sir Robert Peel, and shows that an impartial duty would not destroy, probably would not permanently impair, the cultivation of our colonies; but is it a defence of the government plan, which is not an impartial duty, but a differential one, giving to our colonies a preference of fifty per cent? We admit the justice of the qualified censure which would be implied by such a question. We admit, indeed we have already stated, that the government plan is not that which, if we had been despotic legislators, we should have preferred. We are not sure whether, even in the present state of parties and of public opinion, forced as every government must be to propose, not what is best in itself, but what, with their existing degree of information and intelligence, the people can be induced to sanction, we should have made precisely the same proposal. The great objects of the plan—retention of our foreign markets, reduction of the price of sugar, increase of revenue, repression of the slave trade, and the amelioration and ultimate abolition of slavery—would, we are inclined to think, have been better promoted, if the duty on British sugars had been reduced to 20s. per cent, instead of being left at 24s.; and the duty on foreign sugars had been reduced to 30s. instead of to 36s. These are details, however, on which we speak with diffidence. We throw out the suggestion merely for the consideration of the Chancellor of the Exchequer, whoever he may be, whether Mr Baring or Sir Robert Peel, who will have to present to the House of Commons, now in process of election, a Budget of the same nature as that which the late House rejected. But though we think that Mr Baring's scale of duties might have been improved, we most cordially approve of it, as far as it goes, as a great and beneficial advance in the right direction.

In the first place, coupled with Mr Labouchere's Resolutions, it would have enabled us to retain nearly the most valuable foreign trade which our monopolies have left us—that with Brazil and the Spanish Islands. They could no longer have complain-

---

* Turnbull's *Travels in the West*, p. 565.

ed that their produce was prohibited by enactment in our colonies, or by duties in our home market. On our retention of this trade, the welfare of tens of thousands of our manufacturers depends. In 1839, the last year, for which we find returns, we exported to Brazil more than seventy-five million yards of plain and died cottons, of the value of more than L.1,500,000. The following table shows that our exports to Brazil have, during the ten years ending in 1839, exceeded by 81 per cent those to France ; by 46 per cent those to Russia ; by 800 per cent those to Sweden, Norway, and Denmark united :—

|  | Brazil. | France. | Russia. | Sweden, Norway, and Denmark. |
|---|---|---|---|---|
| 1830 | L.2,452,103 | L.475,884 | L.1,489,538 | L.223,227 |
| 1831 | 1,238,371 | 602,688 | 1,191,565 | 208,001 |
| 1832 | 2,144,903 | 674,791 | 1,587,250 | 192,856 |
| 1833 | 2,575,680 | 848,333 | 1,531,002 | 214,538 |
| 1834 | 2,460,679 | 1,116,885 | 1,382,300 | 219,677 |
| 1835 | 2,630,767 | 1,453,636 | 1,752,775 | 292,413 |
| 1836 | 3,030,532 | 1,591,381 | 1,742,433 | 284,079 |
| 1837 | 1,824,082 | 1,643,204 | 2,046,592 | 276,982 |
| 1838 | 2,606,604 | 2,314,141 | 1,603,243 | 361,536 |
| 1839 | 2,650,713 | 2,298,307 | 1,776,426 | 347,166 |
| Average... | 2,361,443 | 1.301,925 | 1,616,312 | 262,047 |

It would be worth while to make some sacrifices to retain such a trade. The government proposal was, to retain it not only without sacrifice, but by measures immediately and directly beneficial to ourselves. A further result of the government measure would have been, the ensuring that the price of sugar should not rise beyond 34s. 6d. per cwt. When the price was at that rate, or at a rate nearly the same, (34s. 7d.,) the annual consumption of the whole population amounted to $18\frac{28}{100}$ lbs. per head. The consumption during the high price of 1840, was only $15\frac{28}{100}$ lbs. per head. To many of our readers these figures may not convey definite ideas. Their importance will be shown by stating a few facts. The annual allowance per head,

|  | lbs. | oz. |
|---|---|---|
| To persons on board her Majesty's ships is, | 34 | 3 |
| To convicts, | 22 | 13 |
| To the aged in workhouses, | 22 | 12 |
| The well-informed author of 'The sugar Monopoly' estimates the annual consumption of the middle classes per head at | 37 | 0 |

The annual consumption per head at breakfast and
tea, by affluent individuals, is about 52 lbs., and
that on puddings, tarts, &c., about 16 more—together . . lbs. oz.
. 68 0

It will appear from these statements, that with the remarkable
exception of bread, (the other great monopoly which it is the
object of the government to relax, and of the opposition to retain,) sugar is the commodity which the poor and the rich consume in the nearest proportions. A man with L.10,000 a-year,
spends on his house and furniture at least 200 times as much as
a labourer; but he does not use twice as much sugar as a common sailor. Nine-tenths of the expenditure of the rich is for the
purpose of luxury or of ostentation; or, to speak in milder terms,
for the sake of keeping up appearances. Bread and sugar are
used only for health, strength, and comfort. The taxes on these
commodities are those which oppress most severely the bulk of
the people, while their influence on the higher orders is almost
imperceptible. And the opposition has refused even to go into
Committee to discuss a plan for reducing them! We do not accuse the opposition of absolute indifference to the wants of the
people. We believe that, if they thought they could relieve them
without any material sacrifice of income, and without any sacrifice whatever of political power, they would make some exertions
for the purpose. But we do accuse them of inattention to these
wants. We do accuse them not merely of not having voluntarily enquired into them, but of having, under the influence of
avarice or ambition—avarice among the sordid followers in the
party, and ambition among the leaders—refused to allow them to
be exposed.

We will endeavour to obviate the effects of this refusal, by
offering to our readers a few details; and we request their attention to the following extracts from Mr Tuffnell's Report of the
Poor Law Commissioners, on the economy of the labouring
classes in Surrey and Kent. It was made on the 1st March 1841,
two months before the Budget was proposed. These extracts
are rather long; but they contain much instructive matter :—

'I visited,' says Mr Tuffnell, 'their cottages, and obtained specific
accounts of their furniture, dietaries, wages, and other circumstances
that affect their comfort. I will first describe the cottage and mode of
living of a Sussex labourer, whose family is such as to make him one of
the most distressed of his class. He has a wife and seven children, the
eldest of whom is a girl aged twelve, and all the rest happen to be girls,
except one boy five years old.

' On entering, the cottage displays a room about 20 feet long by 15,
paved with brick, and nearly divided into two by a partition; the fire-
place is here, and it forms the sitting-room of the family. The furni-

ture consists of one common-looking deal table, a rather elegant round oak one, with moveable flaps, a mahogany cupboard, and six chairs ; there are curtains to the windows. Adjoining is a pantry, which seems filled with all sorts of cooking utensils, and a bakehouse, where the family bake once a-week, as it is the custom in these parts, bakers being rarely employed. Up stairs there are two bed-rooms, in one of which the man, his wife, and the baby sleep, and in the other, which contains three beds, the rest of the children. They purchase six gallons of flour weekly, which is made into bread or cakes with potatoes. They drink tea made with burnt crusts, China tea being too expensive now. *Since the price of sugar has risen, they have been obliged to give up its use ; but a quarter of a pound is bought weekly to sweeten the pap for the baby.* They have no meat except on a Sunday, when a meat pudding is made ; and none of the family ever tastes beer, except, perhaps, the man gets some now and then from his master. The man is in constant work at 12s. a-week, but sometimes he gets piece-work, and then earns 15s. weekly. The cottage, which is rented at 2s. weekly, is clean and well drained ; its literary furniture consists of two Bibles and a New Testament : there is no Prayer-book, as the inmates are Dissenters. The distress of the family arises from the unusual circumstance that the children are nearly all girls, and hence can earn nothing. Were the eldest or the second a boy, he would probably add 2s. or 3s. a-week to the general income by assisting his father.

' The actual weekly expenditure is as follows :—

|  |  | s. | d. |
|---|---|---|---|
| 6 gallons of flour at 16d. | . | 8 | 0 |
| ½ lb. soap, . . . | . | 0 | 3½ |
| ¾ lb. candles, . . | . | 0 | 4½ |
| 1 lb. butter, . . | . | 1 | 0 |
| ¼ lb. sugar, . . | . | 0 | 2½ |
| 1½ lb. meat, . . | . | 0 | 9 |
| Yeast, . . | | 0 | 3 |
| Starch, pepper, and salt, | . | 0 | 2 |
| 1 lb. cheese, . . | . | 0 | 6 |
| Worsted, cotton, tape, &c. | . | 0 | 3 |
| | Total, | 11 | 9½ |

' Here, and subsequently in the accounts of the weekly expenditure of labourers, I shall not insert the rent or clothing, as I find that these are generally not paid for weekly, but are reserved to be paid off at harvest, or at odd times, when more than the usual wages are earned.

' Here is another wooden cottage, in bad repair, containing four rooms, which cost L.30 to build, and is rented at 2s. 6d. a-week. It is tenanted by a man, his wife, and four children—two boys, a girl, and an infant. They sleep in the two upper rooms ; the two boys in a bed in one room, and the man, his wife, and the baby in one bed in the other, a contrivance being made upon the floor for the girl to sleep. The sitting room is 10 feet square, and contains two plain deal tables, and a very small stained one, a neat corner cupboard, three shelves with earthenware ; a few small ornaments are on the chimneypiece, and above it hang some small prints in black frames.   There is a calico window curtain, two small bits of carpet on the floor, a cradle, four chairs, and an arm-chair. Some swinging book-shelves, with religious books.   Altogether, this cottage has a neat, cleanly, and orderly appearance.   The man's earnings are 13s. a-week, but he is occasionally out of work: the wife, in ill health, earns but little.   The family consume weekly, 5¼ gallons of flour, 3 gallons of potatoes, 1 lb. cheese, ½ oz. of tea, 2 ozs. of coffee, ¼ *lb. of sugar for the infant,* 3½d. worth of milk, ½ lb. of soap, 1 lb. of candles, 1 cwt. of coals.

' I have at former times frequently collected information as to the precise method in which a labourer spends his wages ; and, as the point seems to me very important towards understanding the condition and economy of the poor, I will give several of their dietaries,

' In 1837, an aged man and his wife expended their weekly earnings of 6s. in the following way :—

|  |  |  | s. | d. |
|---|---|---|---|---|
| Bread, 2 gallons | . | . | 2 | 2 |
| Bacon, 1 lb. . | . | . | 0 | 7 |
| Butter, 1 lb. | . | . | 1 | 0 |
| Tea, 2 ozs. . | . | . | 0 | 6 |
| Sugar, 1 lb. | . | . | 0 | 7 |
| Coals, 1 cwt. | . | . | 0 | 11 |
|  |  | Total | 5 | 9 |

' It would be quite impossible for the old couple to live as well at present, in consequence of the increased price of provisions ; *but the tea, the sugar, and the bacon, now disappear from the board, and the money so saved goes to pay the additional cost of the bread.*   At the same period, a man, his wife, and seven children. in Sussex, spent their wages thus :—

|  |  |  | s. | d. |
|---|---|---|---|---|
| 6 gallons of bread | . | . | 7 | 0 |
| 2½ lbs. of bacon | . | . | 1 | 5½ |
| 2½ lbs. of butter | . | . | 2 | 6 |
| 1½ oz. of tea | . | . | 0 | 6 |
| 1¼ lb. of sugar | . | . | 0 | 9 |
| ¼ lb. of candles | . | . | 0 | 3½ |
| ½ lb. of soap | . | . | 0 | 3 |
|  |  | Total, | 12 | 9 |

' The following is the expenditure of a labouring man, with a wife and six children, at present.   The contrast between these two cases is not so perfect as it might be ; as, in the preceding case, the labourer purchased bread ; in the following, flour.   The expense, therefore, of making the bread and baking it, should be added to the account ; and this will more than make up the 6d. difference in the whole sum.   Though there is one less in family than in the last case, it will be obvious how much the increased price of provisions has deteriorated the condition of the family :—

|  | s. | d. |
|---|---|---|
| 6 gallons of flour . . | 8 | 0 |
| Yeast . . . | 0 | 3 |
| 1 lb. of meat and $\frac{1}{4}$ of suet . | 0 | 8 |
| 1 lb. of butter . . | 1 | 0 |
| 1 lb. of cheese _ . . | 0 | 6 |
| $\frac{1}{2}$ lb. of candles . . | 0 | $3\frac{1}{2}$ |
| $\frac{1}{2}$ lb. of soap . . | 0 | $3\frac{1}{2}$ |
| Potatoes . . . | 1 | 0 |
| Worsted, starch, cotton, and tape | 0 | 3 |
| *No sugar.* | | |
| Total, | 12 | 3 |

' I might insert numerous other examples of labourers' dietaries; but I trust the above will be sufficient to show, in some degree, how their wages are expended. They, however, are insufficient, as they do not show the quality of the articles procured. For instance, since the price of corn has risen, many of the labourers have been compelled to resort to an inferior sort of flour, termed " sharps," in order to obtain a sufficiency of food. Tea, were it not an article so subject to adulteration, ought to have materially risen in price, as the importation in 1840, compared with that in 1836, shows a diminution of 17,571,762 lbs. I believe, however, the reason it has not, is, that its place has been supplied by a deleterious mixture, of which some of the medical men make great complaints. *It is now, too, usually drunk without sugar, as the great rise in price in the latter article has caused it nearly to disappear from the labourer's house.*'

We have no similar details from the manufacturing districts; but we know that the manufacturing population has been struggling for the last three years, and is now struggling, with distress far severer than that of the agricultural labourers. In fact, the distress of the latter arises principally from the high prices of the necessaries of life. They have, not, as yet, suffered much either in employment or in wages. The manufacturers have severely suffered in both. Much less work has been offered to them, and a much lower rate of payment for their labour. The accuracy of the representation of the state of the labouring population in Bolton, contained in Lord John Russell's remarkable speech, has not been questioned.

If a mere rise of prices has forced the tolerably well employed labouring classes of Kent and Sussex almost to discontinue sugar, it is impossible that its rise should not have equally affected the consumption of the manufacturers. On the other hand, there is no reason for supposing that the affluent have made the slightest alteration in their habits; or that the middle classes have made any very material change. And we infer that the diminution of consumption from $20\frac{28}{100}$ lbs. in 1831, and from $18\frac{28}{100}$ lbs. in 1837, to $15\frac{28}{100}$ lbs. in 1840, has fallen almost exclusively on the labouring classes; and that their annual consumption, instead of being $15\frac{8}{100}$ lbs. per head, does not really exceed 8 lbs. per head; or, in other words, that their consumption is more than 180 per cent less than that of the pauper or the convict; and more than 312 per cent below that of the common sailor.

Now, the mere possibility of importing foreign sugar at a duty of 36s. per cwt. instead of 60s., would, as we have shown, prevent the price of British sugar from ever rising beyond 34s. 6d. per cwt., the price (including original cost and differential duty) at which foreign sugar can be obtained. This, in the absence of disturbing causes, would enable us to return to the consumption of 1837, $18\frac{99}{100}$ lbs. per head. If assisted by the increased commercial prosperity which would follow from the general adoption of the Budget, it would probably enable us to return to the consumption of 1835—$19\frac{21}{100}$ lbs. per head.

But we believe, in the third place, that the Government plan, taken as a whole, would have enabled our own colonies to supply us with sugar at a price much lower than 34s. 6d. per cwt. The average price of the four years preceding the abolition of slavery, was 27s. $9\frac{1}{2}$d. Now, if it be true that the cost of production of free labour sugar, when not artificially augmented by a monopoly, is below that of slave sugar—and it must be admitted that there is much evidence to that effect—it seems to follow, that when the colonists and their labourers are subjected to competition, they will again be able to furnish sugar at 27s. $9\frac{1}{2}$d. per cwt. And if we are right in our calculation, that Mr Labouchere's Resolutions, if they had become law, would have diminished the cost of production by 4s. per cwt., it seems also to follow that they could furnish it at 23s. $9\frac{1}{2}$d. per cwt.,—a price, it must be recollected, considerably exceeding that of foreign sugar;—exceeding, indeed, that of British sugar in 1831. We are unwilling, however, to push the argument to its utmost extent: instead of assuming that free cultivation is less expensive than slave cultivation, we will assume that it is much more expensive;—we will assume that it adds 25 per cent to the cost of production. On that supposition, the price would be 29s. $7\frac{1}{2}$d. per cwt. That is to say, it would exceed by only 1s. 10d. per cwt., or about a farthing per pound, the price before the abolition of slavery.

In the fourth place, the Government plan, while it increased the comforts of the people and extended our trade, would have benefited the revenue to an amount much exceeding the L.700,000 which Mr Baring, with the caution incumbent on a Chancellor of the Exchequer, relied on. This is proved at once, by the following table annexed to his speech :—

| Years. | Rate of consumption per head of sugar and of molasses, reduced to its equivalent of sugar. | Average price of British Plantation Sugar as advertised in the Gazette. | | Consumption of 1841, population 27,952,727, at the average rate per head of each year. |
|---|---|---|---|---|
| | lbs. | per cwt. | | cwts. |
| | | *s.* | *d.* | |
| 1830 | 19.94 | 25 | 0¼ | 4,976,583 |
| 1831 | 20.11 | 23 | 8 | 5,019,012 |
| 1832 | 19. | 28 | 8½ | 4,741,980 |
| 1833 | 17.99 | 29 | 7½ | 4,489,907 |
| 1834 | 18.31 | 29 | 2½ | 4,569,771 |
| 1835 | 19.21 | 33 | 9½ | 4,794,392 |
| 1836 | 16.58 | 40 | 9 | 4,138,002 |
| 1837 | 18.38 | 34 | 5 | 4,587,162 |
| 1838 | 18.42 | 33 | 7 | 4,597,225 |
| 1839 | 17.16 | 39 | 4½ | 4,274,721 |
| 1840 | 15.28 | *48 | 7¾ | 3,813,550 |
| Av. | 18.22 | 33 | 4 | 5,545,664 |

It appears from this table, that at the price of 34s. 5d. per cwt., the price to which (within one penny) the government plan must necessarily have reduced sugar, the consumption of sugar in 1841 would have been 4,587,162 cwt., instead of 3,813,550, its computed amount, according to the consumption in 1840. The difference between the consumption of 1840 and the consumption of 1841, as it would have been at the reduced price, is 773,612 cwt. ; the difference in revenue, supposing the whole additional supply to have come from our own colonies, would have been L.928,334. Supposing the whole additional supply foreign, it would have been L.1,392,506. The enemies of the measure assume that the whole additional supply would have been foreign; for they cannot suppose that the agriculture of our colonies would be destroyed, or even impaired, by the measure, if its consequences were an *increase* of their exports. Sir Robert Peel, therefore, must have felt convinced that the measure would produce an increase of revenue of at least L.1,392,506, instead of Mr Baring's estimate of L.700,000. And, consistently with this opinion, he did not intimate a doubt that, as a financial measure, the proposed

---

* Some of the figures in this column differ slightly from those which we have already adopted. We believe that ours most nearly represent the real market prices

sugar duties would be successful. In fact, Sir Robert Peel and his
friends, if they were sincere in their fears of injury to our colonial
agriculture, must have expected a much greater gain to the revenue than L.1,392,506. They must have expected—not the continuance of our present amount of colonial imports—but its great
diminution. Sir Robert Peel, as we have seen, maintained that the
measure would occasion the total expulsion of the whites from
Jamaica, and the occupation of the soil by the negroes, without any
trade with England or with any other country. He believed,
therefore, that the importation of colonial sugar would be
diminished by at least the whole annual export of Jamaica—that
export, on an average of the six years that have elapsed since the
abolition of slavery, amounts annually to 907,256 cwt. On that
supposition the addition to the revenue would be, not, according
to the Chancellor of the Exchequer's estimate, L.700,000, or,
according to his data, 24s. per cwt. on 773,612 cwt., but 36s. per
cwt. on more than 907,256 cwt., that is to say, more than
L.1,633,060. We believe Sir Robert Peel's anticipations to be
utterly absurd: we believe that the admission of foreign sugar, at
36s. per cwt., accompanied by Mr Labouchere's Resolutions for
the relief of the colonies, would not exclude from our market an
ounce of colonial sugar : and we have given our reasons for that
belief. We do not believe even that the whole additional supply
would be foreign. But, supposing only one half to be foreign,
the increase to the revenue would be L.1,060,420, even at a
consumption governed by the price of 34s. 5d. per cwt. And of
course as the price fell—and we have shown that, with the fall in
the cost of production, it would fall—the consumption and the
revenue would augment together.

Fifthly and lastly, we believe that the Government plan would
have eminently promoted the extinction of the slave trade, and
the amelioration and ultimate abolition of slavery. This we
must observe is a proposition which Sir Robert Peel holds to be
monstrous—which he maintains 'will never be believed by any
' country on the face of the universe.' Now, as we know it
to be true, and as we think that we can explain the grounds of
our conviction, we will endeavour to show, at least to the people
of _this_ country, that they ought to believe it.

There is no part of our history which throws so much discredit
on our morality at one period, and our ability at another, as our
conduct with respect to the slave trade. For more than two hundred
years we were the most active and most extensive slave traders in
the maritime world. We peopled, not only our own plantations with
slaves, but those of the rest of Europe. We reserved to ourselves
by treaty, the privilege of carrying negroes to Spanish America.

During periods of war, we cut off indeed the supply from the colonies of the enemy while the enemy retained them; but it was only to renew it, in an increased ratio, as we conquered them. In vain did the Jamaica legislature remonstrate against the traffic. We treated them as theorists who did not know what was good for themselves, or for their colony, or for us. The influence of class interests was still stronger in the venal parliaments of the last century, than it is now. The shipowners, whose vessels had been built or fitted for that peculiar trade; the manufacturers, whose goods were adapted only to the African markets; the merchants and the proprietors connected with Demarara, Trinidad, and the other fertile and thinly-peopled districts which we had wrested from Holland and Spain—all maintained that the slave trade was the great field for shipbuilding; the great nursery of seamen; the great outlet of manufactures, and in fact the great source of our prosperity. At length, attention to its horrors was forced on the public. We first regulated the trade: we restricted the number of prisoners who might be lawfully contained within the hold of a vessel of a given tonnage; and we required a given space between her decks. In 1792, the House of Commons resolved that the trade should cease in 1796—but when that time approached, in 1795, it refused to give any effect to that resolution. And there is no reason to believe that, if the Tory government had been uninterrupted, the trade would ever have been discontinued. What the Whigs in opposition, aided by Mr Pitt, could not effect, they would scarcely have effected, if still in opposition, after his death. In 1806, however, they had a brief interval of office—the English slave trade was declared unlawful; and the prohibition was supported by measures so well devised and so honestly executed as to have effected its extirpation.

In the same year it was declared unlawful by the United States of America.

The progress of public opinion, when no longer blinded by interest, was rapid. Up to 1806, we had thought it right to be slave traders ourselves. Eight years after, in 1814, we believed it, and most truly, to be our duty to endeavour to prevent the slave trade from being exercised by any other nation. In that year we engaged with France to act together at the Congress of Vienna, in order to induce all the powers of Christendom to pronounce its universal and definitive abolition. In 1815, we agreed with the United States of America to unite our efforts for that purpose; and in the same year, we obtained from the powers constituting the Congress of Vienna a declaration 'of their ' desire to concur, by every means in their power, in the most ' prompt and effectual execution of this measure: leaving it,

' however, to each separate power to judge how and when it
' should be effected.'

Slowly and painfully, by negotiation or by purchase, we have
prevailed on every maritime power to prohibit the trade. But
mere prohibition is nothing, unless enforced by vigorous measures
of repression; and among these measures one of the most effectual
is an extensive maritime police, to watch the extensive African
slave coast, and intercept slavers on their way to the market, and on
their return. Such a police no foreign nation has been willing,
or perhaps able, to establish. *We* have established one; but,
under the general law of nations, it is powerless against all
except our own subjects. A ship is a floating portion of the
territory whose flag it is entitled to bear. Except in the case of
piracy, which renders it the general enemy of the world, its
crew are amenable to no law but that of their own country, and
punishable by none but their own courts. Under the general
law of nations, we have no more right to interfere with a foreign
slave trader, whatever be the punishment inflicted on slave trading
by the law of his own country, than we have to enter the bazars
of Constantinople or Cairo, and to require that the wretches exposed to sale should be set free. If a British cruiser has a
reasonable ground for suspecting that a vessel is first a British
vessel, and secondly a slaver, she has a right, under the general
law of nations, to detain her; and if the suspicion be well founded,
to send her to a British Court of Admiralty for trial. But such
a case never in fact can occur; for no British vessels are slavers.
Unless, therefore, we had supplied this want of power by treaty,
our cruisers would have been mere spectators of the trade, without the slightest power of interference. Of course we had recourse
to treaties. We obtained from every important maritime power,
except Portugal, the right to search their ships within certain
latitudes, and the right to detain them, as to some powers, if they
appeared to be equipped for the slave trade; and, as to all, if
slaves were found on board, to send them to a Court of Admiralty
for trial; and, if found guilty of slave trading, for condemnation.
From Portugal we obtained a limited treaty, and an express
contract for a complete one;—a contract, however, which we have
not been able to induce her to perform. From the United States
of America, we have obtained no treaty whatever. Her engagements to us on this subject are confined to the vague stipulation
that she will use her best efforts to put down the trade. She
absolutely refuses to allow us to interfere with her vessels; whether
our suspicion of their being slave traders be or be not well
founded. We are grieved at the conduct of Portugal. We are
grieved, surprised, and ashamed at that of the United States.

It is lamentable that a great nation should, from the suspicious
sensitiveness which is the great defect of her character, refuse to
concur in the repression of a traffic which she acknowleges
to be atrocious.   It is strange that she should feel her dignity
injured by granting a reciprocal right of search, in which all ·
the great European powers have acquiesced.   It is disgraceful to
our common origin that, from such petty motives, she should suffer
her flag to be so prostituted.   We trust that the time will
come when she will be influenced by nobler feelings; and our confidence is strengthened by the late message of President Tyler.
But while she adheres to her refusal, we have no more right,
under the law of nations, to detain a slaver entitled to use the
American flag, than we have to destroy the ship-yards in Balti-
more, in which we know that slavers are constructed.   We have
a right, of course, on having reasonable grounds for suspecting
that she is not so entitled, to search her; but this right can be
exercised only in good faith : it cannot be assumed unless reasonable grounds of suspicion exist, or be persevered in, though
the hold be filled with slave shackles, if the ownership prove to
be American.

Such is a brief outline of our efforts to suppress the foreign
slave-trade.   We now proceed to state their result.

That deplorable result has been not merely failure, but aggravation.   We have succeeded in intercepting about one slaver in
three, as appears from the extra premium of insurance on slaves
of about 33 per cent.*   But that success has not prevented the
continuance of the trade, or even its increase.   The amount of
that increase cannot be accurately stated, since an illegal trade
has no statistics.   Sir T. F. Buxton believes it to be 100 per
cent.   ' Twice as many human beings,' he maintains, 'are now
' its victims, as when Wilberforce and Clarkson entered upon
' their noble task.' †   Mr Irving, in his speech on Sir R. Inglis's
motion of the 10th May 1838, makes the increase nearly 200
per cent—that is to say, from an annual export of 70,000 to one
of 200,000.   Without adopting either of these estimates, it is
certain that the trade has increased—has increased very greatly ;
and, up to the last period to which our information extends, has
continued to increase.   And it is equally certain, that by making
it contraband, we have enormously aggravated the sufferings of
its victims.   While the trade was legal, we could require that
the living cargo should have a definite amount of space, ventilation, and food.   It was possible, too, that even the captain of a
slave ship might be a man of ordinary humanity.   But a trade

* Turnbull, p. 369.        † The African Slave-Trade, p. 173.

which is punishable by death or infamy, must be abandoned to the outcasts of mankind. In a voyage which may be a continued chase, every thing is sacrificed to promote the chances of escape. The build most favourable to speed, is that which affords the least accommodation in proportion to its computed tonnage. Into such vessels, measuring sometimes only thirty inches between the decks, the cargo is stowed, in a proportion more than three times greater than the largest which, under any other circumstances, would be considered admissible. We will not disgust our readers by a description of the horrors that ensue.* All the misery of a long life of wretchedness on land, cannot equal that which is concentrated in the weeks of the middle passage. The least of its evils is its mortality of 25 per cent.

The result, then, of our long struggle has been, that there are probably twice as many sufferers as there were when we began it; and that each person suffers more than twice as much. This has been the result of the perseverance of a quarter of a century, and of the profuse expenditure of British life and British resources. We have redressed injuries after the manner of Don Quixote. We have satisfied our own consciences; but it would have been far better for the African race, if, after we abolished the slave trade, they had never seen a British cruiser.

At length it seems time to try some new expedient, and we believe that a new expedient, and a promising one, may be adopted. As yet, the only instrument that we have used has been force; and that force has been applied only in one direction. All that we have attempted has been to hunt down the slaver, and prevent him from landing his cargo. Once landed, it is safe. The African cannot tell his own story; he is instantly confounded with the mass of the slave population; and if one cargo out of three is landed, the importer is covered from loss. If two out of three are landed, which seems to be the real proportion, he obtains a profit of cent per cent. †

It is possible that we may diminish the proportion of successful slavers: it is possible that, by employing more numerous squadrons, with larger numbers of steamers—that is, by exposing a larger number of our sailors to the pestilence of the slave coast, and enormously adding to our already enormous expenditure for the suppression of the slave trade—we may intercept half the slavers. But the half that will escape, will still afford a profit on the whole venture of 50 per cent. We may intercept two-

---

* See Sir T. F. Buxton, p. 96 to 146.
† Turnbull, pp. 368, 369.

thirds—that is, we may intercept twice the number that we now intercept—but one-third even now pays the expense of the whole number that sail ; the price of slaves will rise with the cost of production; slave trading will still continue an advantageous lottery, and, like every other lottery, continue to attract speculators. This was not the means by which we put down the British slave trade, nor do we believe that it will ever destroy the foreign one. We put down the British slave trade by measures enforced within the colonies themselves. We required every slave to be registered ; we gave freedom to those who did not appear on the register ; and we established tribunals and public prosecutors through whom the claim could be established; and we obtained in our West Indian colonies the co-operation of the people. In the Mauritius there was no co-operation, and the slave trade lingered there for years after it had ceased in the West Indies.

Such is the course which we venture to recommend for adoption, or at least for trial, in the only important markets now remaining to the maritime slave-trade, Cuba and Brazil.

The present state of Cuba is remarkably favourable to such an attempt.

' In Cuba,' says Mr Turnbull, ' the proprietors of estates, with their full complement of labourers, and with a fair proportion of women and children, have no sort of interest in the maintenance of the slave-trade ; or rather, I ought to say, that their interest lies all the other way, and that they would greatly benefit by its instant and perpetual suppression. On this subject I have had the means of communicating much at large with many of the most enlightened Creole proprietors, and I believe myself in no danger of falling into error when I say, that I am now speaking their sincere and genuine sentiments in declaring that the highest and the best of them desire, as devoutly as ever did Clarkson or Wilberforce, the immediate, total, and immutable abolition of the slave-trade.

' It is not my business in this place to enquire into their motives, or compare them with those of our own philanthropists. Pecuniary considerations in the one case, may have done what the love of distinction and the interests of party may equally have prompted in the others. It is quite certain that the interests of the proprietor of a well managed and fully peopled estate in the island of Cuba, are all in favour of the suppression of the slave-trade. His land, his slaves, and his produce, would instantly increase in value, to an amount which it is not easy to define. A slave at Havanna would be at least equal in value to a slave at New Orleans, and now the difference is as 300 dollars are to 1500 dollars. Suppose him to have 500 slaves, and their value would instantly rise from 150,000 dollars to 750,000 dollars.

' But it is the policy of the court of Madrid to keep the island of Cuba in her dependency; and this, it is supposed, can only be done effectually by the salutary terror inspired by the presence of a numerous, half-savage, negro population.  The existence of such a population seems at once to justify and require the presence of a peninsular army, which, under the command of a captain-general enjoying the confidence of the court, and zealously aided by a numerous train of public functionaries and *empleados*, produces such a pressure on Creole interests, as to have hitherto deterred the native inhabitants from any open attempt to assert their independence.  These public functionaries, with scarcely an exception, are Europeans by birth, and therefore decidedly opposed to a separation which would instantly deprive them of all their emoluments.*

' It is neither the wish,' he adds in a separate part of his work, ' nor the interest of the Creoles of Cuba, as a body—at least not of the old landed proprietors—to continue the practice of the slave trade.  It is the captain-general, who represents the opinions of the cabinet of Madrid; the subordinate functionaries, the natives of Old Spain, who reap a rich revenue from the trade ; and the actual slave dealers, who embark their capital in the undertaking, that are its real and substantial supporters.' †

Since Mr Turnbull left the island, the disapprobation of the slave trade, which he observed as a feeling, has shown itself in overt acts.  The administration of the present Captain-General has been favourable, perhaps we may say partial, to the Creole and agricultural portion of the community, (which in Cuba is the liberal portion,) in the points in which they have been opposed to the new proprietors and to the mercantile classes ; most of whom are Anglo-Americans, or, what is more distasteful to the Creoles, Spaniards, and to the subordinate officials, who are also Spaniards.  He has given to the Creoles spirit and confidence, which, aided by their far greater numbers and greater wealth, have ensured to them political preponderance.  The first use that they have made of their new power is remarkable.  Two important bodies in Havanna, the Junta de Fomento, and the Ayuntamiento, or municipality of the city, have each petitioned the Queen of Spain to take measures for the immediate and total suppression of the slave trade.  A Memorial to the same effect has been presented to the Captain-General from all the most considerable Creole proprietors.  The contest may be long between the active and concentrated force of the minority which profits by the trade, and the scattered majority which suffers from it, if each be left with its present motives and its own resources.  But if we can strengthen the motives of the Creoles, and weaken those of the slave traders—if we can make the abolition of the trade more beneficial than it would now be to the Creoles, and its retention less beneficial than it now is to the merchants; we shall materially al er the relative force of the two parties.  Now

---

* Turnbull, p. 170, 171.          † Ibid. p. 318.

this we can do by adopting the proposal of the Chancellor of the Exchequer and Mr Labouchere, accompanied, as of course they were intended to be, by the abolition of the strange law which forces foreign coffee to be taken to the Cape of Good Hope before it can be received in England at the ninepenny duty ;—a law which takes ten or twenty per cent from the profit of the planter without the slightest benefit to us. We have already expressed an opinion, that the addition of the British demand to that of the whole world would not occasion a permanent rise in the price of foreign colonial produce. But it would certainly occasion an immediate rise. And it would be not only a new market, but a constantly improving one. The labouring people of the British islands, restored by commercial freedom to regular employment and good wages, would be able at least to double their present consumption. They might even rise to that allowed to the common sailors in her Majesty's navy. In addition to this great and increasing market would be that of our colonies; not so much for sugar as for live stock and provisions. The extent to which these new sources of trade would benefit Cuba, it is impossible to calculate. So great and so numerous are the advantages of commerce, that every fresh market generally becomes far more beneficial than it was expected to be. But that the benefit would be great is certain. Every existing estate would become more valuable. Every proprietor would have a still stronger motive to exclude the rivalry of the new estates, cultivated chiefly by imported slaves; and, from the want of females, incapable of keeping up their labourers except by purchase. On the other hand, the objections to the abolition of that trade, on the part of the mercantile classes, would be weakened. The commercial capital of Cuba, like that of every colony, is small, and fully employed. In order to take advantage of the new modes of employing it which new markets would offer, they must remove a portion of it from its existing employments. And what employment would they quit so readily as the slave trade? It is an illegal employment, and, even in Cuba, a dishonourable one. Avarice, example, and habit, are indeed strange blinders ; but no man can like a business in which he knows that he occasions every year the cruel murder of hundreds or thousands of his fellow-creatures ; and the captivity, degradation, and misery, of three times the number. We cannot doubt, therefore, that even among the merchants of Cuba a large proportion would joyfully embrace the opportunity of removing their capitals from the slave trade to a lawful, and innocent, and honourable commerce with Great Britain and her colonies. And on these grounds we believe that, if the Government had been allowed to carry their

Budget, the party in Cuba, favourable to the abolition of the slave trade, would have been strengthened, and the abolition materially accelerated.

We cannot appeal to public protestations against the slave trade, by any popular bodies in Brazil, similar to those which have been made in Cuba; but we know that there exists on the subject, among the persons most distinguished by their station and influence, a firm and well-directed opinion. Out of the six persons constituting the present ministry, four are decided and open abolitionists; and the motives to abolition, strong as they are in Cuba, are far stronger in Brazil.

The last enumeration which we have seen of the population of Cuba, that taken in 1827, classified it thus :—

| | |
|---|---:|
| Whites, . . . . | 311,051 |
| Free coloured (including Negroes), | 106,494 |
| Slaves, . . . . | 286,942 |
| | 704,487 |

And though the numbers of each class have probably much increased during the interval, Mr Turnbull states his opinion, that the proportions are nearly accurate.*

We have not been able to find any official census of Brazil, but we have received from a trustworthy authority the following approximation :—

| | |
|---|---:|
| Whites, . . . . . | 1,200,000 |
| Free coloured (including Negroes), | 1,250,000 |
| Half-coloured Indians, . . | 200,000 |
| Uncivilized Indians, . . . | 2,000,000 |
| Slaves, . . . . . | 2,200,000 |
| | 6,850,000 |

The whites, then, appear in Cuba to be more numerous than any other single class; and not to be greatly inferior in number to all other classes put together. In Brazil the most numerous class consists of slaves, and the least numerous of whites. The whites do not form one-fifth of the whole population—do not amount to much more than one-third of the coloured population, and are equal only to $\frac{6}{11}$ ths of the slave population. It is impossible that they can see, without alarm, a great annual addition made to a slave population which already so much outnumbers them—an addition, too, consisting almost exclusively of men, and of men not trained to servitude. Brazil has as yet been emi-

---

* Turnbull, p. 230.

nently fortunate.  She alone, of all the colonies planted by Europe, has obtained independence without violent revolution and prolonged civil war.  She is not, like the Spanish settlement on the continent of America, a spoil for anarchy; or, like the Spanish islands, subject to the jealous and vexatious interference of an imported executive and a distant sovereign.  No anti-national interest prevails in her councils; no distant regency endeavours to force her to continue a slave trader, in order that she may continue dependent.  The enlightened must grieve to people a country far larger than Central Europe with an African instead of an European race—with the worst race instead of the best,—the ambitious must regret to see an increase of population productive of national weakness instead of strength, —the humane must deplore the waste of life and happiness,—and the timid, or, to speak more correctly, the prudent, must look at Haiti, and dread the increase of the barbarous part of the community.

We repeat, therefore, our belief, that the motives for desiring the abolition of the slave-trade exist still more strongly in Brazil than in Cuba; and that an additional impulse from this country—such an impulse as the Government plans, if they had been adopted, would have given—would have enabled us to obtain the real co-operation of the Brazilian authorities in putting it down. With such co-operation on the part of Brazil and Cuba, it can be effected—without it, and we have never yet obtained it, all our efforts on the African coast or on the high seas—all our expenditure of life, health, and treasure have produced, and will continue to produce, effects worse than mere failure.  They will *not* materially diminish the amount of the trade, and they *will* materially aggravate its horrors.

A further and last result which we expect from the liberal commercial policy which the present government has proposed, and which, as far as sugar and coffee are concerned, even the immediate successors of that government—if it is to have immediate successors—will undoubtedly carry into effect, are the amelioration and gradual extinction of slavery.  If that policy will enable us—as we have shown that it will—to destroy the slave trade, the amelioration of slavery is the necessary result.  This is too obvious to require detailed explanation.  The inequality of the sexes, one of the worst evils of a slavery kept up by importation, must instantly begin to subside.  We shall hear no more of gangs worked to death and replaced every ten years, as the most profitable mode of consuming them.  The labourers who can no longer be imported, will be carefully preserved and bred.  And this is the only mode by which they can be prepared for emancipation. Men must have been brought up in civilized life, accustomed to its wants and its restraints, to its obedience and its regular labour, before they can exist in it as free members with advantage, or even safety. To give freedom to Africans, and to expect them to become useful labourers, would be absurd. Discontinuance of the slave trade is, therefore, a necessary fore-runner of emancipation; and the success of the experiment in our colonies is mainly attributable to its having been made nearly thirty years after the importation of Africans had ceased. So long an interval may not be necessary in every case; nor is it necessary that so great a change should be always so rapidly completed. But we repeat, that discontinuance of the importation of Africans must always precede emancipation, and precede it by a considerable period; and that the extension of our commercial intercourse with the Spanish colonies and Brazil, as it affords the only means of putting down the slave trade, affords, therefore, the only means of promoting emancipation.

We now conclude, for the present, our remarks on the Budget. We could not say less on the most beneficial measure of the kind that has been proposed during the long period in which we have laboured to advance the cause of commercial freedom. We regret that our limits do not allow us to consider the details of the proposals respecting Timber and Corn. But these subjects, as our readers cannot but recollect, have been frequently can-vassed in this Journal; and having been obliged, in order to do justice to it, to confine our present observations to one of the three grand heads of enquiry presented by the Budget, we thought it the most advisable course to select the one which has been least discussed by the Press, and is the least generally understood.

# The Budget of 1842

*Edinburgh Review* (April 1842)

NINE months ago, we remarked that our financial difficulties, painful as they are in their causes and in their immediate effects, are not without their advantages. We rejoiced that they had forced public attention towards the barbarous Commercial Code which every day tends more and more to diminish our enjoyments, to misdirect our industry, to render our trade hazardous as well as unproductive, and to divide society into hostile sections—intent some on wringing a profit out of the calamities of the country, and others on subverting the institutions under which such an oppression can be favoured or permitted. We rejoiced that they gave to a wise and patriotic Government the means of saying to classes, and even to individuals—' Unless you ' will allow us to increase the revenue by diminishing duties, we ' must tax you. If you wish sugar to continue at 8d. a pound, ' or bread at 9d. a loaf, or timber at 30 per cent beyond its natu- ' ral price—if you wish our manufactures to oscillate between ' periods of feverish prosperity and prolonged depression—if you ' wish to lower the price of labour, while you raise that of sub- ' sistence—if you wish to render employment irregular, while ' you diminish its reward—if you wish to give a temporary sti-

' mulus to rents, by injuring the profits out of which all rent is
' ultimately supported—you must consent to raise as a tax the
' revenue which you refuse as a boon.  If you resolve to prolong
' folly and oppression until they reach the verge of ruin or revo-
' lution, you must contribute the expense of your system by a tax
' on your expenditure or on your income.'

We had no hope, indeed, of the immediate success of these
arguments.  We knew that they would be repelled by the selfishness of many, and by the prejudices of still more ; and be deadened
by the ignorance and apathy of the great mass of the community.
We knew how comparatively small was the number of those who
could estimate the evils to be encountered, or foresee the effect
of the different remedies that might be applied.  We knew that
the party whose unhappy fate is to depend for power on misgovernment, and therefore on error, would proclaim that ' periods
' of distress are necessarily incidental to the state of a manufac-
' turing and commercial people—that our financial difficulties
' were the temporary result of a concession to ignorant impa-
' tience—that the welfare of the whole community may be best
' consulted by continuing to each class of monopolists its accus-
' tomed protection—that cheaper commodities would produce
' lower wages, freedom of commerce lower profits, and extension
' of trade dependence on foreign nations.  And that the first step
' towards improvement must be the refusal of plans mischievous,
' so far as they are not visionary ; and the second step, the expul-
' sion of their proposers.'  We knew that all this would be said,
and we knew that it would be believed; and we fully anticipated, therefore, the rejection of the Whig Budget, and the
accession of a Tory Ministry.

But we then felt, and we still retain, a firm reliance on the
ultimate prevalence of truth.  Firmly convinced that the principles proposed and rejected in 1841, are the only principles by
which the country can be restored to its former, or even be
enabled to retain its present, amount of wealth and of civilization, we then believed, and we still believe, that those principles
must in time be adopted.

It is possible, indeed, that the contest between good and evil
may be protracted.  It is possible that a long period may elapse
during which months of prosperity may alternate with years of
adversity ; during which the value of our currency, the extent of
our commerce, and the comfort of our population, may depend
on the caprices of our variable climate ; during which the baro-
meter may be the regulator of wages and profits, and ten days of
wind in March, or of rain in August, may decide the welfare or
the distress of millions.  But in time the struggle must end.  In

time we shall discover the folly of attempting to be wiser than Nature; and of striving to produce, by a system of alternate relaxation and prohibition—a system so complicated and so uncertain, that its inventor dares not venture a conjecture as to its operation *—the regular supply and steady price which are the spontaneous results of commercial freedom. In time we shall feel the wickedness of exposing millions to privation and want, in order to supply affluence to thousands; and in time the small class which governs us will discover that the permanence of its rule depends on its escaping from the charge of selfish legislation.

We have said that the intervening period may be long; but it is possible, we think even probable, that it may be short; and we are sure that the events of the few weeks during which Parliament has been sitting, have not tended to prolong it.

If the Melbourne administration had pursued the usual course of a declining party—if they had acted in 1841 as they did in 1839, had proposed no measures which they did not fully expect to carry, and had resigned as soon as their working majority was gone—the task of their successors would, for a time, have been comparatively easy. They would have found, indeed, a deficit; but from the twenty-five millions worth of taxes which had been repealed since the peace, there would have been no real difficulty in reimposing an amount sufficient to re-establish the revenue. They would have proceeded, as is the practice of that party, along the beaten road, and taxed houses, or windows, or salt, or leather; and we should have heard of no alteration in the corn law or the timber duties—of no importation of cattle, and unquestionably of no income tax. But the Budget of 1841 was a measure, the importance of which did not depend on its success. A plan which proposed to restore revenue by cheapening the subsistence, and increasing the comforts, and extending and steadying the trade of the country, might be defeated, but could not be disregarded. The contrast between such a measure and the coarse expedient of a mere increase of taxation, would have been too glaring. Sir Robert Peel therefore felt that he must propose a Budget possessing some resemblance, at least in form, to that of his predecessors; and we proceed, as far as the very brief time will allow, to consider how far he has succeeded.

The most mischievous of the abuses against which the Whig Budget was directed, is the gigantic injustice of the Corn Law.

---

* See Sir R. Peel's answer to Lord Worsley, March 18, 1842.

But not only is that law the palladium of the Tory party—it has been, until a few weeks ago, the especial favourite of Sir Robert Peel himself. ' I should like to know,' he said, in his Reply on the want of confidence motion in last June, ' who in this ' House has more steadily stood forward in defence of the exist- ' ing Corn Law than I have done ? '

We are inclined to think, that at this time he intended to retain unaltered the law of which he boasted to have been the steady defender. A short time afterwards, when he addressed the electors of Tamworth at the nomination, he expressly stated that he had come to the conclusion that the existing system should not be altered ; and that our aim ought to be to render ourselves independent of foreign supply. Such must have been his plan, too, when he admitted the Duke of Buckingham to his Cabinet. He must have been aware that such an associate would not allow even the appearance of a breach in the walls which protect his monopoly. Even the speech of the 9th of February last, in which he brought forward the alterations, such as they are, which he now proposes, was that of a man yielding not to conviction, but to popular clamour. It contained scarcely a sentence that might not have been uttered by the fiercest and blindest champion of ' No surrender.' He began by denying the supposed amount of the existing commercial and manufacturing distress, and by main- taining that the distress, whatever it may be, has not been caused, or even promoted, by the Corn Laws, and will not be removed, or even palliated by their modification. Having thus disposed of those who are supported by profits, he proceeded to those who live by wages; and after stating, what is certainly true, that the bulk of the labouring classes in Great Britain are even now in a state superior to that of the bulk of the labouring classes on the Continent, he hinted (for he is too cautious to make such a state- ment in express words) that their superiority arose from the cir- cumstance, that ' in this country meat is dear, corn is dear, and ' most of the leading articles which constitute the means of sub- ' sistence and comfort, are dearer than in the Continental states.' He went on to repeat, that it is of the first importance to the ' permanent interests of the country, that, *as far as is possible*, we ' should be independent of foreign supply ;' and that the foreign supply, if any, ' should be limited in quantity, and should be ' brought in only for the purpose of repairing an accidental and ' comparatively slight deficiency.' On these grounds he deprecated a fixed duty. He deprecated it because it woud not go to the utmost verge of possibility in excluding foreign supply—he depre- cated it because it would substitute a permanent for a casual importation ;—in other words, he deprecated it because it would give us a steady commerce and a settled currency ;—because it would give a regular trade to the merchant, a regular demand to the manufacturer, and regular wages and regular employment to the workman.

Such premises appear to lead to no conclusion except the maintenance of the existing law, or adding to the severity of its restrictions and prohibitions. At length, however, he came to the reasons for a change. These he stated to be, first, that a general impression exists that some change is expedient; secondly, that a duty of 20s. having been found in ordinary seasons nearly prohibitory, a higher duty is a piece of useless insolence ; and thirdly, that under the present law the importation of a whole year is generally concentrated within a short period, and at an inconvenient season, just before the home-grown corn is threshed. Of these arguments, we have no doubt that the first was that which most influenced Sir Robert Peel, but the last was the one on which he dwelt most. ' This consideration alone,' he remarked, ' ought to prevail with those who most approve ' the protection at present afforded, to listen with favour to some ' modifications of the existing law—modifications, in my opinion, ' likely to prove as advantageous to the agricultural interest as ' to any other class.'

These were the motives which he assigned for changing a law, in the defence of which he had for fourteen years ' steadily stood ' forth ;'—motives so narrow and inadequate, that it is painful to believe that he really obeyed them. He supported his proposed alteration by no enlarged views of national welfare—by no plans to extend the trade, or increase the comforts, or relieve the distress, or appease the discontent of the people, or to increase the revenue of the State. Such objects he passed over, not because he is indifferent to them, but because he knew, and indeed avowed, that his proposed measure would not effect them. He avowed, that in proposing merely a shadow of a fixed duty—a duty still perplexed by a sliding scale, though sliding by more regular gradations, and with two intervals of rest—he was leaving the real principle of the existing Corn Law unaltered.

But though he refused to abandon the sliding scale, he might have materially improved the law ; or, to speak more accurately, have materially diminished its mischief by an effectual reduction of duty. He stated the question for the consideration of Parliament to be, ' What was the amount of duty which would give ' a just and satisfactory protection to domestic agriculture?'—a question to be determined, according to Sir Robert Peel, by two considerations ; first, the price which, on the whole, may be considered a sufficient encouragement to the grower ; and secondly, the price at which foreign corn can be introduced. On the second point he said nothing. The first he fixed for wheat at 56s. At this price, therefore, he subjected foreign wheat to a duty of 16s., rising to 20s., its maximum, when the price falls to 50s. ; and sinking to 1s., its minimum, when the price rises to 73s. Instead of the sudden jumps of the present scale, two rests are interposed, one from 66s. to 68s., both inclusive, when the duty is stationary at 6s. ; the other at 54s. and 53s., when it is stationary at 18s. As a further protection to domestic agriculture, he proposed to increase the number of towns from whose returns of prices the averages are framed ;—an increase which, by letting in returns from cheaper markets, is expected to lower the Gazette price by between two and three shillings a-quarter. It must be recollected, therefore, in considering the probable results of the proposed duties, that about two shillings a-quarter will be taken from the apparent price, and therefore added to the duty ; so that when wheat, under the present system of averages, would be stated at 56s. a-quarter, it will, under the new system, be stated at 54s. ; and therefore incur an eighteen shilling, instead of a sixteen shilling duty.

But, even disregarding this new element in the calculation, it is clear that the proposed scale will be, as it is avowedly intended to be, in all ordinary seasons, prohibitory. Sir Robert Peel states the average price of wheat to be 56s., and at that price imposes a duty of 16s. Now, a duty of 16s. has been found from experience to be nearly prohibitory. Out of the thirteen millions and a half of quarters which have been entered for home consumption under the existing law, not a million and a half have been entered at a duty amounting to 16s.

A further, and perhaps a still clearer evidence as to the effect of the proposed duty, may be acquired by examining the question which Sir Robert Peel, after stating its importance, did not think fit to resolve ; namely, the price at which foreign corn may be obtained. On this subject, however, we will not trouble our readers with statements of shipping charges and consular returns. The papers on corn presented to Parliament on the 4th March 1842, (No. 50,) contain information which appears to us to be more satisfactory.

The island of Jersey enjoys a free corn trade. She is not forced to have recourse to the nearest market, lest a cargo from a distant port should find that a sudden rise of duty has changed profit into loss. She can import at the time and from the country which affords the cheapest supply, and her demand is too slight to affect sensibly any market. Under such circumstances, the prices at which Jersey imports may be considered as the most favourable at which corn can be obtained in the British islands. We subjoin the prices of foreign wheat in Jersey since 1828, when the present Corn Law was passed, down to 1841 inclusive, the latest period for which the returns are published; and we have added from the same Parliamentary Paper the average price in England for the same period.

| Year. | English Price. | | Foreign Price. | |
|---|---|---|---|---|
| | *s.* | *d.* | *s.* | *d.* |
| 1829 | 66 | 3 | 68 | 0 |
| 1830 | 64 | 3 | 54 | 0 |
| 1831 | 66 | 4 | 62 | 6 |
| 1832 | 58 | 8 | 57 | 0 |
| 1833 | 52 | 11 | 39 | 0 |
| 1834 | 46 | 2 | 40 | 0 |
| 1835 | 39 | 4 | 36 | 0 |
| 1836 | 48 | 6 | 37 | 0 |
| 1837 | 55 | 10 | 47 | 0 |
| 1838 | 64 | 7 | 55 | 0 |
| 1839 | 70 | 8 | 67 | 0 |
| 1840 | 66 | 4 | 54 | 9 |
| 1841 | 64 | 4 | 51 | 1 |
| | 58 | $9\frac{1}{2}$ | 51 | 5 (within minute fractions.) |

It will be seen, that during that period the average price of foreign wheat in Jersey, which, as we have already stated, represents the most favourable price at which it could be obtained in England, has been 51s. 5d. per quarter; and that the average price in England has been 58s. $9\frac{1}{2}$d. a quarter—a price which Sir Robert Peel considers excessive. At this price he imposes on foreign wheat a duty of 14s., which, added to the average price of 51s. 5d., raises the cost of importing foreign wheat to 65s. 5d., and of course prohibits it. Until British corn has risen to 62s., at which price the duty falls to 10s., and the price and duty taken together, of foreign corn, amount to 61s. 5d.—importation at average foreign prices cannot take place. Indeed it cannot take place even then, since the necessary results of the attempt to import—namely, a rise of the price abroad, and a fall here— would derange so even a balance. We have not the slightest doubt, that if Sir R. Peel's proposition be adopted, it will be under the law of 1842, as it was under the law of 1828. Ninetenths of the importation will be confined to the occasions when the English price exceeds 65s., and the remainder will be sold at a loss by the victims of our perverse ingenuity.

One of the great rules of commercial legislation, indeed of all legislation whatever, is to diminish the empire of chance, to enable men to reckon on the results of their actions, or at least not to disturb the elements of the calculation. The duties which conform best to this rule, are the ordinary *ad valorem* duties. The producer, the importer, and the warehouser, who deals in articles subject to such a duty, may calculate on a steadiness of profit even greater than can always be expected under a perfect freedom of trade; since what he gains or loses by a rise or fall in price, is in some measure balanced by an increase or diminution of duty. A fixed duty, though it contains no such principle of compensation, has the great advantage of stability. One portion of the cost of production, often a very important one, is unalterable. One of these duties, an *ad valorem* or a fixed rate, is adopted, with one exception, in our whole fiscal code; the fixed rate being generally applied to raw produce, the *ad valorem* rate to manufactured articles. The solitary exception—the single commodity as to which the law strives to aggravate the hazards of commerce—the single commodity on which it imposes a duty not *ad valorem*, but *contra valorem*—the single commodity as to which, when the price falls, the law doubles the importer's loss by a proportionate addition to the duty, and, when it rises, doubles his gain by a proportionate diminution of duty—the single commodity to which this monstrous legislation is applied, is the *food of the bulk of the inhabitants of Great Britain.* It is the commodity of which the legislating classes are the principal producers, and the labouring classes the principal consumers. It is the commodity from which the incomes of the former are derived, and on which those of the latter are spent. After this, who can wonder at Chartism?

We have often thought it a question, whether, if we had had to choose between the system of successive, but unforeseen prohibition, and free admission, under which we have suffered ever since 1815, and a permanent prohibition, we ought not to have preferred the latter. Now, of course, with a population increased forty-four per cent, Sir Robert Peel's proposed independence of foreign supplies has become impracticable—at least if the labouring classes are to be allowed to continue the use of wheat; but it was otherwise when the population of Great Britain did not exceed thirteen millions.

The average price of corn would have been somewhat higher— the rate of increase in the towns and manufacturing districts would have been retarded—the productiveness of industry would have been diminished—wages would therefore have been somewhat lower; we should have been a less numerous and a poorer

people.  But, on the other hand, we should have escaped one
of the main causes of the alternations of prosperity and distress,
of panic and confidence, of increased and diminished demand for
labour, which, with an increased rapidity of recurrence, have
been interspersed during the whole of that period.  Our currency would not have been deranged by sudden demands.  The
specie in the vaults of the Bank of England, the narrow foundation on which our vast superstructure of credit rests, would not
have been periodically threatened with exhaustion.  The Bank
would not have been forced, in its struggles to retain the gold
which the imperious demand for food was driving out, to curtail
its issues, to endanger the fortunes of the mercantile world, and to
alter the standard of value by which all men's proceedings are regulated.  Our trade would not have been deranged by being forcibly
attracted in a certain direction at one period, and forcibly repelled at another.  Our work-people would not have suffered at
one period under the demoralizing influence of a sudden rise
of wages, and at another under the still more demoralizing influence of a sudden depression.  We are inclined to think that
we should, on the whole, have been a better and a happier
people.

Of course, we do not mean to prefer the condition of Great
Britain under a supposed prohibition of the importation of corn,
to its condition if importation had been subjected to a moderate
fixed duty.  Such a duty would, indeed, have produced the
effect deprecated by Sir Robert Peel.  It would have occasioned,
except in the rare case of a succession of abundant harvests, a
steady importation.  It would have made us dependent on
foreign nations for a portion of our regular supply.  We should
have had to endure the dependence of the rich on the poor, the
dependence of England on Ireland, the dependence of Sir
Robert Peel himself on his own tradesmen.  But that supply
would have been drawn from the whole world, instead of coming
from the few ports whose proximity now enables them almost exclusively to take advantage of our unforeseen demands.  If it be
true, according to Sir Robert Peel, that the great corn producing countries of Europe, lying in the same latitude with this
country, are affected by the same causes, and therefore partici-
pate in our scarcity, and in our abundance, what can be more
insane than a policy which confines us to the least favourable
markets?  With the whole world competing for our custom,
we should have purchased our supply at the price at which the
producer could afford it; not at that which he could extort from
our necessities.  We should have purchased it for manufactures
instead of for bullion; by extending our trade instead of by

deranging it; by improving instead of deteriorating the welfare of our work-people; by augmenting the public revenue instead of diminishing it; by adding to the Customs without taking from the Excise. Such would have been the results, and such would now be the results of the substitution of a fixed duty for the sliding scale, which Sir Robert Peel has thought fit to grant to the prejudices of his supporters. We are told, however, that a fixed duty could not be maintained. Whether it could be maintained or not, would depend on its amount. A fixed duty of 20s., or even of 15s., certainly could not be supported, and ought not to be supported; but it is equally clear that a fixed duty of 8s., the amount proposed by the late Government, *could* be maintained. In the whole of the fourteen years during which the present Corn Law has existed, there has been only one (1839) in which the average price has been above 66s. 4d.; and there have been only four, 1831, 1839, 1840, and 1841, in which it has been above 66s. 3d. The latter, therefore, must be considered as a price un-usually high. Yet in 1829, at this extravagantly high price, a duty much exceeding 8s. was maintained. In that year, 1,026,803 quarters of wheat were imported, at an average duty of 9s. 3d. per quarter. In the rather dearer year of 1840, when the price was 66s. 4d., a duty of 7s. 2d. a quarter was maintained. 2,011,774 quarters in that year paid that average amount of duty. Under a regular trade, a trade in which the abundance of the West and the South were allowed to supply the scarcity of the East and the North—when America, Hungary, and the Ukraine were admitted on equal terms with the countries in our own latitude, to which Sir Robert Peel confines us—when prudent merchants and corn-dealers could again venture to equalize prices, by reserving the excess of cheap years to supply the deficiency of dear ones—we do not believe that a price of 66s. 3d. a quarter would ever be reached. But if it were reached, the experience of 1829, nearly repeated in 1840, shows that a duty of 8s. could be maintained.

One of the most remarkable features of the long debates which followed Sir Robert Peel's proposal as to corn, was the abandon-ment by the leaders of the Tory party of most of the old bulwarks of monopoly. We were no longer told that the manufacturers are dependent on the agricultural market; and that it was their inter-est to pay an extra price for their bread, in the hope that a portion of that extra price would be laid out in the purchase of cottons and woollens. Sir R. Peel disclaimed all wish to prop up rents, or to defend the interests of any particular class. He left it to Sir E. Knatchbull to contend, that ' the duty of corn should be ' calculated in such a manner as to return to the landed interest

' full security for their property, and for the station in the country
' which they had hitherto held;' and to be rewarded by indignant
cheers from one side of the House, and by shame and silence on
the other. Even the old fallacy, that wages depend on the price
of corn—fall as it falls, and rise as it rises—was only hinted at by
Sir R. Peel. He left that *falsism*, if we may be allowed to coin
a term to designate what is both true and false, to be formally
asserted only by his subordinates. He left to Lord Granby to
maintain, that ' the experience of all Europe shows that the
' certain consequence of making food cheap is to lower wages ;' to
Sir Francis Burdett to affirm, that ' to the labouring classes the
' price of corn does not signify one straw ;' to Mr Stuart Wortley
to state, that ' if the price of corn were reduced, masters would
' reduce wages ; that if sixpence a-week were saved to the artizan
' in corn, the diminution of wages would amount to 2s. 6d. a-
' week :' to Mr Gladstone to talk of ' the fallacy of cheap bread;'
and to Lord Mahon to argue, that ' the price of wheat being at
' Warsaw about 22s. a-quarter, the people were *therefore* mise-
' rable and uneducated; and being in Amsterdam from 58s. to
' 63s. a-quarter, the artizan and labourer were there, as a natural
' result, in a comfortable condition.'

When such an error as this is maintained by men with the
knowledge and sagacity of Mr Gladstone and Lord Mahon, and
almost countenanced by Sir Robert Peel himself, it may be worth
while, pressed as we are by questions equally important and still
more urgent, shortly to expose it. It is easy to refute it directly.
For this purpose it is necessary only to remind the reader, that
wages depend on the supply, on the one hand, of labour, and, on
the other hand, of the commodities intended for the use of the
labourer. If the supply of the commodities intended to be used
by the labourer is diminished, he is forced to work more hours
for the same wages; to send his children, and perhaps his wife,
to the factory ; in short, to increase the supply of labour. If the
supply of those commodities be increased, he can support himself by less exertion ; he can keep his wife, and perhaps his
eldest girl, at home ; in short, he can diminish the supply of
labour, and he does so. All this is clearly stated by Mr Milne,
Mr Wood, Lord Mansfield, and Lord Lauderdale, in the evidence
taken by the Committee of the House of Lords on Grain and
the Corn Laws in 1814. We extract a portion of Mr Milne's
evidence—the evidence of a man of great practical experience,
both in agriculture and in manufactures.

' As a proprietor of land, have not you attended to the expense of
agricultural labour in Scotland ? I have.

' Have you not also had large concerns as a manufacturer ?    I have.
' Where?    At Aberdeen.
' In what line ?    Both in the cotton and linen manufacture.

' Can you state to the committee the effect, as far as your observation
has gone, of the rise or fall of grain on the value of agricultural labour
in Scotland?

' In Scotland, both agricultural labour and manufacturing labour are
considerably affected by the rise and fall of grain and provisions.  I have
always considered, that when grain and other provisions rose, both manufacturing and agricultural labour fell ; on the contrary, when provisions
and grain fell, manufacturing and agricultural labour rose.  The reason is
obvious.  Supposing there are in any one parish 100 labourers, who are
able to do the work of that parish : if provisions rise, those labourers will
do double work ; of course, there being only a certain demand for labour,
the labour falls : if provisions, on the contrary, fall, those labourers do
much less work, probably not one-half ; you must, therefore, seek more
labourers ; this makes a demand for labour, and labour rises.

' When you say that the labourer will do double work, do you not
mean that the rise in the price of grain, and the difficulty of obtaining
the same quantity, will urge him to do such a quantity of work as will
enable him to have the usual enjoyments ?

' Certainly ; and very often it goes further than that, that he does too
much work, and works beyond his strength, when grain is very high ; at
other times he is idle, when grain is low.

' Can you state to the committee any particular instance of agricultural work that you may have contracted for, in a dear year and a cheap
year ?

' I can state a very strong instance that happened to myself last year.
I wished to enclose a farm at the latter end of the year 1812, or the
beginning of 1813 ; I sent for my bailiff, and told him that I had en-
closed, about five-and-twenty years ago, a good deal of land ; that the
enclosure at that time cost me 3s. per ell of 37 inches ; that a neighbour
of mine, two or three years ago, had made similar enclosures, which cost
him 5s. per ell ; that I thought he had paid too much, and that I ought
to have it cheaper :—the answer I got from my bailiff was, that provisions
were very high, that the labourers were doing double work, and that of
course there was less demand for labour, and that he could do those
enclosures last year at a cheaper rate than I had ever done them, and he
actually executed this enclosure at about half-a-crown an ell.  He again
came to me, and told me that I had proposed to him to do some ditching
and draining upon another farm, which I did not intend to do till about
a twelvemonth after, from the circumstance of not being fully in possession of the whole farm ; he requested I would allow him to do it that
season, as he could do it so much cheaper, and that a great many labourers were idle from having a little work, in consequence of those who
were employed doing double work ; I desired him to go on with that
labour likewise, and he actually contracted for very large ditches at sixpence an ell, which I do not think I could now do under from one shilling to eighteenpence, in consequence of the fall in provisions.

' Can you give the committee any information respecting the effect of the price of provisions on manufacturing labour ?

' When provisions are likely to fall, I have always been in the habit of giving orders to look out for more hands, imagining that more hands would be wanted to do the same quantity of labour ; and when provisions got high, I never had much fear of getting plenty of hands, because they did more work.'

It may be said, however, that these are only temporary and immediate results, and that ultimately the supposed accordance between corn and wages would show itself. Has it shown itself in Ireland, where wages are one-third of the English prices, and corn is cheaper only by the expense of transport? Has it shown itself in the United States, where labour is worth a dollar a day, and wheat 40s. a quarter? But it may be asked, must not the labourer live? Of course he must ; but not necessarily on corn. He may rise to meat, or sink to potatoes. Increase the supply of provisions, and he will live better. Add to that increase, improved trade and more regular employment, and he will live better still. Diminish the supply of provisions, and he will live worse. Increase the evil by a diminishing trade and irregular employment, and he will live worse still. But with the example of Ireland on the one side, and of America on the other, never talk of the ' fallacy of cheap bread;' or of ' wages rising and ' falling with the price of corn.'

On a matter, however, of such importance, it may be proper not merely to refute the error, but to show the causes which have occasioned able men to be entangled by it. The first and great cause probably is the fact, that high wages and a high price of provisions, and low wages and a low price of provisions, are in most countries coexistent ; so a man who lives in a palace is generally wealthy, and a man who lives in a cottage is generally poor. But it would be rash to infer that wealth is occasioned by inhabiting a palace, or poverty by dwelling in a cottage. A high price of corn is not the cause, but the effect of high wages, and a low price of corn is not the cause, but the effect of low wages ; just as a palace is the result, not the cause of wealth, and a cottage is the result, not the cause of poverty.

No principles are better established—no principles, indeed, are more true—than that the general price of corn must correspond with the price of that portion of the whole supply, which is regularly furnished at the greatest expense; and that the price of that portion consists entirely of the wages of the labourers who produce it, and the profits of the farmers who advance those wages. If the wages of a labouring family in one country are £40 a-year, and profits are ten per cent, the corn raised by that family's labour during a year must sell for £44. If in another country wages are L.20 a-year, an equal quantity of corn raised by the same labour may be sold for L.22. Halve wages in the former country, and double them in the latter, and prices will at least be reversed.

Again, in every corn-eating country, the great consumers of the corn are the labourers themselves. If wages rise, the principal commodity on which their wages are expended has a double tendency to rise; first, because it costs more to produce it; secondly, because the fund for purchasing it is increased. If wages fall, the principal commodity on which wages are expended has a double tendency to fall; first, because it costs less to produce it; and secondly, because the fund for purchasing it is diminished. As a general rule, it may be laid down, that high wages produce a high price of provisions, and low wages a low price of provisions; just as wealth is the cause of good clothes, and poverty is the cause of rags.

The principal exceptions to this rule are, the case of a fertile inadequately peopled country, in which the productiveness of agricultural labour makes up for its high price, as in the example of America; and the case of a country in which corn is raised, not for the use of the labourer, but for that of the more opulent classes, or for exportation. Such is the state of Ireland, and of Poland when our ports are open. In such a country as the valley of the Mississippi, though labour is dear, corn may be cheap, because little labour will produce a large quantity; in such a country as Poland, though labour is cheap, corn may be dear, because it will fetch a high price in England. A third exception might be afforded by an opulent manufacturing and commercial country, which should choose to purchase with the produce of its skill, its machinery, and its capital, the corn grown by the cheap labour of its less advanced neighbours, or from the fertile lands of less densely peopled regions.

Two accidental circumstances have concurred, the one in England, the other both in England and Scotland, to give currency to the error which we have been exposing. One was the maladministration of the unreformed English poor-law. In the pauperized districts, and there were few agricultural districts uninfected by pauperism, wages and employment were not a matter of contract, but of right, on the part of the labourer, and of duty on the part of the farmer or the overseer. The labourer was treated like a slave, paid not according to his services but his wants, and entitled not to a certain sum of money, but to the money, whatever were its amount, which would purchase a certain quantity of bread for each member of his family. Of course, under such a system the expense to the farmer of his plough-

men, and of the horses which his ploughmen drove, was governed by the same causes. The wages of one rose and fell with
the price of bread; just as the keep of the other rose and fell
with the price of hay. Even now, though the scale has disap-
peared, its traces remain. The labourer with a family accustomed to wheaten bread, when its price rises beyond his means
at his usual wages, threatens to enter the workhouse unless his
wages are raised. The farmer is frightened at the probable increase of rates and submits; and infers that wages depend on the
price of fine wheaten bread.

The other circumstance which promoted the error in question
was the depreciation of the currency during the Bank Restriction Act. While the pound sterling gradually sunk till it was
worth only 14s., of course, both wages and provisions had a tendency to rise, and, so far as that common cause affected them,
to rise in precisely the same proportions. They did not, indeed,
rise in the same proportions; as provisions were enhanced by a
series of seasons the most calamitous on record, and by the obstacles opposed by the war to importation. In any ordinary
state of things, wages would therefore have had a tendency to
fall; but the stimulus given to trade and manufactures, by our
enjoying the monopoly of the world, prevented their fall; and the
alteration of the standard in which they were estimated gave
them the appearance of rising. Every rise in the price of provisions, therefore, was followed by an apparent rise of wages ;
and among those who were ignorant of the real circumstances of
the case, that is to say, among 999 out of every 1000 persons,
the two ideas became connected as cause and effect.

Notwithstanding Sir Robert Peel's refusal to offer even a conjecture as to the revenue to be obtained under his Corn Bill, we
have considered that bill as part of his financial scheme. We have
done so on two grounds. First, because we cannot but believe
that some revenue will be obtained, though a much smaller and
more irregular one than would have been derived under a rational
system. And secondly, because his management of an article
which, under his predecessor's plan—the plan on the rejection of
which his power is founded—would in last September have produced an additional revenue of more than L.700,000, must be
considered as a financial measure. Like his alterations on the
duties on coffee and on timber, it may be a measure for the
diminution, not for the increase of the revenue, but still it is a
measure of finance.

We now proceed to consider the remainder of his Budget, so
far as he has thought fit to explain it.

We join in much of the praise which has been bestowed on his speech of the 11th of March. The arrangement is good, the statements are clear, there are many passages of powerful reasoning, and a few that rise to eloquence. We have no doubt that it will survive its occasion, and be long read as one of the best productions of a great artist. Indeed, when it shall be read merely as a study, it will appear a much better speech than it does now; for its great defect will then be unperceived. It will not be seen that it is a piece of elaborate sophistry. It will not be seen that the whole argument rests on one great palpable misrepresentation.

Sir Robert Peel first showed that, comparing the current revenue with the current expenditure, there is a deficit in the present year of rather more than two millions and a half; and that it is not an occasional but a permanent deficit, and must be remedied, therefore, not by temporary, but by permanent expedients. He then proposed to go through the possible expedients exhaustively.

Loans he of course rejected : they are mischievous palliations.

He then rejected further taxation on the articles of subsistence; believing that we have arrived at the limits of such taxation. The proof which he offered was, that the additional five per cent imposed in 1840 on the customs and excise, produced an increase of only one-half per cent. He stated that to raise the post-office duties would arrest a great experiment, which has not yet been fully tried; that to revive the taxes on salt, leather, or wool, or to impose a tax upon gas, would interfere with various compacts and commercial arrangements ; and that further taxes on locomotion would prevent the labourer from carrying his only capital to the best market.

At length he came to consider the possibility of augmenting revenue by reduction of taxation ; a subject which, probably because he felt it to be the portion of his premises most palpably false, he reserved to the last.

Having stated that in the cases of tobacco, hemp, sugar, malt, soap, paper, and advertisements, a reduction of duty had been followed by a diminution of revenue, he inferred that such must be the result of every reduction. And having, as he assumed, proved that every other mode of increasing the revenue is objectionable or inefficient, he proposed an Income tax.

Sir Robert Peel's proposition, that increase of revenue cannot be obtained by an alteration of duties, depends of course on the assumption, that the existing duties are in every case those by which the largest revenue can be obtained. In fact, it is only a different mode of stating the same proposition. But on looking through our existing tariff, or the tariff now proposed to Parliament, it will be seen that there is scarcely a single article of any importance on which different rates of duty are not imposed, depending on the place where it is produced, or from whence it is imported. Now it is obvious that, when different rates of duty are imposed on the same commodity, one only can be that by which the largest revenue is obtainable. Of the four rates imposed on coffee, 1s. 3d.—1s.—9d.—6d., one only can be the most productive. And when we find that the duty of 1s. 3d. produced in 1840, only L.671, and that of 9d. L.544,653, or nearly a thousand times as much ; it seems strange to suppose that no revenue could be obtained by a reduction of the former. When a duty on sugar of L.3, 3s. produced a revenue of L.7647, and a duty of L.1, 4s. produced L.3,717,369, would a reduction of the former be unproductive ? If a duty of L.2, 16s. 6d. per load on Baltic fir timber produced L.331,325, and a duty of 11s. 6d. on Canada fir timber L.304,540, is it not obvious that one or the other, or both must be wrong ? Again, if out of 3,500,000 lbs. of silk, exported from France to England, only 1,800,000 pay duty,* so that the expense of paying duty and of smuggling appear to be nearly equal,—is it not probable that a small reduction of duty would turn the balance in favour of the fair trader, and increase both the revenue and the consumption ?

But the relief wanted is, it is urged, *immediate.* Well, would not a diminution of differential duties afford immediate relief ? If our warehouses are filled with commodities, excluded from our market by prohibitory duties, would no revenue be obtained by such a reduction as would admit them to be entered for home consumption, instead of being re-exported to countries enjoying a wiser financial system ? It is perfectly true that, when a duty imposed for the purpose of revenue is reduced, the immediate effect is loss, and the ultimate gain remote. But when a differential duty is reduced, the whole result is gain, and the gain is immediate.

The fallacy of Sir Robert Peel's argument is so gross, that it almost implied disrespect for his hearers. He affirmed that the plan proposed by the late Government would not afford any immediate relief; and his reason was, that no immediate increase of revenue followed the reduction of duties on tobacco, hemp, sugar, malt, soap, paper, and advertisements; though the two measures had, in fact, nothing in common. The duties on tobacco, hemp, sugar, malt, soap, paper, and advertisements, were revenue duties. They had been originally imposed at the amount sup-

---

* See Mr Porter's evidence, Committee on the Import Duties, 2536, export.

posed to be most productive. The presumption therefore was, that the reduction would occasion a loss. The duties which the late Government proposed to reduce, were duties originally proposed, not for the purpose of revenue, but of exclusion. They were duties for the purpose of excluding foreign sugar, foreign timber, and foreign corn. The presumption therefore was, that their reduction would produce a gain. And experience had shown that on one article, and in one month, it would have produced a gain of more than L.700,000. To confound things not only dissimilar but opposed, simply because they bear the common name of reduction, was worthy neither of the audience, the occasion, nor the speaker. And yet it was upon this fallacy that his whole argument rested; for he admitted that the expediency of an income tax depended on its *necessity*—on its being the only resource except a loan. The truth being, that we have to choose, not between an income tax and a loan, but between an income tax and cheaper bread, cheaper sugar, and cheaper coffee; and a nearer approach to equality in the burdens imposed on Canadian and Baltic timber.

We have said that the wide and bold principles of utility on which the rejected Budget of 1841 was founded, rendered it necessary that the Budget of 1842 should bear some resemblance to it. Sir Robert Peel therefore has his amended tariff. A very few years ago, such words from a Tory minister would have been ominous. They would have portended aggravated taxation and still more rapacious monopoly. But though, at length, we have rounded the corner, though we have left behind, never we trust to return towards it, the extreme point of fiscal misgovernment, the difference between the Whig and Tory tariff is as great as the improved intelligence of the times will allow. The Whig tariff proposed great improvements with respect to a few great articles. The Tory tariff proposes small improvements in a great many small articles. The Whig tariff proposed to improve the revenue by nearly two millions. The Tory tariff proposes to reduce it by about L.1,200,000. The Whig tariff was framed on the principle of diminishing differential duties; the Tory tariff not only perpetuates and extends them, but establishes them as the general and fundamental basis of the British customs. Whether a commodity, supposed to be capable of being exported from our colonies, have or have not been hitherto subjected to a differential duty—whether it have or have not hitherto entered into colonial trade, even if it be an article which, from its obscurity, has been left unenumerated—the monopoly of the British market is endeavoured to be secured to it by differential duties; never less than a 100 per cent, and often amounting to 500 per cent. We must say that the mere establishment of this most mischievous principle, appears to us far to outweigh the advantages, considerable as they are, offered by other portions of the scheme.

And yet the loss which this principle will occasion is one of the pretexts for the income tax. By raising the duty on colonial timber, and lowering that on foreign timber, until the advantage given to colonial timber was only 150 per cent, the late ministry expected to *add* L.600,000 a-year to the revenue. By abolishing the duty on Canadian timber, while a duty, amounting in many instances to more than 50 per cent on the value, is retained on foreign timber, Sir Robert Peel expects to *take* L.600,000 a-year from the revenue. This difference, L.1,200,000, is nearly half of the deficiency of the year. In the same spirit, while the duty on colonial coffee is to be reduced to 4d. a pound, that on foreign coffee is to be fixed at 8d. Sir Robert Peel estimates the consequent loss at L.170,000 a-year. Now, when we recollect that foreign coffee can be furnished so much more cheaply than colonial coffee—that in the face of a differential duty of 50 per cent, and the further expense, amounting to about one half-penny a pound, of being sent round from the Cape of Good Hope, it supplies more than one-third of our consumption, and nearly one-half of our revenue—there can be no doubt that if, instead of increasing the differential duty from 50 to 100 per cent, we abolished it, and imposed on all coffee the duty most productive of revenue, we might substitute a gain for a loss.

The coffee of Hayti, grown by freemen, and fully equal in quality to the average of what we consume, might be obtained in this country, all expenses except duty paid, at rather less than fivepence per pound. It is sold at that price on the Continent of Europe. Our present tariff subjects it to a duty, including the expense of the voyage to the Cape, of about 190 per cent. Under Sir Robert Peel's tariff, it will remain subject to a duty of 160 per cent. For what purpose is this enormous duty retained, while that on British Colonial coffee is reduced by one half? For the purpose of revenue? No. Sir Robert Peel expects a heavy loss on the whole transaction. To repress slavery, or the slave trade? No. The bulk of the coffee excluded by our present tariff, and by our proposed differential duties, is free grown. For the benefit of the proprietors and mortgagees of coffee estates in the British West Indies? *This*, of course, is the real motive ; but we do not believe that the object will be attained. The effect of the monopoly given to our colonies has been a competition for labour, which, operating on an untrained population, has produced among the negroes idleness, irregularity, carelessness ;—in short, every quality that can make a labourer unprofitable; and, among the planters, a blind strug- gle to retain their existing cultivation—fruitless in most cases, and, where it has been effected, absolutely ruinous.* The reduc- tion of the duty on colonial coffee by more than 33 per cent, will of course raise the price in bond—that is to say, the price extra the duty ; since the dealer would be able to pay for it two- pence a pound more than he now pays, if he continued to sell it at the same price; and to pay for it a penny a pound more than he now pays, if he should reduce the price to the consumer by a penny a pound.

The natural result seems to be, that the increased demand should produce increased cultivation—increased supply, a fall of price, and an increased consumption. This is the result expect- ed by Sir Robert Peel. Paradoxical as it may appear, we be- lieve that the result will be diminished cultivation—diminished supply—no reduction of price, and, of course, no increase of con- sumption. And we found our expectation on the double mono- poly, which is the object of Sir Robert Peel's differential duties. The monopoly possessed by the negro against the planter, in all our principal colonies, makes increased cultivation impossible. Irregular work for a few days in the week, and a few hours in the day, gives the labourer all that he requires. His present idle and insubordinate habits are the result of a fund for the pur- chase of labour, larger than, with the existing habits of the la- bourers, can be beneficially employed. Increase that fund, as must be the necessary result of a rise in the price of coffee in bond, and the disproportion between the amount of wages offered by one party, and of labour offered by the other party, will be aggravated. The negro will act with respect to coffee as he has acted with respect to sugar. He will do less work for the same wages. Cultivation will decrease instead of increasing ; the loss to the revenue will be aggravated by the loss to the consumer ; and the friends of slavery, and of the slave-trade, will triumph in an additional instance of the failure of emancipation.

Some of the other errors and abuses of the proposed tariff will have a more extensive effect; but perhaps there is none that is more glaring than the proposal as to coffee. Such a wanton destruction of revenue looks almost like a determination to ren- der an income tax necessary.

We feel some doubt, too, as to the propriety of abandoning, without enquiry, export duties amounting to L.108,000 a-year.

---

* See Mr Burney's excellent observations on the Island of Trinidad.

Sir R. Peel says that such duties are contrary to a sound principle of legislation. Of course *all* duties are mischievous, and are defensible only because a revenue is necessary ; but we own that we see no reason for considering an export duty as more mischievous than an import duty. In fact, all duties on imports are also duties on exports. As all steady trade is barter, and as foreign nations can purchase only as far as they sell, every restriction on importation, is a restriction on the exportation of the British commodity, with which the foreign commodity would directly or indirectly have been purchased. The only difference is, that where a direct tax is laid on exports, the inconvenience is concentrated on the producer whose commodity is taxed. He is aware of the fact, and complains. When a tax is laid on imports, the inconvenience is diffused. The aggregate of the consequent interruption of exportation may be considerable; but the share of each producer is small, and perhaps unperceived even by himself. If the export duties in question can be shown to be specifically injurious, let them be abandoned.

But we shall feel great difficulty in believing them to be specifically injurious, until we find them specifically complained of. It is to be observed that, according to Sir Robert Peel's statement, a large part of them must fall almost entirely on the foreign consumer. He states, that they arise in part ' from the export of ' woollens and yarns *to countries with which we have no reciprocity* ' *treaties.*' If this were true—if these export duties on woollens and yarns were imposed only on goods exported to countries with which we have no reciprocity treaties, the purchasers in those countries would unquestionably bear the whole burden. Our manufacturers and traders could not deal with them, on terms less profitable than those which they exact from others, and therefore must charge them with the duty as an addition to the price. But we believe that Sir Robert Peel, whose acquaintance with the laws of the customs is but recent, has committed an error. We believe that those duties are not affected by our reciprocity treaties, and apply as much to one foreign country as to another. If, however, he has not committed an error, he has furnished an irresistible argument against his own proposal.

On the other hand, we approve, so far as the question is merely an economical one, of the proposed export duty on coals. And when we consider that those whom it will affect are few and united—the most dangerous sort of enemies with whom a minister can have to contend—we admire the courage of the proposer. It has always appeared to us, that to export a commodity incapable of reproduction, on the *abundance,* not merely the *possession*—we repeat, on the *abundance*—of which our national existence depends, and which we are consuming at home on a rapidly increasing ratio—and to export it to our manufacturing rivals—is a preference of immediate to ultimate good, resembling that of the Dutch garrison who sold powder to their besiegers. It has been said that the principal export consists of small coals, and that if it is interrupted they will be wasted at the pit's mouth. We do not believe that this would now be the result. Small coals mixed with pitch constitute Grant's patent fuel, now extensively employed in Steam-Boats; and which, if the abundance of small coal reduce its price, must come into general use. Again, small coal, mixed with clay, forms one of the most efficient and most lasting kinds of fuel; as those who have visited Liege or Aix-la-Chapelle, where scarcely any other fuel is used, must have observed. For the last century, we have been wasting our coal with the recklessness with which our Scottish ancestors wasted their forests.

On economical grounds, therefore, we are grateful to Sir R. Peel for his interposition.

But the question is not purely economical. It has its political side. Our manufactures, and with our manufactures, our wealth, our power, and probably our constitution, are dependent on the importation of raw produce. Up to the present time, duties on the exportation of raw produce have been rare. Are we wise in setting an example of them? The restrictions of our different commercial codes have generally found zealous imitators. Are we sure that what we are now proposing will not be copied? Have we ascertained how far an export duty on coals may affect our pending negotiations with France? France is our principal customer for coals, and, with her irritable suspiciousness, is not unlikely to believe that the whole object of Sir R. Peel's Budget is to deprive her factories and steam-vessels of coal. The absurdity of this suspicion would not, in such a country as France, diminish its prevalence; or prevent its exercising an unfavourable influence on our commercial treaty. We do not offer these suggestions as conclusive against the proposed duty, but as matters to be deliberately considered by the public. The Cabinet of course has already considered them.

It is a strong proof of the rashness and inconsistency with which Sir Robert Peel's tariff has been framed, that the indirect effects of many of its provisions neutralize their direct influence; and sometimes convert what is apparently beneficial into evil. The export duty on coals is perhaps an instance. The admission of cattle, sheep, and fresh provisions, is perhaps another. Taken by itself, this innovation deserves the highest praise. It overthrows at once one of the strongholds of the landed mono-

poly. It is beneficial to commerce, to navigation, to the revenue, and indeed to the whole community as consumers. But
when we consider it, not as an insulated measure, but as connected with the proposed Corn Law, our praise must be qualified
till it almost approaches to censure. At the price which he considers the average price, 56s. a quarter, he imposes on wheat a
duty of 16s., or more than 27 per cent. He admits cattle, sheep,
and meat, at duties not exceeding 9 per cent. As far as differential duties, amounting to 300 per cent, can effect the purpose,
he encourages tillage, and discourages pasture. As manager of
the affairs of the public, therefore, his conduct is precisely the
reverse of that followed by every man in the management of his
own affairs. The great object of every landlord is to prevent
the conversion of pasture into tillage. For this purpose, land-
agents and conveyancers accumulate all the resources of their
ingenuity. We have no doubt that every lease granted by Sir
Robert Peel contains an express reservation of £10 a-year of additional rent for every acre of pasture ground broken up—express
clauses that this additional sum shall be considered as a rent, not
as a penalty, and not be relievable against, at law or in equity;
and further clauses enabling the landlord, not merely to compel
payment of the additional rent, but further to re-enter and eject
the tenant. Of all rural crimes, this seems to be the most
heinous. But the act which he forbids and punishes as an individual, as a legislator, he bribes every tenant to commit. The
great fault of British agriculture, and particularly of English
agriculture, is the preponderance of white crops. This error—if
what is knowingly done in the hope of immediate profit at the
expense of the inheritance ought to be called an error—not only
retards the improvement of our second-rate soils, but is one main
cause of the increasing irregularity of our harvests. Much of the
land now under the plough in England is productive only in
extraordinary years. Five years out of six it is cultivated at a
loss. The sixth, perhaps, comes a lucky season, when the harvest is good locally, but bad generally, and a prize is drawn—but
a prize probably which does not make up for the previous blanks.
It would be much better for landlord, tenant, and consumer, if
such land were employed to produce the steady moderate return
of pasture, instead of being an instrument for gambling in tillage. When we consider Sir Robert Peel's Corn Law and Cattle
Law as one measure, and add to them his proposed exemption
from income tax, of tenants under £300 a-year, and the consequent temptation to subdivide farms and waste capital, we doubt
whether any other modern statesman has devised a system so
mischievous to the agriculture of a country.

We ought to add, that the copy of the proposed tariff which we are forced to use, is that which was first delivered. It is said to contain many typographical errors, which are to be corrected in a subsequent edition. We trust that the tripling the duty on oil-seed cakes is one of these errors. We trust that the subjecting the important articles of butter, cheese, eggs, and meat, and bark, to differential duties of 400 per cent, is another. We trust, too, that either this cause, or the commercial treaties still pending, may be the explanation of the numerous *ad valorem* duties of 30 per cent, and 25 per cent, which we see scattered through the tables. And, on the whole, although we cordially approve of many of the details, we close the schedules with deep regret, that, in the present state of political knowledge, a British Minister should believe that such a tariff is worth purchasing with an income tax.

We do not mean to express any fixed abhorence to an income tax, or to affirm even that it ought to be confined to a period of serious European war. If a real reform of the tariff were proposed to us—a reform which should not leave out or mismanage such commodities as butter, cheese, hops, sugar, coffee, and corn—a reform which should sweep away protective and differential duties—a reform which should prefer the interests of millions to those of thousands—and if it were found that such a reform would produce a temporary loss of revenue—for such a reform, we should be ready to pay the price, the heavy, but not the extravagant price, of a temporary income tax.

But the tax to which, for such a purpose, we would submit, would be a very different one from that which is now proposed.

In the first place, it would include all who could be held able to pay it. Every tax, to be just, must either be self-imposed, or be proportioned to the means of the payer. Taxes upon consumption which do not affect the necessaries of life, conform to the first of these rules—they are self-imposed. ' In the price of ' threepence-halfpenny,' says Adam Smith, ' now paid for a pot ' of porter, the different taxes may amount to three-halfpence. ' If a workman can conveniently spare these three-halfpence, he ' buys a pot of porter. If he cannot, he contents himself with a ' pint, and as a penny saved is a penny got, he gains a farthing ' by his temperance. He pays the tax as far as he can afford to ' pay it, and every act of payment is perfectly voluntary—what he ' can avoid if he chooses to do so.' A tax deducting an equal per centage from the revenue of all permanent property, conforms to the second rule; it is proportioned to the means of the payer. But taxes on the necessaries of life are unjust, since they take

as much from a family with L.30 a-year, as from a family with
L.300 a-year. Taxes upon ground rents, on the devolution of
personal property, on the conveyance of land, or on legal proceedings, are equally unjust. They select particular classes for
taxation. Taxes imposed on persons possessing a given amount
of property or income, and excluding others, except on the ground
of inability to pay, are equally unjust, and far more dangerous.
There are no marked divisions in society depending on the nature
of property. Proprietors of ground rents, lands, or funds, are
interspersed among men of every condition. But society is
divided, according to the amount of property, into marked classes,
—the poorer being always the more numerous. To hold out any
one class as the subjects of exclusive taxation, is to hold out
a minority as the objects of legal plunder. Sir Robert Peel proposes to exempt all incomes under L.150 a-year, that is to
say, to exempt more than nine-tenths of the community. The
return of the number of persons receiving dividends in 1838—
the last year for which we have seen it—states that out of
188,498 such persons, 172,096 received an amount not exceeding L.100 a-year; 10,001 an amount between L.100 and L.200
a-year; and only 6401 an amount exceeding L.200 a-year.*
We have no doubt that the persons with incomes between
L.150 or L.250 a-year, far exceed in number all whose incomes
are larger. Are *they* not likely to demand exemption? When
once an injustice has been committed, when once a line has been
drawn, depending on the arbitrary will of the legislator, what
security have we that it will be adhered to? What security
have we that it will not be gradually pushed up, until the opulent
become what they were in the Greek republics—mere trustees
for the State? The proposed exemption may be a clever party
measure; it may render the tax a favourite with the ten-pound
householders, and with all who are below them; it may gratify
their hatred of the middle classes, and of the aristocracy; but,
in the pursuit of immediate popularity, Sir Robert Peel has entered on a course in which it will be difficult to stop, and ruinous to
advance. This is his first movement towards the revolutionary
party which infests both sides of the House; and ranges itself,
according to each member's constituency, under the ultra Tory
or ultra Radical banner. We presume that he has well weighed
its consequences.

In the second place, the tax to which we would submit must
be confined to that portion of income which can fairly be called

---

* Porter's *Tables*, Part ix. p. 5.

revenue; that it is to say, to the portion which can be spent without impairing the capital. If a man has lent L.20,000, to be repaid to him with interest by four annual payments, can he be said to have an income of L.6000 the first year, L.5750 the second, L.5500 the third, and L.5250 the fourth?* Can his real annual income be said to be more than L.1000 ? Yet, as far as we are at present acquainted with Sir Robert Peel's plan, he will be taxed, in the first place, as if his whole receipts were income; and secondly, the income arising from the L.5000, paid off and reinvested by him every year, will be again subject to taxation; so that, in fact, he will be taxed every year as if his income were L.6000 a-year; that is to say, six times more than if he had lent his money on mortgage at five per cent, and ten times as much as if he had purchased a landed estate with it. What can be said of the fairness of a tax which, the value of the property in each case being the same, taxes one man L.18 a-year, and the other L.180 ?

Of course, we would carry our principle further. Can the merchant, who derives a profit apparently high from a hazardous business; the professional man, who, if he were to spend all that he gains during his few years of eminence and health, would leave his family beggars; the clergyman and the public officer, a third of whose income is employed in insuring his life, or in effecting an accumulation which is to serve as an insurance ;—can any one of these be said to possess, as a means of expenditure, all that is called his income ?

But it may be said, that to attempt to obviate all these anomalies would give a great deal of trouble, and diminish the productiveness of the tax. Suppose that it would. To refuse enquiry because it would cost trouble—to refuse redress because it would cost money—to commit blind wholesale injustice, in order to save the annoyance of having to investigate, and the expense of having to exempt; this again is a conduct to which the term revolutionary, in the most hateful sense of that word, must be applied. This is a conduct which would have been revolting if it had been suggested by a demagogue to an assembly of the people; or by a committee of public safety to a national convention. It could scarcely have been excused, if it had been offered as a sudden expedient to a struggling nation, to meet an unexpected emergency. It is now proposed to a British Parliament

---

* See Mr Attwood's speech, March 23, 1842, where he states this to be his own case ; the very government which imposes the tax being his debtor.

by a Conservative minister, after six months of deliberation, to
supply a voluntary deficiency.

Nor is the excuse, so far as the difficulty of the investigation is
concerned, founded on fact. The case of precarious or temporary investments seems to present no difficulty whatever. We
know that money cannot, as a general rule, be safely invested so
as to produce interest at more than 4 per cent. Whatever is
received beyond this is a compensation, generally an inadequate
compensation, for risk. Let the income derived from all money
investments be calculated at 4 per cent on the sum which they
cost; or, when that cannot be ascertained, at 4 per cent on their
value. There can be no difficulty in this; and we cannot suppose
that the most rapacious financier who has ever oppressed a nation
would venture to object to it, on the mere ground that it would
make the tax somewhat less productive. The case of professional men, including clergymen and public officers, is less susceptible of accurate adjustment; but the supposition that such
men in general put by, and that under a sense of obligation, one
third of their professional income, is, we believe, rather under the
truth. That the amount must vary according to circumstances;
that an old bachelor may venture to spend more than the man
with a family; a man with an independent fortune more than
one whose profession is the only fund from which a provision for
ill health, or for children, is to be accumulated—all this is obvious; but the impossibility of minute discriminating justice is
no excuse for universal indiscriminate injustice. What we
should suggest, if we were framing an income-tax, would be, that
such incomes should be rated at two-thirds of the incomes derived from investments. So that under the proposed rate they
would pay L.1, 18s. 10d. and a fraction per cent, instead of
L.2, 18s. 4d.

With respect to the incomes derived from trades, the data
are more doubtful. We suggest, as the nearest approximation
at which we have been able to arrive, that the average gross
profits of successful trade may be taken at 10 per cent on the
capital employed; and that of this amount 4 per cent may be
considered as interest, 3 per cent as the remuneration for trouble,
and 3 per cent as the compensation for occasional loss—leaving
the average net profit 7 per cent, or about double what can be
obtained from the funds. On large capitals the compensation
for trouble may be smaller, and that for risk larger; the additional trouble taken by the smaller capitalist enabling him to
diminish his risk. If we assume, as we are justified in doing,
that the trader ought to lay by from the three per cent, which he is
supposed to receive for his trouble, one-third—the amount supposed to be reserved by professional men—his real income, the

income which he can afford to spend, will be 6 per cent on his capital. We should suggest, therefore, if we were proposing an income tax, that traders should be assessed at a supposed income of 6 per cent on their capital; or, if they did not think fit to declare their capital, then, at six-tenths of their declared incomes. The extra profit, which is a mere compensation for risk, cannot be fairly taxed, unless the State return to the trader, when he has sustained a loss, what it took from him when his speculations were successful.

The objection which has been raised by Sir Robert Peel,[*] that, if the tax is to depend on the tenure of the income, provision must be made for the case of a jointress, or for that of the tenant for life of an estate which, on his death, is to go to a distant relation, scarcely deserves an answer. The instances in which property is settled on a person for his life, without power to make a provision out of it for his children, are almost too rare for calculation; those in which it can be subjected to a jointure, and yet not charged for the benefit of children, are still rarer. And if it were thought fit to provide for them by assessing the income of such a tenant for life, or of such a jointress, as if it were a professional income, where would be the difficulty?

But modify an income tax as we will, it has this inherent vice, that it is, to a considerable extent, a tax upon the creation of capital. And yet it is remarkable that this vice has often been considered as a merit. It has been often said in its praise, that it affects the hoards of the miser. Those who use such language cannot know of what the hoards of a miser consist. They consist of ships, of docks, of canals, of railways, of farm buildings, of farm stock, of reclaimed lands, of mills, of machinery; in short, of all that produces wealth and enjoyment—of all the sources of employment to the people, rent to the landlord, and revenue to the Government. Every man must spend every shilling of his income, but he may spend it productively or unproductively. If a man with L.2000 a-year spends the whole unproductively, he gives the whole of it every year in exchange for commodities or services for his own enjoyment. If he spend half of it productively, or, in common language, if he save half of it, he employs that half, either himself, or through the agency of some person to whom he lends it, or whom he pays for managing it, in creating new sources of future revenue. Such a man, at the end of twenty years, has added L.20,000 to the capital of the country—an addition which would not have existed if, instead of paying men to drain or to plant, to erect steam-engines, or to

* See his speech, 24th March 1842.

sink mines, he had paid them to wait behind his chair, or attend to his hothouses, or his hounds. Now, if the man with L.2000 a-year, whom we have supposed to save half his income, be sub-jected to a tax falling on his expenditure, the only consequence will be his personal inconvenience. He has so much less to spend, the Government so much more. He may be forced to discharge a footman—the Government is enabled to engage a soldier. But if the tax fall on the portion of his income which he saves, it forces him to discharge, not a footman, but a man whose services created every year a capital exceeding his wages. He is forced to withdraw a workman from a farm-yard, a rail-way, or a manufactory. Suppose such a man to be taxed 50 per cent on his income, and to pay the tax one-half out of what he had been accustomed to spend, and the other half out of what he had been accustomed to save, the L.500 a-year paid out of his expenditure, if it were paid for twenty years, would not affect the capital of the country ; but the L.500 paid out of his sav-ings would take L.500 from what would have been the capital of the country the first year, L.1000 the second, L.1500 the third, and so on, more and more, during every year that it lasted. For this reason, because they fall principally on unproductive expen-diture, we prefer the assessed taxes to all other forms of direct taxation. If any other form of direct taxation be necessary, we prefer a direct tax on every man's declared expenditure.

Such a tax would have little tendency to diminish the accu-mulation of capital : to a certain extent, indeed, it would have a tendency to promote it, since many men would save in order to avoid the tax. It would have the further advantage of being, to a considerable extent, self-imposed. Its assessment, too, would be far less painful. Few persons would feel much objection to declare their expenditure, or to suffer it to be notorious ; be-cause its notoriety would neither affect their credit nor injure their vanity ; and, so far as professional men and traders are concerned, expenditure is more easily ascertained than income.

We have said nothing of the vexatious procedure by which the proposed income tax is to be assessed or enforced ; nor of the evasion, fraud, and demoralization which it will in-troduce ; nor of its tendency to drive British property into foreign funds, and British subjects into foreign countries ; nor of the danger of promoting extravagance, or even war, by a source of revenue so easy of increase. We have omitted these, and many other branches of the subject, not because we undervalue their importance, but simply because we cannot discuss them, at pre-sent, as we could wish.

The same reason prevents our adverting to the details of the debate upon the Budget, so far as it had proceeded at the

time of writing these pages, in the House of Commons. It
is a striking exhibition of the predominance of Sir Robert Peel
over his immediate associates, a predominance as marked in
1842 as it was in 1835. Whether he is equally absolute in the
Cabinet, is a different question—a question which a comparison
of the measures which he brings forward, with those which he
must be supposed to wish to bring forward, would lead us to
decide negatively. But in the House it is clear, that either from
choice or from necessity, (we suspect from necessity,) he represents every department, and refuses to be encumbered by assistance. Another remarkable characteristic of the debate, has been
the superiority of the Opposition. Their cause, without doubt,
gives them a great advantage; but it might have been expected
that they would have had to buy their victories in discussion a
little dearer.

Before we quit this part of the subject, we must express the
regret—which we believe to be general throughout the country
among all who are opposed to an income tax—that this part of
the Budget was not met, by Lord John Russell, with an immediate expression of decided hostility. The vigorous supporter of
the repudiated Budget of the preceding year, would have been
guilty of no inconsistency—no impropriety—in opposing *in toto*
the Budget of 1842. But that the Income tax section of it—
that a proposal calculated to startle, and to meet a hesitating
and grudging acquiescence even under the pressure of an expensive war for a just cause—should not have encountered,
when brought forward in peace, and under no alarming destitution of other expedients, the instant resistance of the clear-sighted
and firm-minded leader of the Opposition, seems to us truly sur-
prising. The prudence and candour of his nature may have
here seduced him into a great practical error. It may be that he
was unwilling, without consulting his party, to follow his own
impulses, and act on his own judgment. The result has been
most unfortunate. The interposition of a whole week between
the announcement of the measure and of the resistance, led to a
suspicion that it was possible that it might be acquiesced in. It
seems to us very clear that the public ought not to have been
allowed, for a single day, to contemplate such a possibility. We
now know that it was not contemplated by the leaders of the
Liberal party; and we think that, in such a cause, they might
have ventured to assume the responsibility of answering for the
opinions and conduct of the whole body of their supporters.

It is scarcely possible that this paper should come into the
hands of any one who, not having heard, has not read, Lord
Brougham's very cogent speech, in the House of Lords, on the
17th of March. It will be seen that we differ from his Lordship

as to the necessity of an income tax ; but, as to the general evils of such a tax, and as to the specific mischief and injustice of the details of the present measure, we are delighted to find ourselves supported by his high authority. In one respect, indeed, he goes further than we do. We have suggested that incomes derived from personal exertion should pay at two-thirds of the rate of incomes derived from property. Lord Brougham proposes that they should pay only one-third. We tax them, therefore, twice as heavily as he does. We leave the public to decide between the two plans, and should not be dissatisfied if the difference were divided. But we think that Lord Brougham's proposal, of which we were not aware until the passages containing our own had been completed, proves that we have not been too liberal in our exemption.

Before concluding, we will, in despite of the ridicule which generally follows unconsummated predictions, hazard one.

We are convinced that if the income tax be persisted in, it will ultimately be fatal to the present Administration. We believe that it will be carried. We believe that a combination between the country gentlemen, who think that they are raising a bulwark around the corn-law ; the planters, who think that they are securing the sugar-law ; and the members whose constituencies rejoice in it as a blow to the aristocracy, will force it through the House. But when once it has come into operation—when the painful exposure and the humiliating discussion have been undergone—when men have felt what it is to tremble at the knock of a tax-gatherer, and to deprecate the suspicions of a commissioner—when the pain of loss has been embittered by that of degradation ;—a detestation of the tax will arise which all the discipline of the Tory party will be unable to control. Unfortunately for that party, the eminent person who leads it is not distinguished for political foreknowledge. He has often yielded to circumstances, but always too late. If he should perceive the signs of the gathering storm in time to change his course—if the working of his new Corn Law should be such as to convince his followers that an alteration productive of a steady price, and a steady revenue, is expedient—if a treaty with Brazil should give him a fair pretext to add a million and a half to the revenue from sugar—if he can open his budget for 1843 by a promise that the income tax shall expire before 1844, and it shall be believed that he will perform that promise;—he may be able, to a certain degree, to skin over the wound which its introduction has inflicted on his influence among his real supporters. Many of them, indeed, are lost to him irretrievably. Some detest the injustice of his measure, others are frightened at its democratic tendency, and all writhe under its severity. It is probable that he is not aware—no minister, perhaps, ever is aware—of the deep and bitter feeling of distrust and dissatisfaction which he has roused. He never will again be popular with his own party, and he has too much experience not to know the value of the praise with which his fiercest enemies have endeavoured to blind him. He knows well with what motives and with what sincerity he is called bold, direct, and honest. Still, however, while they believe it to be their interest, a large portion of the Tory party may continue to serve under him against the Whigs. But they will make no sacrifices in his defence. They will volunteer no expensive contest for him. They will not endanger their seats in his service. They will refuse no pledge against an income tax. If his power imply a continuance of that tax, his majority, strong as it may now appear, will have crumbled away long before the period which he has ventured to assign for the duration of the tax shall have expired.

# Free Trade and Retaliation

*Edinburgh Review* (July 1843)

THE

# EDINBURGH REVIEW,

## JULY, 1843.

### *N⁰.* CLVII.

Art. I.—1. *The Budget: A Series of Letters on Financial, Commercial, and Colonial Policy.* By a Member of the Political Economy Club. Nos. 1 to 6. 8vo. London: 1841.

2. *A Letter to the Right Hon. Sir Robert Peel on the Condition of England, and the Means of removing the Causes of Distress.* By R. Torrens, Esq., F.R.S. 8vo. London: 1843.

3. *Postscript to the above Letter.* By R. Torrens, Esq. London: 1843.

ONE of the great obstacles to the progress of the Moral Sciences is the tendency of doctrines, supposed to have been refuted, to reappear. In the Pure and in the Physical Sciences, each generation inherits the conquests made by its predecessors. No mathematician has to redemonstrate the problems of Euclid; no physiologist has to sustain a controversy as to the circulation of the blood; no astronomer is met by a denial of the principle of gravitation. But in the Moral Sciences the ground seems never to be incontestably won; and this is peculiarly the case with respect to the sciences which are subsidiary to the arts of administration and legislation. Opinions prevail and are acted on. The evils which appear to result from their practical application lead to enquiry. Their erroneousness is proved by philosophers, is acknowledged by the educated public, and at length is admitted even by statesmen. The policy founded on the refuted error is relaxed, and the evils which it inflicted, so far as they are capable of remedy, are removed or mitigated. After a time new theorists arise, who are seduced or impelled by some moral or intellectual defect or error to reassert the exploded doctrine. They have become entangled by some logical fallacy, or deceived by some inaccurate or incomplete assumption of facts, or think that they see the means of acquiring reputation, or of promoting their interests, or of gratifying their political or their private resentments, by attacking the altered policy. All popular errors are plausible; indeed, if they were not so they would not be popular. The plausibility to which the revived doctrine owed its original currency, makes it acceptable to those to whom the subject is new; and even among those to whom it is familiar, probably ninety-nine out of every hundred are accustomed to take their opinions on such matters on trust. They hear with surprise that what they supposed to be settled is questioned, and often avoid the trouble of enquiring, by endeavouring to believe that the truth is not to be ascertained. And thus the cause has again to be pleaded before judges, some of whom are prejudiced, and others will not readily attend to reasoning founded on premises which they think unsusceptible of proof.

About three hundred years ago, men believed in the existence of an infallible Church, possessing a right to require assent to her doctrines, and the aid of the civil magistrate to silence opposition. The corruptions and the persecutions which followed this opinion, led a few strong-minded men to doubt, and ultimately to deny its accuracy. The right of private judgment, the duty of free enquiry, and at length that of toleration, were established in every Protestant country. But scarcely has the victory been apparently gained, when the conflict has recommenced. Catholic Emancipation and the repeal of the Test and Corporation Acts, the crowning triumphs over bigotry and intolerance, were the signals for the appearance, among our southern neighbours, of a sect, now rapidly increasing, whose doctrines reproduce those of Hildebrand and Dominic. We are again told, that our belief ought to be the result of obedience, not of enquiry; or, if of enquiry, of enquiry not as to what is proved by evidence, but as to what is asserted by the Church. We are again told of the duty of acquiescence, and of the danger and presumptuousness of investigation, and the civil governor is again urged to repress the crimes of schism and heresy.

Again, fifty years ago it was believed that the State could supply the want of charity among the rich, and of diligence and economy among the poor. It was believed that by means of an agent, possessed of inexhaustible resources, called ' the Parish,' the whole population of England, whatever were their numbers or their conduct, could be insured a comfortable subsistence; that wives need not suffer for the faults of their husbands, or children for those of their parents; or any persons indeed, except rate-payers, for their own. Throughout the southern districts this opinion was acted on. The overseer, or, on his refusal, the magistrate, undertook to repeal the penalty inflicted by nature on idleness, improvidence, prodigality, and dishonesty, and consequently to annul the rewards which she offers to industry, providence, and conscientiousness.

The discouraged qualities withered; the fostered ones spread with rank luxuriance. The working population became idle, insolent, and dishonest; they ceased to reproduce the fund from which their wages, or what was now substituted for wages, their relief, was to be afforded. Poor-rates began to absorb first, the rents of the landlord, and at length the profits of the farmers; the labouring population, trained to believe that their incomes depended not on the demand for their labour, but on the fears of the overseer, or the favour of the justice, broke out into systematic outrage and rebellion; and England seemed on the eve of events more resembling those of the revolution in St Domingo, than any that are recorded in modern history. Moral philosophers now pointed out the impossibility of uniting the immunities of slavery and the virtues of freedom. They showed that no improvement was to be hoped while idleness obtained the reward of diligence—while improvidence affected not the imprudent or the extravagant individual, but his parish—and while misconduct at most only transferred the labourer from the farmer to the overseer. Attention was drawn to their reasonings by the reduced value of some estates, by the abandonment of others, and by the fires and insurrections which terrified the south of England in the frightful autumn of 1830.

The short-sighted policy, the false humanity, and the base and selfish thirst for power and for popularity, which had fostered the existing abuses, were denounced by all except a few literary or political demagogues. It was acknowledged that the labourer can be a useful, or even a safe member of society, only while his welfare depends on himself—that independence cannot be made honourable except by making pauperism disgraceful—and that employment can be made an object of desire only by making relief an object of aversion. The act which embodied and gave effect to these principles was passed by acclamation;

and whatever might be the dangers to which the social system of England remained exposed, it was supposed to have escaped those which accompany or follow a profuse system of compulsory charity.

Not ten years have elapsed, and almost all the experience of the preceding half century seems to be forgotten. The Work-House is termed an oppression ; the Home Secretary refers triumphantly to the extension of out-door relief. The House of Commons listens with apparent assent to the reprobation of a dietary which gives meat only once in a week, being about ten times as often as it is enjoyed by the independent labourer ;* the Government thinks itself forced to dismiss more than half of the assistant Commissioners, on whose presence the whole maintenance of the reform depends, and whose number, when at the highest, was grossly inadequate ; and the public opinion of England seems to be resuming all those errors which, ten years ago, disgusted by their folly and alarmed by their mischief.

Those who have read the publications, the titles of which are prefixed to this article, will anticipate that we take as a third instance ' the Mercantile System.' That system is well explained by Joshua Gee, who, in the earlier part of the eighteenth century, published a book entitled,—' The trade and navigation of ' Great Britain considered ; showing that the surest way for a ' nation to increase in riches is to prevent the importation of such ' foreign commodities as may be raised at home, and that this ' kingdom is capable of raising within itself and its colonies ma- ' terials for employing all our poor in those manufactures which ' we now import from such of our neighbours who refuse the ' admission of ours.'

' To take,' says this author, ' the right way of judging of ' the increase or decrease of the riches of the nation by the trade ' we drive with foreigners, is to examine whether we receive ' money from them or send them money; for if we export more ' goods than we receive, it is most certain that we shall have a ' balance brought to us in gold and silver, and the mint will be ' at work to coin that gold and silver. But if we import more ' than we export, then it is as certain that the balance must be ' paid by gold and silver sent to them to discharge that debt. ' A nation may gain vast riches by trade and commerce, or, for ' want of a due regard and attention, be drained of them. I am ' afraid the present circumstance of ours carries out more riches

---

* See the Debate of the 23d February 1843.

' than it brings home. Whereas formerly great quantities of bul-
' lion were brought into this country by the Balance of Trade,
' and coined into money: the tables are turned, and as fast as we
' import bullion it is sent away to pay our debts. So, many
' places endeavour to keep out our manufactures, and still con-
' tinue to export their linen, hemp, flax, iron, potash, timber,
' &c., to us, which draws a very great treasure annually out of
' this kingdom. We send our money to foreign nations, and by
' employing their poor instead of our own, enable them to thrust
' us out of our foreign trade; and by imposing high duties on our
' manufactures, so to clog the importation of them that it amounts
' to a prohibition.' *

For more than two hundred years the Mercantile System reigned
with almost undisputed authority. At length it was shaken by
the French Economists—it was conclusively refuted by Adam
Smith—it was abandoned by the scientific and literary public
throughout Europe, and by the mercantile public in Great Britain. Turgot and Pitt were among the first statesmen who acknowledged the erroneousness of the theory, and endeavoured to
amend the practice to which it had given rise. The revolutionary wars arrested in each country the improvement of commercial
legislation; and in France it does not seem to have recommenced
on the return of peace. But in Great Britain the Mercantile, or,
as it was afterwards called, the Protective system, became unpopular even among those who were supposed to profit by it. Thus,
the principal commercial men of London presented, on the 8th
of May 1820, that celebrated petition, in which they affirmed,
' That the maxim of buying in the cheapest market, and selling
' in the dearest, which regulates every merchant in his individual
' dealings, is strictly applicable as the best rule for the trade of
' every nation. That although, as a matter of mere diplomacy,
' it may sometimes answer to hold out the removal of particular
' prohibitions or high duties as depending on corresponding con-
' cessions, it does not follow that we should maintain our restric-
' tions where the desired concessions cannot be obtained. That
' our restrictions would not be the less prejudicial to our capital
' and industry, because other governments persisted in preserving
' impolitic regulations.' And they ended by an earnest protest,
against ' every restrictive regulation of trade not essential to the
' revenue; against all duties merely protective from foreign com-
' petition; and against the excess of such duties as are partly for
' the purpose of revenue, and partly for that of protection.'

---

* Pp. 173, 215; 10, 100.

Lord Liverpool gave the celebrated answer, that he agreed in every sentiment expressed in this Petition; and that, if he were forming a Commercial Code, such should be its fundamental principles.

Unfortunately no change can be made in commercial legislation without immediate injury to individuals. No well-informed person doubts that, if no corn laws had existed, the landed proprietors of Great Britain would have been much richer than they now are. Less land would have been employed in producing corn, and more applied to raising green crops, meat, and the produce of the dairy and the garden; the wealth and population of the country, and consequently the demand for their produce, would have been much greater; and they would have enjoyed the advantage which the proximity of a town gives to the neighbouring country. But, mischievous as the corn laws have been, even to those who expected to profit by enacting them, it is not probable that they could be repealed without exposing some persons to immediate loss; and the same remark applies to almost all the monopolies created by the Mercantile System. Although those who enjoy such a monopoly, or, as it is usually called, such a protection, seldom profit by it; that is to say, are seldom richer, and often are poorer than they would have been if no such monopoly had existed, and they had not been seduced to divert their capital and industry from their natural courses, yet they almost necessarily lose by being deprived of it. Their fixed capital, their established connexions, and their peculiar knowledge or skill, lose a part of their value, or perhaps the whole. The advantage of the change is diffused over the general mass of consumers, the evil is concentrated on a comparatively small knot of producers; and it is difficult to estimate the power of an active minority opposed to that defenceless unenergetic body, the community at large.

The attempt to extricate the commerce of the country from the restrictions which centuries of unwise, or fraudulent, or oppressive legislation had imposed, and which never wanted their fierce defenders, was arduous, and its progress was necessarily slow. That progress, however, was felt to be beneficial, and Free Trade gradually became popular every where, except within the walls of Parliament. The landlords who constitute the House of Lords, and form the great majority of the House of Commons, have always attached a preposterous importance to their legal monopoly. They exaggerate the immediate evils of its removal, and even believe that they are gaining by its existence; and, with the bitter angry selfishness which is apt to inflame those who are forced to confess to themselves that they gain by a public oppression, they endeavour to defend all other monopolies as outworks to their own. They fought the battle with a courage and a pertinacity which would have been honourable in a good cause, but with weapons which threw additional disgrace even on a bad one. Every commercial improvement was opposed by misrepresentation, by sophistry, by appeals to the passions of the many, and to the interests of the few ; and, where these failed, by dogged, unblushing resistance. The leaders of the Tory party, however, urged on by the educated portion of the community, and immeasurably superior in knowledge and public spirit to the mass of their parliamentary supporters, carried on their reforms with the degree of vigour—it must be confessed a very moderate one—which they thought consistent with the main object of all their policy, both foreign and domestic, the stability of their own Administration. Though, at the close of their long reign, not much appears to have been done—though their principal improvements were reciprocity navigation treaties, and the substitution of nearly prohibitory duties for absolute prohibitions—yet some progress towards a better system was made, and, as we have already remarked, that progress was felt to be beneficial.

The Whig Ministry, which, during less than eleven years, effected more for the benefit of the empire than had been done, or attempted, or apparently even desired, by their predecessors during a rule of half a century, after many important but partial improvements, at length ventured to propose an extensive system of commercial reform. They failed, as was foreseen by every one who was acquainted with the prejudices and the interests which they dared to oppose. But their sacrifice of office was not made in vain. Their successors have indeed thought themselves obliged to maintain some consistency in error : as respects Corn and Sugar, they have thought themselves forced to make the country pay the penalty of their factious opposition to what they know to be right ; but on almost all other questions, the principles avowed by Sir Robert Peel and Mr Gladstone differ little from those of Lord Lansdowne and Lord John Russell. And for putting those principles in practice, they have an advantage of which it is scarcely possible to overrate the value. The liberal policy of the Whigs was constantly thwarted by the Opposition ; that of the Tories is actively supported by it. To the Whigs the Opposition was a drag ; to the Tories it is a stimulus. Formerly there was an engine at each end of the train—one pulling it forward and the other pulling it back. Now, while the engine in front is pulling, the engine behind is pushing. We may regret that those who sowed should not be allowed to reap ;

but such is the ordinary course of events. By separating success from merit, by imposing on one set of men the sacrifice and the labour, and giving to another the credit of the result, Providence seems to tell us that higher motives than any that man can offer, ought to actuate those who assume the responsibilities of government. We firmly believe that the motives on which the late Ministry acted were a conviction, that the commercial reform which they introduced would be greatly and extensively useful, and that its introduction by a Government, must, sooner or later, lead to its becoming law. We believe that both these opinions were well founded; and that their authors will ultimately receive, in the adoption and success of their measures, the only reward on which disinterested statesmen can reckon.

It is under these circumstances, when the expediency of Free Trade is admitted by the leaders of all the great political parties, by every writer above the rank of the mere daily or weekly journalists, and even by the merchants and manufacturers, whom Adam Smith stigmatized as its enemies—when it is also admitted that retaliating restrictions, though they may sometimes be useful weapons, are always mischievous in themselves—it is under these circumstances that Colonel Torrens comes forward to reproduce, not in words indeed, but in effect, the Mercantile Theory;— to recommend, in substance, the practice of which that theory was the pretext;—to maintain that, if the Whig Ministers had been permitted to carry their measures, the results would have been the insolvency of the Bank, and a ruinous commercial revulsion, terminating in a permanent contraction of the currency, and a fall of prices, which would have rendered it difficult, if not impossible, to collect a sufficient sum to pay the public creditor;—that the adoption of the Whig Budget would have been the greatest calamity which could have befallen the country, and might possibly have led to revolution.*

When such opinions are deliberately put forward by a man of Colonel Torrens's reputation in Political Economy, we feel that they cannot safely be disregarded. If he is right, all that has been done by the late Mr Huskisson and by his successors is wrong; the theory of Adam Smith and of Say, and the practice of Lord John Russell and Sir Robert Peel, are equally erroneous; and all who have acquiesced in the one or promoted the other, among whom we ourselves venture to claim a place, must beg pardon of God and of man for having done their best to ruin their country. The commercial policy of the seventeenth century

---

* *Budget, or a Series of Letters,* &c., p. 27, 28.

must be resumed. The Balance of Trade must again be the subject of anxious attention. Duties must be opposed to duties, and prohibitions to prohibitions, until, in Mr Gee's words, ' we export more goods than we receive, and have a balance ' brought to us in gold and silver.' But if he is wrong, it is important that his errors should be exposed before they are adopted by those to whose real or supposed interests they are favourable. Nothing spreads so rapidly, or is eradicated with so much difficulty, as a scientific error defending a practice which powerful classes wish to maintain. It is propagated by thousands who are satisfied with the conclusion, and never think of enquiring into the truth of the premises or the accuracy of the inference. Its very erroneousness, by rendering the reasoning obscure, gives to it an appearance of abstruseness and profundity. We have no doubt that if ' the Budget' were to remain unanswered, it would be proclaimed in all the strongholds of monopoly to which British literature penetrates—in Parliament, in Congress, in the ' Algemeine Zeitung,' and in the Councils of the ' Zollverein,'—that Adam Smith and the modern Economists have been refuted by Colonel Torrens ; that free trade is good only where reciprocity is perfect ; that a nation can augment its wealth by restraining a trade that was previously free ; can protect itself against such conduct on the part of its neighbours only by retaliation ; and, if it neglect this retaliatory policy, that it will be punished for its liberality by a progressive decrease of prices, of wages, and of profits, and an increase of taxation. We will state these startling propositions in Colonel Torrens's own words, both to avoid the danger of misrepresentation, and because we do not think we could state them with greater clearness or brevity :—

' First—When commercial countries receive the productions of each other duty free, then (the efficacy of labour being the same in each) the precious metals will be distributed amongst them in equal proportions, and the general scale of prices will be the same in each.

' Second—When any particular country imposes import duties upon the productions of other countries, while those other countries continue to receive her products duty free, then such particular country draws to herself a larger proportion of the precious metals, maintains a higher range of general prices than her neighbours, and obtains in exchange for the produce of a given quantity of her labour, the produce of a greater quantity of foreign labour.

' Third—When any country is deprived of that command over the precious metals which is due to the efficacy of her labour in producing articles for the foreign market, by the hostile tariffs of other countries, she may recover her due command over the metals, by imposing retaliatory and equivalent duties upon the importation of the productions of the countries by which the hostile tariffs are maintained.

' Fourth—When, from foreign rivalry and hostile tariffs, a country begins to lose a portion of her former command over the precious metals, and to experience a contraction of the currency, a fall in prices, in profits, and in wages, and a falling off in the revenue ; then, the lowering of import duties upon the productions of countries retaining their hostile tariffs, instead of affording relief, would aggravate the general distress, by occasioning a more rapid abstraction of the metals, and a deeper decline in prices, in profits, in wages, and in the revenue, accompanied not by a diminution, but by an increase in the real extent of taxation.' *

Colonel Torrens does not weary his reader with facts. His whole proof consists of the following intellectual diagram.

He supposes two countries, which he distinguishes by the names of Cuba and England, to be equal in territory, fertility, population, amount of capital, and general efficiency of labour. That they have each a metallic currency amounting to L.30,000,000, and trade only with one another—England having in commodity A, which he calls cloth, and Cuba in commodity B, which he calls sugar, an irresistible superiority. While trade is free, A and B will alone be exchanged ; Colonel Torrens assumes, on what ground we know not, that equal values of each must be exchanged, and supposes that exchange to consist of 1,500,000 cwt. of sugar, worth 30s. per cwt., against 1,500,000 bales of cloth, worth 30s. per bale.

He now supposes Cuba to impose on cloth a duty of 100 per cent, and England not to retaliate. The result, he says, will be a proportionate diminution of the consumption of cloth in Cuba. England will export only 750,000 bales of cloth instead of 1,500,000—will receive for them only L.1,125,000 instead of L.2,250,000, and, still continuing to import 1,500,000 cwt. of sugar, must pay annually the balance of L.1,125,000 in money. ' Thus, ' then,' he says, ' a new distribution of the precious metals between ' England and Cuba would follow as a necessary consequence. The ' circulation of Cuba would be increased to L.31,125,000, that of ' England contracted to L.28 875,000.' He goes on to state, in words, or in substance, that there must be in the two countries an alteration in the money prices of commodities, corresponding with the altered distribution of the precious metals; and therefore, when the increase of the circulation in Cuba raised the price of sugar there, the price of sugar imported from Cuba must also rise in the British market; and when, in England, the contraction of the currency depressed the price of British fabrics, the price of British fabrics must fall in Cuba. In Cuba the consumption

---

* *The Budget,* p. 28.

of cloth would be increased by a twofold cause—the fall in its price, and the increased quantity of money applicable to its purchase. In England the consumption of sugar would diminish in consequence both of its rise in price and the diminution in the quantity of money. England would go on paying to Cuba a balance, partly in money and partly in cloth, until the circulation of England should be reduced to L.20,000,000, and that of Cuba increased to L.40,000,000; and in consequence the price of cloth should have fallen from 30s. to 20s. per bale, and that of sugar risen from 30s. to 40s., and the exportation from England of 1,500,000 bales, worth 20s. per bale, would discharge the debt incurred to Cuba, by the purchase of 750,000 cwt. of sugar at 40s. per cwt., and therefore no further transmission of the metals would be required. He adds that :—

'The import duties imposed upon British goods would be paid, not by the consumer in Cuba, but by the producer in England. Before the imposition of the import duty of 100 per cent, England sent to Cuba 1,500,000 bales of goods, and brought back 1,500,000 cwt. of sugar. In consequence of the imposition of the duty, England sends out as before 1,500,000 bales of goods, but obtains in return only 750,000 cwt of sugar. Thus, one-half of value of her exports—one-half of the commodities which she formerly received in return for the produce of her industry, is taken from England, and paid as a tribute into the treasury of Cuba. The consumers of cloth in Cuba, who formerly paid L.2,250,000 for 1,500 000 bales, will now pay L.3,000,000 for the same quantity; viz. L.1,500,000 original, and L.1,500,000 duty. But no part of this duty will, in point of fact, be paid by them, because the import duties, by altering the distribution of the metals, increase the amount of money in their hands from L.2,250,000 to L.3,000,000, while reducing the cost price of the 1,500,000 bales of imported goods which they have to pay for, from L.2,250,000 to L.1,500,000. The consumers of British goods in Cuba, though the nominal payers of L.1,500,000 into the treasury of Cuba, would, in reality, be able to command exactly the same quantity of such goods as before. The ultimate incidence of the import duty imposed upon British goods, would be upon the British producers. The wealth of England would be *decreased* by the amount of the duty—the wealth of Cuba would be *increased* by its amount.

' The loss of wealth occasioned by her receiving a less quantity of foreign produce in exchange for the same quantity of exported goods, would be the least portion of the evil inflicted upon England by the change which has been described. Under the circumstances assumed, the abstraction of the precious metals, the contraction of the circulation, the fall in the money price of all domestic products, the increase in the value of all fixed salaries and charges, and the augmented pressure of the debt, would concur in creating a crisis more calamitous than any that has actually been experienced. National bankruptcy and revolution would be the probable results.

' It will be abundantly obvious, that for the evils resulting from the causes now described, the appropriate remedy would not be a reduction of import duties in England. Under the circumstances supposed, relief might be derived from increased taxation. An *ad valorem* duty of 100 per cent imposed upon the sugars of Cuba, would relieve the country from the payment of a foreign tribute of equal amount, would bring back the metals which had been abstracted, restore the circulation to its former amount, raise the price of all domestic products, lighten all fixed charges upon land and industry, and mitigate the pressure of the debt.' *

We need not fatigue the reader by stating Colonel Torrens's demonstration of his last positions. It consists simply in the assumptions, that the duty on sugar would diminish its consumption in England by one half; that Cuba must annually pay in money the balance between her import of cloth and her now diminished export of sugar, until the former distribution of the precious metals, and the former prices of cloth and sugar, were restored; and England and Cuba had again their respective currencies of L.30,000,000 each, and the exchange of 750,000 bales of cloth against 750,000 cwt. of sugar, balanced the accounts between the two countries.

It will be observed that Colonel Torrens assumes, first, that a country can exclude foreign commodities without diminishing the efficiency of its own labour ; and secondly, that the value in any country of the precious metals, depends solely on their quantity there—rises precisely in the proportion in which the quantity is decreased, and sinks precisely in the proportion in which it is augmented.

We believe that if he had considered more patiently either the causes which affect the efficiency of labour, or those which regulate the value of the precious metals, he would not have modified, but abandoned, the greater part of his conclusions. We attach great importance to both these subjects, particularly to the latter ; as we believe it to be a branch of Political Economy which has not as yet received due attention. We shall venture, therefore, to consider it somewhat at length.

We shall begin, however, by some remarks on the simpler question—the influence on the productiveness of labour of commercial restrictions.

It has been admitted from the time of Dr Adam Smith, that the productiveness of labour depends on its division; and that the extent of that division depends on the extent of the market. It is admitted, too, that these principles apply as much to districts as to individuals, and to nations as to districts. No one has perceived this more clearly, or has explained it more fully, than

---

* *Budget*, p. 30, 31.

Colonel Torrens himself, in his earlier publications. In some respects indeed, and in some cases, the territorial division of labour, to use a term which, we believe, was first applied to international commerce by Colonel Torrens, is more beneficial than even domestic interchange. It is obvious that the advantages derived from the increased productiveness of labour, are principally enjoyed by those who consume the commodities on which that labour is employed. Where the producer is himself a consumer, he obtains a double advantage. He profits by the additional supply both of his own commodities, and of those produced by others. If coals can be produced with half the labour which they previously cost, the collier, consuming largely himself what he produces, finds himself, at a less expense, better warmed than before. But an invention which should diminish by one half the labour necessary to produce a given quantity of lace, would confer no permanent benefit on the lace-makers. If the consequence were that the demand for lace were more than doubled, their wages might rise for a short interval; until the increase in the number of hands employed in their trade reduced its profits to the former level. If that demand were less than doubled, their wages might fall until their numbers had been diminished; but when this disturbance was over, their wages would remain the same, and, as they consume no lace, they would then be entirely unaffected by the change. This is nearly the state of the bulk of the manufacturers of an opulent country. Each workman consumes no part, or a very trifling part, of what he produces, and profits almost exclusively by the improvements made by his neighbours.

A great nation, on the other hand, is almost always the principal consumer of its own products. Even of British cotton fabrics, the largest production of any single finished manufacture, and the largest export that the world has ever seen, the British islands consume not only more than any other single country, but more than all the rest of Europe put together.

Again, the inhabitants of the same district enjoy nearly the same natural advantages. The benefits which they derive from the division of their labour arise almost exclusively from the use of machinery, and the increased dexterity and assiduity of each workman, as his field of operation is confined. International commerce adds the still greater benefits arising from varieties in soil and climate. When a Londoner buys his beer from a great brewery, instead of brewing it himself, he gains perhaps twenty per cent. But when he imports claret from Bordeaux, he gains 3000 per cent. He might brew his own beer at a guinea a barrel instead of 16s. He could not make his own claret at ninety guineas a dozen instead of three. If an individual were to cover with glass one of the southern slopes of the Hampstead hills, and establish there a great manufactory of English Sherry, we should be almost inclined to appoint a committee on his estate. When a Government commits acts the same in kind, its conduct excites no surprise, and little blame. It seems almost a matter of course. In many parts of the Continent where the climate resembles that of England, the British traveller is struck by a sort of cultivation which he never saw at home. The sunniest slopes, the richest bottoms, are covered by a bright green lettuce-like plant, on which more manure and more attention are bestowed than on any other product, except perhaps the vine. He finds that this is tobacco, and that in order to raise it at five times the cost of importing it, the best land is sacrificed in countries where there is not room for a hedge, and labour, where it cannot be obtained even to keep the communications between the villages passable. As he proceeds further eastward, he finds two great empires, each with a thin population—with a vast extent of fertile and imperfectly reclaimed territory, with indefinite powers of increasing their agricultural and mineral wealth,—directing the whole energy of their governments to projects for forcing their boors and miners to become cotton-spinners and weavers; and devoting to manufactures, which can be supported only by prohibitions mounted on prohibitions—by prohibiting the produce of the Zollverein, which itself can manufacture only by prohibiting the produce of Great Britain—the capital and the industry which are wanted for the ordinary trades of a civilized country.

It is a great mistake to suppose that a country which rejects the territorial division of labour, suffers merely by the greater dearness of the commodities which it is forced to produce instead of importing them. It incurs a further, and in many cases a greater, injury—in the general diminution of the efficiency of its own industry, occasioned by the misdirection of capital and the diminished division of labour. To what extent might not the agriculture of Austria be carried, if she would devote to roads and canals, and the improvement of the instruments of industry, the productive power which she is now wasting on mills and factories? But Joseph II., the founder of her commercial policy, belonged to the school of Colbert, the.Emperor of China, and their pupil Colonel Torrens. He thought, that by restricting foreign trade he could bring money into the country, and resolved that his empire should no longer be tributary to foreigners. That a sovereign surrounded by manufacturers, eager to become monopolists, should have fallen into such errors, is not strange—that Colonel Torrens should have done so, is almost unaccountable.

He states that his imaginary Cuba, after having excluded one half of all her previous imports, will retain all her previous productive powers. He forgets that she must immediately withdraw from other pursuits a portion of her capital and her industry, in order to produce at home a portion of what she formerly imported; or, if he does not forget this, he does not perceive that the general diminution of the division of labour which must be the consequence, must produce the further consequence of a general diminution of the efficiency of labour. Taking his hypothesis as he has laid it down, namely, that England and Cuba were, when Cuba first laid her duty on English cloth, precisely equal in wealth and in productive power as to every commodity except cloth and sugar; the result would be, that after Cuba had forced herself to misapply a portion of her capital and labour to the making cloth, she would, in some branches of industry, become inferior to England. Both the English producer and the Cuba consumer would find it profitable that certain commodities previously made in Cuba should be supplied from England. The labour and capital previously devoted to them in Cuba might be employed in the production of cloth; and part of the labour and capital previously devoted, in England, to the production of cloth for Cuba, might now be devoted to the production of these substituted articles. In such a case, no money need pass, and Colonel Torrens's vast superstructure falls.

He is entitled, however, to amend his hypothesis, and to suppose that the 100 per cent duty is imposed in Cuba upon every English commodity except money. Under such circumstances, Cuba would be forced to withdraw from other employments labour and capital, to be employed in making cloth, and could not supply their place by importation; and England would have to find an employment for the labour and capital now no longer wanted to make cloth for Cuba, and could not find it in the production of any other consumable commodity for that market.

The result, in each case, appears to us to be clear. The second of the two great errors, of which we have accused Colonel Torrens, consists in his having omitted to state it.

It is obvious that the capital and labour in England, which could no longer be employed in their accustomed trade of supplying cloth for the Cuba market, would be employed in the new trade of procuring and exporting the precious metals to Cuba; and that the capital and labour which would now be wanted in Cuba, in order to make the cloth formerly imported from England, would in fact be obtained by applying to that purpose the capital and labour formerly employed in procuring the precious metals. In short, that the result of the restrictions laid by Cuba on her commerce with England, would be to turn some of the English clothiers into miners, and some of the Cuba miners into clothiers.

The possibility of such a result, however, is not alluded to by Colonel Torrens. He does not admit that either of his two imaginary countries, which, it is to be recollected, represent the whole commercial world, could increase its stock of money except by taking from that of the other. He does not admit that the value of the currency of either is connected with its cost of production. He seems to suppose that some unknown agent has thrown into the commercial world a certain amount of the precious metals, incapable of increase or diminution, and depending for its value on its quantity.

Many of our readers may think that no answer need be made to the theory, that the local value of the precious metals depends on what Colonel Torrens calls their distribution; that is to say, on the comparative amount of them in each country. But that theory is favoured by Mr Ricardo in some unguarded passages, particularly in his chapter on foreign trade—a chapter containing the germ of most of the errors which have expanded themselves so vigorously in the writings of Colonel Torrens. It is maintained in express terms by the late Mr Mill; with the addition that any increase or diminution of the rapidity with which the money of a country circulates, produces the same effects as the increase or diminution of its quantity.* An opinion so supported cannot therefore be safely neglected.

Yet it is an opinion that seems refuted as soon as it is explicitly stated. No one will maintain that gold and silver differ from the other metals, except in their greater scarcity and durability; or that their attributes are changed the instant they are divided into portions of a given weight and authenticated by a stamp. But if we were asked, why does one ton of copper generally exchange for five of lead—we should immediately answer, for the same reason which causes one bushel of wheat generally to exchange for two bushels of barley; namely, that it costs as much in wages and profits, or, to use another nomenclature, in labour and abstinence, to produce one ton of copper as five tons of lead, and one bushel of wheat as two bushels of barley.

There is probably more than fifty times as much gold in use in Europe as there is platina; but yet gold is five times as valu-

---

* Mill's *Elements of Political Economy*, 3d edition, s. 7.

able as platina. There is about forty-seven times as much silver as there is gold; but gold is not quite sixteen times as valuable as silver. Again, it is probable that silver changes hands ten times as often as gold ; but no one seriously supposes that this cause affects the comparative value of the two metals. Cost of production, the cause which decides the value of any other commodity not the subject of a monopoly, must decide the value of the precious metals.

We will endeavour to show in detail how this takes place under the simplest circumstances.

We will suppose an insulated society of 10,000 families, having an abundance of fertile land, and using manufactures so rude, that the trifling capital employed by them may be disregarded, and so equal in fortune and rank, that the relations of landlord and tenant, and capitalist and workman, shall not exist. We will suppose gold alone to be their money, and that it is obtained by washing alluvial deposits without any expensive machinery or skill, and always in the same ratio to the labour employed.

The cost of producing gold would, under these circumstances, always remain the same ; and its value in labour, or, in other words, the amount of labour which a certain quantity of it could purchase, would always correspond with its cost of production ; except for short intervals, when any sudden increase or diminution in the demand for it, should occasion the existing supply to be for a time relatively excessive or deficient. Under such circumstances, the value of all other things would be estimated by comparing their cost of production with that of gold. If the labour of a family employed for a year, could gather from the washing-places fifty ounces of gold, and, by equal exertion, gather from the spontaneous produce of the fields fifty quarters of rice, the rice and the gold would be of equal value, and a single quarter of rice would be worth an ounce of gold. If the same labour could produce, in the same time, one hundred ounces of gold instead of fifty, a quarter of rice would be worth two ounces instead of one ; or if the same labour could gather one hundred quarters of rice instead of fifty, a quarter of rice would be worth only half an ounce instead of a whole ounce ; but while a year's labour could produce just fifty ounces of gold, the yearly income of each family, however employed, supposing their diligence, strength, and skill equal, would be of the value of precisely fifty ounces of gold.

The quantity of gold produced would depend partly on the quantity wanted for plate—including, under that word, all use of gold except as money—and partly on the quantity wanted for money. The quantity wanted for plate would of course depend on the prevailing fashions of the country; the quantity wanted for money would depend on causes numerous and complicated. We shall explain them at some length, as the question—what are the causes which determine the quantity of money which a community shall possess?—is important, and by no means easy of solution.

It is obvious, in the first place, that the whole quantity of money in a community must consist of the aggregate of all the different sums possessed by the different individuals by whom it is constituted. And what this quantity shall be, must depend partly on the number of those individuals; partly on the value in money of the aggregate of their respective incomes; and partly on the average proportion of the value of his income which each individual habitually keeps by him in money. The two first of these causes do not require much explanation. It is clear that, *cæteris paribus*, two millions of people must possess more money than one million. It is also clear that, *cæteris paribus*, a nation, the value of whose average aggregate income amounts to L.100,000,000 sterling a-year, must possess more money than one whose annual income is only L.50,000,000.

But the causes which determine what proportion of the value of his income each individual shall habitually retain in money, are less obvious. Briefly, it may be said to depend, first, on the proportion to his income of his purchases and sales for money; and secondly, on the rapidity with which they succeed one another; but such a statement is too concise to be intelligible without further explanation.

Exchange, as it is the principle cause, is also one of the principal effects of improvement. As men proceed from a primitive to a refined state of society, as they advance from hunters to shepherds, from shepherds to agriculturists, from villagers to townspeople, and from being inhabitants of towns depending for their supplies on the adjacent country, to be the citizens of a commercial metropolis using the whole world as one extensive market;—at each of these stages man becomes more and more a dependent being—consuming less and less of what he individually produces, until at last almost every want, and every gratification, is supplied by means of an exchange. Our ancestors lived on their own estates, fed their household from the produce of their own lands, and clothed them with their own flax and wool, manufactured within their own halls. Food and clothing were the wages of their domestic servants; and their tenants, instead of paying rent in money, were bound to cultivate the lord's demesne; to supply him certain quantities of corn or live stock; and to serve under his banner in public or private war. The services of the Church were obtained by allowing the priest a tenth of the annual produce; and the demands of the State were limited to the maintaining roads and bridges, defence of castles, and attendance in war for forty days, with adequate provisions. Under such circumstances, the Barons and their dependents—and these two classes comprised the bulk of the community—might pass years without having to make a sale or a purchase. Exchanges they made, where one party gave services or produce, and the other party food, clothing, shelter, or land; but these were all made by barter. The yeoman, who cultivated his own land and used the manufactures of his own family, might, in fact, live without even an exchange; nor could the serf, though he received maintenance in return for labour, be said to make an exchange, since he had no more power to enforce, or even to require any stipulation than any other domestic animal.

The same circumstances must, however, have occasioned what money there was in the country to circulate very slowly; or, in other words, to change hands very unfrequently. A man who, in such a state of society, received a sum, might not find for a long time an advantageous opportunity of spending it; and he would have many reasons for not parting with it, even on what might appear advantageous terms. Where property and person are so insecure as they were among our ancestors, every one must feel anxious to have some means of support if he should be forced to quit his home, or to witness the destruction of his less portable property. Again, the demands for money, when they did come, were great and unforeseen. The knight was in constant danger of having to pay a ransom; the tenant of having to assist in raising that ransom; and the Crown, from time to time, required a subsidy or an escuage.

Under such circumstances, it is probable that each individual, or, to speak more correctly, each person managing his own concerns, might on an average receive in money one fiftieth part of the value of his annual income. But it is likewise probable that what he did so receive he might retain on an average for four years. The aggregate sum in his possession would not exceed a month's income; a very moderate hoard, where the motives for hoarding were so powerful. We are inclined to think that the average proportion of their incomes, which our ancestors hoarded, during the first two or three centuries after the Conquest, was much larger. It is impossible otherwise to account for the importance attached to treasure trove, which seems to have formed a material portion of the royal revenue; and now probably does not afford, except from ancient deposits, L.1000 a-year. The whole money of the country would, under such circumstances, change hands only once in four years.

It is probable that in this supposition—which is not without resemblance to the state of England under the Norman and Plantagenet lines—we have stated the extremes both of absence of exchange, and of slow circulation of money, that could take place in a community entitled to be called civilized. We will now suppose the country to be at peace, and secure within and without; and all the peculiar motives for hoarding to be removed. Instead of a month's income, each family might retain only a week's. Instead of once in four years, the whole money of the country would change hands every year; and L.100,000 would perform all the offices of money as well as L.400,000 did before.

In the case which we have supposed of an insulated community consisting of 10,000 families, the quantity wanted would depend partly on the cost of producing gold, and partly on the rapidity of its circulation. The rapidity of circulation being given, it would depend on the cost of production. It is obvious that twice as much money would be required to effect every exchange, if a day's labour could obtain from the washing places thirty-four grains of gold, as would be necessary if a day's could obtain only seventeen. And the cost of production being given, the quantity of money wanted would depend on the rapidity of its circulation.

We have supposed 10,000 families of equal incomes. We will now suppose the cost of producing gold to be such, that a family could gather 118 grains, or what we call a guinea, per week, or about 17 grains per day. Now, if the habits of the community were such, that each family lived from hand to mouth, and purchased every day the day's consumption, (an impossible supposition, but one which may be used as a mere illustration,) it is obvious that no family would at an average possess more or less than 17 grains of gold; 170,000 grains, therefore, would be the precise quantity wanted for the purposes of money, and all the money would change hands every day. Let us now consider what would be the consequence if their custom were to make their purchases half-yearly instead of daily. At first sight we might think that the rapidity of circulation would be retarded in the proportion of 1 to 182½; and, consequently, that rather more than 182 times as much money would be necessary. Such would be the case if each family were, on one and the same day, to make all their purchases for the ensuing half a year's consumption. But if we suppose them to lay in their stocks of different articles at different times, and on an average to make their purchases and sales, and of course to receive their incomes, on 36 different days during each year; the quantity of money wanted, instead of being 182 times, would not be much more than ten times the former quantity. Each family would, at an average, instead of 17, possess rather more than 170 grains of gold, the whole quantity wanted would rather exceed 1,700,000 grains of gold, and would change hands nearly ten times in a year.

But though any alteration in the rapidity of circulation would much affect the quantity wanted, it would not, except during short periods, affect the value of money while the cost of production remained unaltered. Whether 170,000 or 1,700,000 grains were wanted, still, while a day's labour would produce neither more nor less than 17 grains of gold, 17 grains of gold would, except during comparatively short intervals, be the price of every commodity produced by the labour of a day. We say, except during comparatively short intervals; because though the causes which limit the supply of gold are supposed to be unalterable, those which give it utility, or, in other words, which create the demand for it, might be increased or diminished; and during the interval between the diminution or increase of the demand, and the increase or diminution of the supply in the market, the value might rise above, or sink below, the cost of production.

The primary cause of the utility of gold is, of course, its use as the material of plate. The secondary cause is its use as money. And in the absence of any disturbing cause, the labour employed in producing gold, would be just enough to supply the annual loss and wear of the existing stock of plate and money. Suppose, now, that a change of fashion were to occasion a sudden demand for an increased quantity of plate—the introduction, for instance, of the Roman Catholic forms of worship, and a belief in the meritoriousness of adorning every altar with golden candlesticks—that demand would be supplied partly, by melting and converting into candlesticks some of the existing plate and some of the existing money, and partly by employing on plate all the current supply of gold, a part of which would otherwise have been used as money. The whole quantity of money being diminished, the average quantity possessed by each family must be diminished. A less portion would be offered on every purchase; all prices (except that of plate) would fall; and the monied incomes of all persons except the gatherers of gold would be diminished. This, of course, would occasion much more labour to be employed in gathering gold until the former amount of money were replaced.

If, after this had taken place, the use of plate should suddenly diminish—if, for instance, Protestant forms of worship should supplant the Roman Catholic—the consequences would be, of course, precisely opposite. The candlesticks would be melted down, and the sudden supply of gold would sink its value. Part of that additional supply would probably be used as plate, of which each family could afford to use a little more—the rest would be turned into money. The whole quantity of money being increased, each family would have rather more; rather more would be offered on every exchange; all prices (except the price of plate) would rise, and the money incomes of all persons except the gatherers of gold would be increased. The gathering of gold would, of course, cease; until the gradual loss and wear of plate and money, uncompensated by any annual supply, should have reduced the quantity of gold below the amount necessary to supply the existing demand for plate and money. On the occurrence of that event, it would again become profitable to gather gold; and the price of every thing would again depend on the proportion of the labour necessary to its production, compared with the labour necessary to obtain a given quantity of gold. Similar and equally temporary consequences would, of course, follow any causes which should increase or diminish the demand for gold, by diminishing or increasing either the use of money in exchange, or the rapidity of its circulation.

Our principal object in this discussion has been to show, that the value of money, in so far as it is decided by intrinsic causes, does not depend *permanently* on the quantity of it possessed by a given community; or on the rapidity of its circulation, or on the prevalence of exchanges, or on the use of barter or credit, or, in short, on any cause whatever excepting *the cost of its production.* Other causes may operate for a time; but their influence wears away as the existing stock of the precious metals within the country accommodates itself to the wants of the inhabitants. As long as precisely 17 grains of gold can be obtained by a day's labour, every thing else produced by equal labour will, in the absence of any natural or artificial monopoly, sell for 17 grains of gold; whether all the money of the country change hands every day, or once in four days, or once in four years; whether each individual consume principally what he has himself produced, or supply all his wants by exchange; whether such exchanges are effected by barter or by credit, or by the actual intervention of money; whether there be 1,700,000 or 170,000 grains in the country.

In many respects, our insulated community of 10,000 families is a miniature of the whole commercial world. The whole commercial world may be considered as one community, using gold and silver as money; and ascertaining the value of other commodities by comparing their cost of production with the cost of obtaining gold and silver. And though many causes may alter the quantity of the precious metals possessed by any single nation, nothing will permanently alter their value, so far as that value depends on intrinsic causes, unless it affect the cost at which they are obtained.

The causes which actually decide what shall be, at a given period, the cost of obtaining the precious metals in the countries in which the mines, streams, and sands which afford them are situated; or, in other words, which decide what, at a given period, shall be the poorest mine that shall be worked, or the least productive soil or sand that shall be washed or sifted, form the subject of an interesting enquiry, on which our limits will not allow us at present to enter. We hope to recur to it hereafter; but we shall now confine ourselves to the causes which regulate the supply of gold and silver in the countries which, having no natural deposits, obtain them by commerce. Such countries bear a still stronger resemblance to our supposed insulated community of 10,000 families. The rest of the commercial world is the silver mine, or the auriferous sand, to which each of them resorts in order to supply her annual consumption; and her gatherers of the precious metals are those who export her commodities.

During thirteen years, from 1829 to 1841, both inclusive, France imported 385,885,880 francs, or L.15,435,435 sterling of gold; and 1,969,600,513 francs, or L.78,784,020 sterling of silver; and exported 356,132,082 francs, or L.14,245,283 sterling of gold, and 619,656,625 francs, or L.24,786,265 sterling of silver;—showing that she requires for her own consumption, in plate and money, an average annual supply of both metals to the amount of 106,130,591 francs, or L.4,245,223 sterling.*

We have no official data showing the annual supply required by the British islands. Mr Jacob, in 1831, estimated the annual consumption of the precious metals in Great Britain, for all purposes except money, at L.2,457,221 sterling.† This estimate is treated by Mr M'Culloch as excessive.‡ But when we consider that Ireland is excluded, and that, during the twelve years that have since elapsed, the population of the British Islands has augmented by more than three millions, and our exports have risen from thirty-seven millions to fifty-one millions, it probably rather falls below than exceeds the present consumption in Great Britain and Ireland. If we add to this about L.200,000

---

* See, for the statistics of French commerce, the yearly official publication entitled, *Tableau général du Commerce de la France.*

† Jacob on the Precious Metals, Vol. ii. p. 299.

‡ *Dictionary of Commerce,* Art. Precious Metals.

as the annual waste by loss and wear of money, the annual consumption of the British islands may be taken at L.2,700,000.

From whence do France and the British islands obtain their supplies? From the whole commercial world. The annual export of British and Irish produce and manufactures, exceeds in value fifty millions sterling. The annual export from France of French produce and manufactures, exceeds in value thirty millions sterling. There is no portion of this great export of which the exporter, if he thought fit, might not receive the price in gold or silver. In fact, he almost always does receive it in gold or silver. There is much inaccuracy in the common statement, that the commerce between two countries, when the values which they reciprocally give and receive are equal, resolves itself into barter. It has a tendency to do so, because such a result is beneficial to all parties; but this arrangement is often defeated by local difficulties, or by the ignorance of one person as to what has been done or is doing by another—an ignorance which occasions almost all the errors by which commerce is deranged. The goods which are exported from Hull to Stettin are sold for Prussian thalers—those exported from Stettin to Hull are sold for English sovereigns. The English exporter wishes to convert his thalers into sovereigns; the Prussian exporter to convert his sovereigns into thalers. The ultimate resource is, that the Englishman has his thalers sent to him, and sells them for sovereigns to a London bullion merchant; and the Prussian receives his sovereigns, and sells them for thalers to a Prussian bullion merchant. But this is a very expensive process. The voyage may take a month or more; the freight and insurance on bullion are considerable; and coined money is almost always worth something more than the mere metal which it contains. The best expedient of course is, that the Prussian and English debt, so far as they are equal, should be exchanged; and, if the Englishman and Prussian are correspondents, this is done of course. But one debt may be much larger than another; or the two exporters may have different agents, who may not be acquainted with each others' transactions. In this case, the Prussian who has to send money to England will naturally endeavour to effect it by sending commodities. Supposing the expense of sending corn or bullion to amount to 10s. per L.100, and the voyage to take a month, a profit of 10s. per month, or at the rate of six per cent per annum, would be obtained by sending goods, which would sell in Hull for merely what they cost in Stettin. If he could not send commodities, he would endeavour to find some one to whom money was due in England, who would take his Prussian money, and transfer to him his English debt.

It would be worth his while even to pay, as a premium, any thing less than ten shillings per cent—the supposed expense of remitting coin or bullion ; and this premium might induce some one else to send commodities to England. If he could not make the proposed arrangement at Stettin, he might be able to make it at Dantzic, or Berlin, or Leipzic. Or if money were due to him in Vienna, or in Paris, or even in New York, by persons to whom money was due in England, it might be worth his while to direct his debtors in Vienna, or Paris, or New York, to discharge their debts to him by discharging his debts to his English creditor, and thus prevent the transit of money.

It is in this manner, by the exchange of debts and credits, that the commerce of the world is carried on, and with a comparatively small transmission of the precious metals. But, though the international circulation of the precious metals is comparatively small, it is positively great. We have seen that during thirteen years ending in 1841, France, while she imported gold and silver of the value of L.94,219,455 sterling, exported gold and silver of the value of L.39,031,548 ; all of which was exported merely to come back to her—the greater part being constantly passing and repassing between London and Paris. The expense, indeed, of sending money from Paris to London is so slight, that it may be supposed that no great effort is made to avoid it. But even between England and China, where it costs an expensive and dangerous voyage, and a loss of six months' interest, vast sums go and return.

It is notorious that, during the last five years, we have received eight or nine millions of ounces of silver from China. In that period we have exported to China 122,840 ounces in 1837 ; 125,197 in 1838 ; 947,256 in 1839 ; 322,446 in 1840 ; 127,797 in 1841 ; 1,040,194 in 1842 ; and 164,000 ounces in the first ten weeks of 1843. During that time, there can have been seldom less than half a million of ounces on the sea, going backwards and forwards merely between England and China. And yet, what we send to China does not amount to one twentieth part of our annual exportation of the precious metals. From the beginning of 1837 to the 10th March 1843, we exported 2,062,247 ounces of gold, and 87,555,117 ounces of silver, of the aggregate value of L.29,918,653, besides the amount recorded in the custom-house ;—an amount which may be very large, as there is no penalty on non-entry.* What we imported during that time is not recorded ; but according to Mr Jacob's estimate—

---

* Parliamentary Return, 17th March 1843. No. 56.

which appears to us, as we have already stated, to be rather below than above the truth—that we annually consume L.2,700,000 by the wear and loss of plate and money, our importations cannot have amounted to less than L.43,318,653, or more than eight millions sterling a-year. A sum equal, according to Mr Jacob's estimate, to the whole metallic currency of Europe, (L.313,388,560,) enters France in less than fifty years; and the British islands in less than forty years. When the precious metals are in this state of constant motion—when every commercial country is every day receiving and parting with them at a thousand inlets and a thousand outlets—to suppose that one nation can drain another, is as rational as to suppose that the level of the British Channel could be altered by enlarging or contracting the Straits of Dover.

Without doubt it is in the power of a nation, not by commercial, but by monetary regulations, to increase or diminish the amount of its metallic money. If we were to make silver instead of gold the British standard, we might reverse the existing proportions of the British currency. From thirty millions of gold and ten of silver, we might constitute it of thirty millions of silver and ten of gold. By issuing unconvertible government notes to effect all the larger payments, and copper coins for all the smaller ones, and rendering the use of gold and silver money penal, we might banish both metals from our circulation. Or, by prohibiting the issue of notes and copper coinage, or by internal commotions restrictive of credit, and consequently of the banking operations which depend on credit, we might render our currency exclusively metallic; and require 80 millions of metallic money instead of 40. But those measures would affect the value of the precious metals only so far as they affected the cost of obtaining them. Whether our currency consisted of 30 millions, or 10 millions, or 60 millions of sovereigns, the value in Great Britain of each sovereign would always depend on the amount of British labour necessary to obtain one.

France, with a population of 34 millions, is supposed to possess a currency of more than 120 millions sterling.* The British islands, with a population of 28 millions, possess a currency of only 40 millions. There is much less division of labour in France than in England; and consequently there are

---

* Chevalier. *L'Amerique du Nord.* Vol. 1. Note 20. M. Leon Faucher estimates the specie of France at 3,500,000,000 of francs, or about L.140,000,000 sterling. See his able Pamphlet, entitled *Recherches sur l'Or et sur l'Argent.*—P. 59.

much fewer exchanges in proportion to the population. The
general scale of prices is much lower, and consequently each
exchange, in which money is employed, can be effected with
less money. But the effects of the causes which tend to diminish the quantity of the precious metals in France, are more
than counterbalanced by those which tend to increase it. In
the first place, the general want of credit occasions the use of
money in exchanges, in a proportion, perhaps, ten times as
great as in England; and secondly, money is exclusively employed in France as a safe, though unproductive investment.
The French peasant accumulates specie until he can buy a patch
of land—the only investment which, from the tradition of centuries,
he believes to be secure. The English labourer either expends
all that he earns, or lends his savings to the Government, through
a Savings' bank, or to a neighbour, or employs them in some
retail trade. Perhaps half the money of France does not change
hands once in ten years. In England there is scarcely a hoard,
except the specie in the vaults of the bank. But though France
has nearly three times as much money in proportion to her
population as England, gold and silver are more than one third
dearer in France than in England. It costs a Frenchman more
labour to obtain two ounces of silver, than it costs an Englishman to obtain three. If France could rely on internal and external tranquillity—if mutual confidence and commercial habits
could be established among her people—if every town had its
bank of deposits and circulation, and every village its Savings'
bank—60 millions might perform all the operations for which
120 are required. The remaining 60 millions might be exported, and send back the materials, and implements of agriculture, and manufactures, in which France is now so lamentably
deficient. The distribution of the precious metals, to use Colonel
Torrens's expression, would be altered; but would France be a
sufferer by the change? Would rents or wages fall? Would it
cost more labour to obtain an ounce of silver than it does now?

Colonel Torrens states with perfect truth, that the main cause
which renders the value of money, in relation to labour, different
in different countries, will be found to be the different degrees of
' efficacy with which, in different countries, labour is applied.'—
(*Budget*, p. 24.)—Yet, in the next page, he assumes that the
value of money depends on its quantity, and may be lowered by increasing that quantity, and raised by diminishing it:
' Let us assume,' says he, ' that labour is applied with equal
' effect in England and in France; that, in consequence, the
' metals are distributed in equal proportions throughout the two

' countries; and that the commerce carried on between them
' consists in the interchange of hardware, worth in England
' £1,000,000, for wine, worth in France £1,000,000. This
' being the previous state of things, let us assume further, that
' while England receives the wines of France duty free, France
' imposes a duty of 50 per cent upon British goods. The effects
' of this duty would be to alter the distribution of the metals
' in favour of France, and, consequently, to raise prices in that
' country, and to lower prices in England. The process would
' be as follows :—In France, the price of British goods would
' be increased by the amount of the duty, and their consumption
' in that country diminished in a corresponding degree ; while in
' England, in the first instance, the price of French wines would
' not be enhanced, and the consumption would, consequently,
' continue as before. The result of these changes would be, that
' England could not now send to France such a quantity of hard-
' ware as would pay for the wine she received, and would be com-
' pelled to discharge a portion of her foreign debt by a transmis-
' sion of bullion : this would raise prices in France, and depress
' prices in England. In England there would be less money
' applicable to the purchase of wine, and the consumption would
' diminish. In France, there would be more money applicable
' to the purchase of hardware, and the consumption of British
' goods would gradually increase ; and these processes would
' continue until the quantity of hardware sent to France again
' became sufficient to pay for the quantity of wine received, and
' until no further transmission of the metals should be required.
' But when the commerce between the two countries should thus
' be restored to a trade of barter, the precious metals would no
' longer be equally distributed between them, and the scale of
' prices would be higher in France than in England.

These hypothetical illustrations, in which every element is imaginary, and the words France and England, hardware and wine,
might be replaced, and perhaps advantageously, by A and B, X
and Z, are often instructive. But the writer who uses them incurs one of two dangers : either that of fatiguing his readers by
an enumeration of all the supposed circumstances which may affect the conclusion—an enumeration which it is as difficult to follow, and to bear in mind, as it is to master the *dramatis personæ*
of a new play ; or that of omitting to state some of the essential
conditions.

Colonel Torrens has avoided the former of these errors. His
illustrations are simple. They seldom contain more than three
or four suppositions. But he has fallen headlong into the latter.

By not considering the precious metals as the subjects of waste and supply—by not considering the mode by which the stock is kept up—by not considering the influence of commerce on the efficiency of labour, and by confining his attention to two, or at most three countries, and not considering the manner and the degree in which the changes in their mutual intercourse would affect their commercial relations with other nations—he has been able to extract from his assumed premises consequences which we believe to be not merely unlike those which would be the real results, but absolutely opposed to them. He has inferred wealth from conduct which would produce poverty; and a rise of prices from causes which would make them fall.

We will not, however, fatigue the reader by opposing to Colonel Torrens an hypothesis as abstract as his own, and more complicated. We will take the British islands and France as they are, and endeavour to show what would be the actual results to each country, of a change in the French commercial code which should suddenly diminish by one half our exports to France. And we hope that those among our readers to whom our arguments may appear trite, will be interested by some of our facts.

In the year 1841—the last for which we have either French or English returns—France, according to the French return, imported from the British islands, including their European dependencies, merchandize of the value of 144,048,592 francs, and precious metals of the value of 65,402,822 francs. Of the merchandize she re-exported 42,140,718 francs, and retained for home consumption 101,907,874 francs; of which 77,784,894 francs consisted of materials of industry, 7,939,894 francs of raw consumable produce, and the remaining 16,183,086 francs, of complete manufactures. During that year she exported to the British islands merchandize of the value of 163,892,613 francs, and precious metals of the value of 20,876,485 francs. Of the merchandize, 56,401,681 consisted of foreign commodities re-exported; and the remaining 107,490,932 were French productions.

To avoid dealing with such cumbrous figures, we will call her exports to the British islands of French productions, and her imports for home consumption, each four millions sterling; three-fourths of the imports consisting of the materials of industry. Supposing France now to impose duties reducing her British imports by one half: the first result would be, that French capital and French labour must be diverted from their previous employment, to produce at home what was previously purchased from abroad. On looking through the detailed statement of the importations from the British islands, it will be seen that scarcely any commodity is mentioned, the use of which could be dispensed with, or without great inconvenience diminished. If we suppose that the supply could be produced at home at an additional expense of only 50 per cent, it would cost three millions to produce what could have been imported for two millions. L.20 a-year is a high amount for the wages of a French family ; at that rate of wages, and assuming nine-tenths of the cost to consist of the wages of labour, it would require the labour of 108,000 families, or about 540,000 persons. All this labour, and the capital necessary to set it in motion, must be taken from other employments. To what extent this would diminish the general division of labour in France, and the general efficiency of French labour, it is of course impossible to say; but that it would diminish both cannot be doubted.

In the next place, the increased cost of production of large classes of commodities, comprising many of the most important materials and implements of agriculture and manufactures, would occasion a further, and probably a still more severe blow to the industry of France. The loss annually inflicted on the agriculture alone of France by the high duties on British iron, is estimated by an eminent French authority at 49,522,000 francs, or about two millions sterling.*

In 1841, France imported for home consumption, merchandize of the value of 804,557,931 francs, and imported in gold and silver 186,980,851 francs ; she exported French products of the value of 760,653,561 francs, and in gold and silver 72,892,083 francs. In round numbers, her imports of merchandize may be called L.32,000,000 sterling, and her exports L.30,400,000 ; her imports of gold and silver L.7,500,000 sterling, and her exports L.3,000,000. About 45 per cent of her importations were the produce of the countries immediately adjoining her ;—England, Belgium, and the dominions of the King of Sardinia, (which alone furnished more than 33 per cent,) Germany, Spain, and Switzerland ; and the same countries received about 47 per cent of her exports. It is obvious that among countries so much resembling one another in climate, soil, and civilization, as France and the group of nations which surround her, a slight difference in the cost of production must decide, as to many commodities, which shall be the exporting and which the importing country.

---

* M. Annison. *Examen de l'Enquête sur les Fers*, cited by Mr Macgregor. Commercial Tariffs, France, p. 140.

The diversion of a portion of the industry and capital of France from their former employments, in order to produce at home half of the commodities which she formerly imported from England, and the general diminution of the efficiency of her labour, would make it the interest of many French consumers to purchase abroad much of what they formerly purchased at home : it would make it the interest of many foreign consumers to purchase at home, or in other markets, much of what they formerly imported from France. Nearly one-fourth of the exports of French products consists of cotton and woollen manufactures ;—commodities with respect to which she has no natural advantages, and in which Britain, Belgium, Germany, and America are her formidable rivals. An addition of one thirty-second part to the imports into France, and a diminution by one-thirtieth of her exports, would take from her more than the two millions of specie which, according to the Mercantile Theory, she was to have gained by the exclusion of British commodities. But it is clear that she would lose much more. We have seen that the value of money, in relation to labour, in different countries, differs according to the efficiency with which in each country labour is applied. As French labour became less efficient, its value would fall in the general market of the world—a less sum than before would perform the functions of money. As the value of gold and silver with relation to labour rose, or, in other words, as it required more labour to purchase a given quantity of either, her population could no longer afford. to use the same quantity of plate. She would require less of the precious metals than before, and she would obtain less. Her national debt, her taxes, and her fixed payments, would rise in value; and all the effects which, according to Colonel Torrens's supposition, ought to occur in England, would take place in France. There would be a change in the distribution of the precious metals; and, what is really important, there would be in France a change in the cost of obtaining them. France would not only have fewer commodities, but less gold and silver; and, to obtain a given amount of either the one or other, would cost every Frenchman more labour than it does now.

Let us now see what would be the effects in England. From the year 1825, the earliest for which we have regular returns, until 1841 inclusive, England has exported to France, in coin and bullion, the average annual sum of 95,563,294 francs, or L.3,822,531; and has imported from France, in corn and bullion, the average annual sum of 36,273,840 francs, or L.1,450,953. As soon as the change in the French tariff took place, and the export of commodities from England to France fell from L.4,000,000 to L.2,000,000, her imports continuing to be L.4,000,000, it would be necessary that England should either increase her annual remittance of coin and bullion to France by L.2,000,000, or cease to receive the 1,400,000, which she now receives, and increase her remittance by only L.600,000. As the greater part of the bullion which England annually imports is imported only for the purpose of re-exportation, she might either direct to France a larger portion than she now directs to her of her exports of the precious metals, or she might order her foreign correspondents to send to France, instead of to herself, L.600,000 out of the eight or nine millions of gold and silver which she now annually receives.

Such a change would produce a slight disturbance in the bullion trade—one of the most trifling businesses in the empire; and this slight and transient disturbance would be the whole amount of its effect on the British money market. Instead of draining us of our gold and silver, doubling our debt, halving our wages, and making us pay to the French treasury an annual tribute of L.2,000,000 sterling, it would merely give some trouble to the clerks of half a dozen dealers in a trade which probably does not employ 500 persons!

The only real injury which England would suffer, would be, that the L.2,000,000 of commodities formerly sent to France, must now receive a different destination; or the labour and capital formerly devoted to them a different employment. Of course, this would be an inconvenience. Every forced change in the channels of trade is an inconvenience. But there are grounds for believing that in this instance the inconvenience would not be great or permanent. In the first place, England would find herself in an improved situation in all the markets in which France was formerly her competitor. The efficiency of labour, and consequently the power of exporting commodities, having diminished in France, the English exporter would every where meet his French rival on better terms;—might divide a trade of which he previously had only a small share, and monopolize one which he previously divided. And, as all manufacturing superiority has a tendency to increase—the greater quantity being in general produced at a less proportionate expense, and the less quantity at a greater proportionate expense—it is difficult to say to what extent the relative superiority of English over French manufacturing industry might be carried. The new or enlarged outlets might be sufficient to absorb the whole L.2,000,000 worth of commodities excluded from the French market. We will suppose, however, that they dispose of only one-half. The labour and capital previously engaged in producing commodities of the value of L.1,000,000, would have to seek a new market.    We may assume 9-10ths of their cost to have consisted of the wages of labour, the wages of a British manufacturing family to be about L.36 a-year, and the capital engaged to have been equal in amount to the value of the commodities produced by it in a year.

On these data, which we believe to represent fairly what actually takes place, the commodities in question employed a capital of about L.1,000,000, and the labour of about 25,000 families, constituted of about 125,000 persons. If there were any thing peculiar in the machinery or in the skill required for the production of commodities for the French market, the contraction of that market must diminish, and might destroy the value of that peculiar skill or machinery; just as peace diminishes or destroys the value of the skill and machinery employed in producing some military articles.    But there is no such peculiarity.    Our exports to France are not the results of any manufacture especially adapted to French use; they are merely a part of the commodities which we produce for our own consumption.    Yarns, linens, silks, and minerals, amount to more than eighty per cent of them.    The only result of the diminution of our trade with France, would be a rather larger supply of these commodities in the market than before. But unless we believe in the possibility of a general glut—unless we believe that every body can have too much of every thing— we cannot believe that the produce of the labour of 25,000 families, or of L.1,000,000 worth of capital, would want a market. Every year more than double that number of families are added to our population, and several millions to our capital.    All these new-comers must be fed, clothed, lodged, and warmed.    Nine-tenths of them are employed in producing commodities and services, to be exchanged against those which they require themselves.    Not only the home market but the foreign market is constantly expanding itself.  Notwithstanding those hostile tariffs from which Colonel Torrens fears our commercial dethronement —notwithstanding the aid which we afford to such tariffs by our own senseless or corrupt legislation—the exports of the British islands augment more rapidly than either the population or the capital.

We have been permitted to extract from the proof sheets of the forthcoming volume of official tables, the following statement of the declared values of British and Irish produce and manufactures, exported during the fifteen years ending with 1841 —the last year for which the accounts are made up.    Confining ourselves to the *millions,* they stand thus:—

| | | | | |
|---|---|---|---|---|
| 1827, | . | L.37,000,000 | 1835, | . L.47,000,000 |
| 1828, | . | 36,000,000 | 1836, | . 53,000,000 |
| 1829, | . | 35,000,000 | 1837, | . 42,000,000 |
| 1830, | . | 38,000,000 | 1838, | . 50,000,000 |
| 1831, | . | 37,000,000 | 1839, | . 53,000,000 |
| 1832, | . | 36,000,000 | 1840, | . 51,000,000 |
| 1833, | . | 39,000,000 | 1841, | . 51,000,000 |
| 1834, | . | 41,000,000 | | |

The details of that table show what changes may occur in particular branches of foreign commerce, without disturbing its general advance. They show that, in the years which it comprehends, our exports to particular countries frequently varied backwards and forwards by more than a million a year. But if we take periods of five years, the aggregate advance is progressive and great. A change, indeed, like that which occurred in our commercial relations with the United States of America, between the years 1836 and 1837, when our exports in one year, and to one country, fell from twelve millions to four, is a serious calamity; especially if aggravated, as it was on that occasion, by a bad harvest and a sliding corn-duty. But a change merely equal to the one which we have supposed—a change affecting our exports to one country only to the extent of a million, might occur almost without being perceived.

We will now consider the probable result, if England were to adopt the retaliatory measures recommended by Colonel Torrens and others, and impose additional duties on French commodities, which should diminish by one half the L.4,000,000 worth which she now imports from France. It is obvious that England would suffer evils the same in kind as those which were inflicted on France, when she imposed duties which reduced by one half her imports from England. England must now produce at home, or import from a less advantageous market, substitutes for the L.2,000,000 worth of commodities which she previously received from France. Her wants would be worse supplied and at a greater expense. Her labour and capital would be less concentrated on the employments in which they are most efficient. The raw materials which she now imports would be dearer. The diminution in the division of her labour, and the increased price of some raw materials, would somewhat diminish the efficiency of her labour. She would be a less formidable rival to France, and to all her other competitors, in third markets. She might, perhaps, export less gold and silver to France, but she would be able to import less from other countries. The wages of labour, and with them the general ability to use plate, would diminish. Instead of increasing her stock of the precious metals, she would diminish it. In short, the results of the measure would, as in the case of France, be precisely the reverse of those which it was intended to produce. But though the results in each case would be the same in kind, they would be different in degree. The imports from England into France consist principally of the materials and instruments of production; and of that production which is most useful to the mass of the community. Those from France into England consist principally or finished commodities; and those commodities are principally for the use of the opulent classes—a comparatively small minority even in England. Forty-two per cent, or nearly one-half, consist of silk, cotton, woollen, and linen goods, all of them of the finer kinds. The wines and brandies, amounting to 12 per cent, are also for the consumption of the higher classes. Grain and eggs, the former of which amounted, in 1841, to $9\frac{8}{10}$th per cent, and the latter to $5\frac{3}{10}$th, and madder, which constituted $3\frac{9}{10}$th—altogether 19 per cent—are the principal French commodities which the bulk of the British community consume. The customhouse war which we have supposed, like the customhouse war which now unhappily exists between the two countries, would be far more mischievous to France than to England. But that it would be mischievous to England—and, which is the important question, that the evils inflicted on England by the restrictions imposed on her commerce by France would not be diminished, but would be aggravated by retaliation— we think has been satisfactorily proved. That, under the peculiar circumstances of our commerce with France, the evils produced by that retaliation would not be great, perhaps would not be sensible, is probably true. It is enough for our argument if we have shown that the tendency of retaliation is to produce evil. It is a sufficient objection to a proposed remedy if it can be shown that its tendency, however slight or remote, is to exasperate the disease. It need not be shown to be *mortal*, or even perceptibly hurtful.

Since the preceding observations were written, Colonel Torrens has published a Postscript to his Letter to Sir Robert Peel, in which the expediency, or rather the necessity, of retaliatory tariffs is maintained, but on different premises. In his previous publications, he defended that necessity on the ground that the nation which imposed the lower duties would lose her command over the precious metals. We have shown that this ground fails. He now leaves the precious metals out of the question, and maintains that if two countries, which may be called England and Cuba, exchanged only two commodities—England being the sole producer of commodity A, called cloth, and Cuba the sole producer of commodity B, called sugar—it would be advantageous to either to retaliate a duty imposed by the other. We believe this to be true; but we believe it to be one of those barren truths from which no practical inferences can be drawn. It is true only on the supposition that each country possesses, against the other, a strict monopoly;—a monopoly unaffected by the existence of any third market or of any third commodity, capable of serving as a medium of exchange. Each is supposed to be willing to receive only one commodity, and to be incapable of obtaining it from any source except the one other country to which its commerce is confined. The prices of the two commodities in question would be governed, not by the general and permanent regulator of price, cost of production, but by the occasional and disturbing causes, demand and supply. Any diminution of supply, the demand not having been previously diminished, would raise the value of either commodity; any diminution of demand, the supply not having been previously diminished, would sink it, and *vice versa.* In the supposed case, if England wanted more sugar, she could get it only by sending more cloth; and, as the increased supply would lower the price, she would have to give more cloth than before for a given quantity of sugar. If she wanted less sugar, she would send less cloth; the diminution in its supply would raise its value, and she would have to give less cloth than before for a given quantity of sugar. If the English Government were to lay a duty on the export of cloth, —that is to say, make every exporter pay for the permission to export it—the export would diminish, the value would rise, and the Cuba people must give more sugar than before for a given quantity. If the English Government were to impose a duty on sugar—that is to say, make every consumer of sugar pay a tax for the permission to use it—the consumption would diminish, the value would fall, and the Cuba people must give more sugar for a given quantity of cloth. By a retaliatory duty on the export of sugar, or on the import of cloth, Cuba might neutralize these effects, and the result might be to make sugar and cloth exchange again in the same proportions, though in diminished quantities.

But when Colonel Torrens attempts to deduce *practical* inferences from this hypothesis; when he affirms that, in real life, the terms of international exchanges are determined not by cost of production, but by demand and supply;* when he asserts that the country which imposes the highest duties will have her demand for the product of other countries diminished in a greater

---

Postscript, p. 6.

proportion than that in which the demand for her own productions is diminished in other countries, and that the effect will be an alteration in the terms of the international exchanges to the advantage of the country imposing the highest duties, and to the disadvantage of the country imposing the lower duties;*—in short, when he seriously urges us to act as if his hypothesis represented the actual state of things, we utterly dissent from, and repudiate his doctrine.

In order to show the grounds of our dissent, we will endeavour to state more clearly than we think has been done by Colonel Torrens, the principles on which international exchange depends. And we shall begin by explaining the term ' cost of production,' and by showing that it is the real governor, not only of domestic, but of international, commerce.

Every thing which can be produced at will, is subject to two different costs of production; the one the *minimum*, below which price cannot permanently fall; the other the *maximum*, beyond which price cannot permanently rise. The first, which may be called the cost of production to the producer, or seller, consists of the sum of the sacrifices which must be made, or, in other words, the sum of the wages and profits which must be paid or retained by the producer, in order to enable or induce him to continue to produce;—including, of course, the wages of his own labour, and the profit of his own capital. The second, which may be called the cost of production to the consumer, or purchaser, consists of the sum of the sacrifices which must be made by the consumer, if, instead of purchasing, he produce for himself. The amount of the interval between these two extremes is one of the measures of the advantages derived from the division of labour. A good shoemaker can make a pair of shoes in a day; he could not make a coat in a fortnight. A good tailor can make three coats in a week; he could not make a pair of shoes in a month. So far as the price of a commodity is not affected by any natural or artificial monopoly, it coincides with the cost of production to the producer. Were it lower, he would cease to produce. Were it higher, his employment would afford more than average wages or profits; and rival producers would crowd into it, and undersell one another.

That this is true with respect to domestic commerce, is obvious; it appears to us obvious, that it is equally true with respect to international commerce. The English spinner sells his yarns to the French importer at precisely the price which he charges to his English customer. The French weaver sells

---

* Postscript, p. 7.

his silks to the English importer at precisely the price which he charges to his French customer. In many cases, neither the one nor the other knows for what market he is producing, or to whom he is selling. He produces the quantity for which he expects to get a remunerating price—a price which will repay the cost of production; that is to say, the cost of the raw material, the interest and wear and tear of his machinery and other fixed capital, the wages of his work-people, and a profit to himself, at the current rate of the country, for the time which elapses between his advances and his returns. He sells to a broker, and seldom knows whether his product is to be consumed in England, or America, or France. But it may be said, what is it that decides what shall be the wages of the work-people, which, in fact, appear to be the positive principle on which price depends, the other elements being mere ratios? Why are the wages of an English cotton-spinner four ounces of silver a-week, and those of a French cotton-spinner only three? For precisely the same reason that an English cabinetmaker earns 6s. a-day, and an English carpenter only 3s.—the comparative efficiency of their labour. The produce of the cabinetmaker's day's work is worth a little more than 6s., and therefore he gets 6s. The produce of the carpenter's day's work is worth only a little more than 3s., and therefore he gets only 3s. An English cotton-spinner receives more silver for a day's work than a French cotton-spinner, because he produces in a day a larger amount of yarn, and of a better quality. The products of the labour and capital of all the French and all the English manufacturers are competitors in the general market of the world. The prices at which those products sell, determine the whole sum which is paid for the result of a given amount of the labour of each country—assisted by a given amount of its capital, advanced for a given time. The relative proportions in which labour and capital have concurred in the production, and the current rate of profit, determine in each country how much of the price of each commodity is to go to the labourer, and how much to the capitalist. If this exceed average wages or profits, other capitalists or labourers crowd in; if it be less, the production is, in time, discontinued. There is, in reality, no difference between the principles which regulate foreign, and those which regulate domestic exchanges. Why does a given sideboard sell in England for twenty guineas? Because the materials cost a sum which we will call four guineas, and the wages of the workmen fourteen, and the rent of the workshops and salerooms two guineas, making together twenty guineas; because this sum was advanced for two years, and because the current rate of profit is ten per cent per annum. Why did the wages amount to fourteen guineas? Because two workmen were employed at two guineas a-week each for three weeks and a half. Why were their wages two guineas a-week? Because the efficiency of the labour of an average English labourer bears the same proportion to the efficiency of the labour of a cabinetmaker which the week's wages of an average English labourer—that is to say, the gold which his week's labour is worth in the general market of the world—bear to two guineas. If the value of the produce of English labour were to double in the market of the world—or, in other words, if the produce of the day's work of an average English labourer could purchase in the general market of the world twice as much gold as it can now—all other circumstances remaining unaltered, sideboards would double in price; if it were to fall, they would fall in the same proportion; and this although the supply continued the same. But if twice as many sideboards were required, they would not cost more a-piece. If only one half the number were required, they would not cost less. Indeed, under the operation of the general rule, that every increased supply of a manufactured commodity is produced at a less proportional expense, it is probable that twice as many sideboards would cost less than twenty guineas a-piece; and only half that number more. So, if France habitually purchased from England twice as much yarn as she now takes, she would not buy it at a dearer rate. If she habitually required only half as much, she would not get it cheaper. We say habitually, because a sudden and great alteration in the demand of France, might, for a time, raise or depress wages or profits in the spinning trade, and thus affect the cost of production. But this effect must cease as soon as the capital and labour employed in spinning yarn had been proportionally increased or diminished. , And the probability is, that the price would then rise or fall in a direction opposite to that of the supply—a larger quantity selling at a cheaper rate, or a smaller quantity at a dearer.

But if France will take from us only half the yarns which we previously supplied to her, how are we to get the silk which we previously received in exchange for our yarns? If a butcher will take no physic from an apothecary, how is the apothecary to get meat? The services performed by coin in facilitating domestic interchange, are performed in international exchange by bullion; that is to say, by gold or silver, valued according to weight and fineness, not form;—a commodity which every nation possesses, which every nation accepts, and which from its facility of transport, and the identity of the qualities of every portion of it, has less peculiar local value than any other object of exchange. But would England suffer no inconvenience from the refusal of

France to take more than half the yarns which she previously imported ? Precisely the same inconvenience in kind which the apothecary suffers when the butcher, having been previously his patient, recovers. While the butcher was ill, the value of the drugs and of the meat, mutually supplied, may have been equal, and the apothecary may have paid for his meat without sending money. He must now send money. The amount of the inconvenience would depend partly on the proportion which the profit derived by him from the butcher's custom bore to his whole income ; and partly on the facility with which he could devote, to the supply of other customers, the capital and labour previously employed in obtaining this profit from the butcher.

To a certain extent, the same causes decide what is the amount of inconvenience which the loss of a customer occasions to a nation. If the Isle of Wight were to lay prohibitory duties on all British commodities, the general prosperity of British commerce would be unaffected. If England were to prohibit the produce of the Isle of Wight, that island would be seriously injured. If all Europe were to do so, the island would be ruined. So the commerce of Britain would be seriously injured, if prohibitory duties should diminish by one half her exports to America. She employs in supplying that hemisphere probably more than L.40,000,000 of capital, and the labour of more than 400,000 families, and derives a profit of more than L.4,000,000 a-year. One half of this great amount of capital and labour must now receive a different destination ; and years might elapse before it could find new markets equally advantageous. But if Europe and America were to combine absolutely to exclude the produce of China, that vast empire would suffer no material loss. It is probable that the whole trade of China with Europe and America, does not employ one three hundredth part of her population, or one thousandth part of her capital. The trade of Britain with America employs, at least, a twentieth part of her population, and at least a tenth part of her commercial and manufacturing capital.

There is, however, one difference between individuals and nations, when considered as producers and sellers, which materially affects the degree in which they are respectively affected by the conduct of one another. An individual seldom produces more than one or two kinds of commodities—a nation can produce all the different raw products which are not denied to her by her soil or climate, and all the manufactured commodities of which she can import the materials. An individual, if the demand for his peculiar product is diminished, can seldom indemnify himself by directing his capital, his industry, and his skill, towards a different branch of production. If the demand for the drugs and services of the apothecary be diminished, he is not likely to better himself by turning farmer or manufacturer; but for that very reason he has to fear the competition only of those who are engaged in the same business as himself. He is not afraid of being opposed by the butcher, or by the shoemaker. A nation can turn her capital, industry, or skill, towards an almost indefinite variety of employments. If one market, or one sort of exports, become less profitable, she can resort, probably not without immediate loss, but still she can resort to another; but, again, for that very reason she has a rival in every other member of the community of the commercial world. Her own customers are her competitors in her own markets, and in every third market. As every nation, by excluding totally, or even partially, the products of a neighbour, diminishes her own productive power, she becomes a less formidable rival to the nation whose products she excludes. If France were to abolish her duties on British yarns and British iron, she would increase the demand for some kinds of British industry. On the other hand, the vast addition which the use of British iron and British yarn would make to the agricultural and manufacturing powers of France, would materially increase the productiveness of her industry. France is even now, perhaps, our most formidable rival in our best markets, and in some of the products in which we most excel—cotton goods, linens, and woollens. Is it certain that we should be gainers by the change? Is it certain that the demand for British industry would not be as much diminished in one quarter as it would be increased in another?

Our own opinion is, that we *should* be gainers by the change. France would, in two different ways, become a better customer to us. In the first place, she would take more of our produce— she would enable us to direct more of our industry and capital towards the employments in which they are most successful. She would increase the productiveness of British industry; and at the same time, by coming in as an additional purchaser, raise the value of its products in the general market of the world. She would be a greater bidder for our produce in the auction in which all commodities are sold. In the second place, her own industry in the production of the commodities which we import from her would be more productive. Though her labourers would be better paid, their labour would be more efficient, and the produce of a given amount of labour would be more abundant and better. France would purchase more British yarn and iron ; and by the improvement in her industry, would be able, without loss, probably with a greater profit than before, to give for every cwt. of either, more cotton goods, silks, woollens, eggs, and wine, than she now gives. We believe that these advantages would more than compensate the inconvenience which we should suffer by finding her in every third market, and indeed in her own, a more powerful competitor. But we cannot believe that our gain would be clear.

The plausibility, such as it is, of the errors contained in Colonel Torrens's Postscript, depends, in the first place, on his exclusion of the use of money. By that exclusion alone, he is able to represent international exchange as depending on demand and supply, instead of on cost of production. If France would receive in exchange for her silks nothing but yarn, she might force England to increase the proportionate supply of yarn, in order to obtain a greater or even the same supply of silk. But money the French Government has not the will, or even the power, to exclude, or to subject to more than nominal duties. The French weaver has neither the will nor the power to refuse to sell his silks for money, at the cost of their production. The refusal, therefore, of France to receive yarn, would (as we have shown, at a greater extent perhaps than so obvious a statement required) affect the trade between England and France only by converting it from a direct into a roundabout trade—only by forcing us to alter the destination of the capital and labour now employed in producing yarn for the French market; and to send to France a larger portion than we now send of the bullion which is constantly passing through our ports, or under our control. And, in the second place, this plausibility depends on the assumption that the supposed customhouse war is carried on between the British empire on the one side, and the whole remainder of the commercial world on the other. His England represents the British islands and their dependencies; and his Cuba every other portion of Europe, Asia, Africa, and America. The whole of Cuba is tacitly assumed to enjoy free trade, as between all its different members; but to agree to impose duties of two per cent on all British commodities. What would be the measures to be adopted if all the world were to constitute itself into a Zollverein against the British empire, is a question scarcely requiring serious enquiry. In the first place, there is no motive to such a conspiracy; and in the second place, the mutual jealousies of the different nations, and the wants of their respective exchequers, would make the mere attempt impossible, even if there were a motive. And while all our neighbours are wasting their own productive powers by diffusing, instead of concentrating their industry, though they are less profitable as customers, they are less dangerous as rivals.

It must not be inferred from the preceding details that we necessarily disapprove of all retaliatory duties; or that we recommend an unconditional abolition of all which we have imposed. We believe, indeed, that every one of the duties by which a foreign nation attempts partially or wholly to exclude our produce, is more injurious to herself than to us. We believe that every one of them has in a certain degree the compensating effect of rendering that nation a less formidable rival in third markets. But we believe that in every separate case we suffer from them; and, in the aggregate, suffer considerably. We have no doubt that, if there were no other resource, we should much diminish that suffering by abandoning wholly the protective system, and levying duties only for the purposes of revenue. We believe that by doing so we should increase the productiveness of our labour; we should diminish, or perhaps destroy, the rivalry of many of our competitors in third markets; and that thus, without perhaps affecting, what is perfectly unimportant, the distribution of the precious metals, we should increase our command over them.

But it certainly would be much better if we were not only to renounce our own follies, but to induce our neighbours to renounce theirs. ' There may,' says Adam Smith, and we agree with him, ' be policy in retaliations of this kind, when there is ' a probability that they will procure the repeal of the high ' duties complained of. The recovery of a great foreign market ' will generally more than compensate the transitory inconveni- ' ence of paying dearer during a short time for some kinds of ' goods. To judge whether such retaliations are likely to pro- ' duce such an effect, does not perhaps belong so much to the ' science of a legislator, whose deliberations ought to be governed ' by general principles, which are always the same, as to the ' skill of that insidious and crafty animal, vulgarly called a states- ' man or politician, whose councils are directed by the momen- ' tary fluctuations of affairs.' *

' But,' he adds, and here also we agree with him, that, ' when ' there is no probability that any such repeal can be procured, ' it seems a bad method of compensating the injury done to cer- ' tain classes of our people, to do another injury ourselves, not ' only to those classes, but to almost all the other classes. This ' may no doubt give encouragement to some particular class of ' workmen among ourselves, and, by excluding some of their ' rivals, may enable them [for a very short time] to raise their ' price in the home market. Those workmen, however, who

---

' suffered by our neighbour's prohibition, will not be benefited
' by ours. On the contrary, they, and almost all the other
' classes of our citizens, will thereby be obliged to pay dearer
' for certain goods. Every such law imposes a real tax upon
' the whole country, not in favour of that particular class of
' workmen who were injured by our neighbour's prohibition,
' but of some other class.' *

But, after all, the practical question for a British statesman is
the policy not of retaliation but of persistence. It is not, whether by inflicting, or by threatening to inflict restrictions on the
commerce of foreign nations, we should endeavour to persuade
them to remove, or to relax, those which they have imposed
upon ours; but whether, after having by our exactions, by our
prohibitions, by our sliding scales, and by our differential duties,
provoked foreign nations to retaliatory schemes, we ought or
ought not to retrace our steps. The British reader of Colonel
Torrens might suppose that we are the innocent victims of an
Anti-Anglican conspiracy. A foreign economist would tell a
different story.

We will compare the British tariff with that of a nation which
is supposed to be distinguished by the exclusiveness of its commercial system, namely, with that of France. In 1841, the
value of the imports of France for home consumption amounted to 804,557,931 francs; the duties on them amounted to
129,679,125 francs—being L.16, 2s. 4d. per cent. And this
includes the imports from her own colonies and dependencies.
It may be supposed that British commodities were unfavourably
treated. The value of the commodities imported by France for
home consumption in 1841, from the British islands and their
European dependencies, was 101,907,874 francs; the duties on
them amounted to 11,288,996 francs—being L.11, 1s. 6d. per
cent. These estimates, however, require some correction; in
consequence of the valuation of foreign commodities having been
made in 1816 and 1817, and not subsequently revised. Since
that period, many of them might have altered in value, and some
of them must have fallen. If we take 10 per cent from the value
of the whole bulk of the commodities imported, it will leave the
French tariff not quite 18 per cent on the average value of the
commodities imported for home consumption, and not quite $12\frac{1}{3}$
per cent on British commodities. Let us now turn to the British tariff. As the greatest part of our duties are imposed according to quantity, it is difficult to state, with accuracy, what pro-

* *Wealth of Nations*, Book iv, cap. 11.

portion they bear to the value of the commodities imported. But we will endeavour to give a rough approximation.

For the ten years ending with 1840, the last included in Mr Porter's published tables, the average gross revenue of the customs amounted to L.21,941,764 a-year. If we had a return of the real value of the imports from which this revenue was derived, we could, of course, state the average *ad valorem* amount of our duties. But we have none. We have, however, an account of the real value of our exports. Their average annual value during these ten years was L.45,244,407. With these exports we purchased every year not only the commodities liable to duty, but also L.2,700,000 of gold and silver, which amount, as we have shown, is annually consumed in the British islands, on the wear and loss of coin and plate. After deducting the exports which went to purchase this sum of L.2,700,000, there remains an annual export of the value of L.42,544,407, with which our imports, exclusively of gold and silver, were purchased. The imports, of course, on their arrival in the British islands, were worth more than this sum; as the expenses of carriage and the importer's profit must be added. To cover these expenses and this profit, and any other inaccuracies which may have crept into our estimate, we will make the large addition of 20 per cent. On these data, the imports on which, the average annual sum of L.21,941,767 was paid for duty, were of the average annual value of L.51,053,288; making the average amount of our duties L.42, 19s. 6d. per cent on the value of the commodities imported—including, as we have done with respect to France, the imports from our own colonies and dependencies. But it may be said that we have taken into the account only the duties imposed by France, and not her prohibitions. Do we impose no virtual prohibitions? A duty of L.42, 19s. 6d. per cent is, with respect to the vast majority of commodities, as effectual a bar as the most express prohibition. Or it may be said that this was the state of things under our old tariff, and does not represent what now exists. In fact, however, the new tariff has made no material alteration. The most important articles which it has affected are corn, coffee, and timber. On corn it has practically raised the duty from 5s. 10d. per quarter, the average duty previously paid, to 8s. per quarter. Coffee and timber it has left subject to duties of nearly 150 per cent; and the amount of both is too small to lower the aggregate percentage of our duties as much as the increase of the duty on corn has raised it.

Now, when this is the state of the commercial relations between France and the British islands—when France imports for home consumption L.4,000,000 worth of our products, at an average duty of less than 18 per cent—Colonel Torrens ventures to assert that the import duties imposed by France, limit our exports to that country to an inconsiderable extent,* and to advise us, by the prompt adoption and rigid enforcement of a retaliatory system, to give the French producers a lesson on the evils of protection.†

There are few nations with whom a British negotiator must not carefully avoid all allusion to retaliation, and certainly France is not among those few. Colonel Torrens, however, goes further still. In his patriotic blindness to the conduct of his own country, he recommends us to oppose differential duties to the tariffs of Cuba and Brazil‡—countries whose staple commodities we tax at 150, 300, and 3000 per cent!

If we believed, with this writer, that, under existing circumstances, to open our ports is charlatanry, and that to reduce our duties without requiring corresponding reductions, is ' to ' make ourselves tributary to foreign states ;'§—' to relinquish ' the lever which might move them to concession, and to grant ' a bounty on the continuance of restrictions on our trade ;' ‖—if we believed this, we should feel all the apprehensions which he expresses, and more. We should tremble for the prospects of our country, if we believed that a hostile conspiracy was shutting us out from the rest of the commercial world, and that the value of our labour and our command over the precious metals were rapidly diminishing. We should despair, if we believed that restrictions still more vexatious, duties still more oppressive, and prohibitions still more numerous, were the remedy. That our situation is not without difficulty or without danger—that we cannot be extricated by any Minister who wants the knowledge of what is right, or the decision necessary to compel his ignorant or selfish followers to submit to its adoption—that the vessel is not in seas in which she can be navigated by an irresolute captain, disunited officers, and a mutinous crew ; all this we believe, and indeed fear that we may have tired our readers by repeating. If we further believed that there is no course less objectionable than that which has led to the shoals and quicksands to which we have been steering—if we believed that to retreat is still more dangerous than to advance—we should endeavour to shut our eyes to the signs of approach to unavoidable ruin, and only hope that we might not be in life at the time of the catastrophe.

---

* Letter to Sir R. Peel, p. 21.     † The Budget, p. 67.
‡ Postscript, p. 27.     § Budget, p. 61.     ‖ Ibid. p. 62.

It is because we know that the evils which we are suffering, and the dangers which we are fearing, are self-inflicted and self-created—because we know that they are to be remedied or averted, not by concessions to be wrung, or rather attempted to be wrung, by entreaty, or menace from foreign rivals, but simply by consenting to purchase what they are eager to sell—because we know that our industry will be re-animated when it is unfettered, and prosperous when it ceases to be misdirected, that we feel hope; it is because we know that these opinions are rapidly spreading and gaining strength throughout the nation, that we feel confidence.